Office of Government Commerce

Service Strategy

London: TSO

TSO

Published by TSO (The Stationery Office) and available from:

Online
www.tsoshop.co.uk

Mail, Telephone, Fax & E-mail
TSO
PO Box 29, Norwich, NR3 1GN
Telephone orders/General enquiries: 0870 600 5522
Fax orders: 0870 600 5533
E-mail: customer.services@tso.co.uk
Textphone 0870 240 3701

TSO Shops
16 Arthur Street, Belfast BT1 4GD
028 9023 8451 Fax 028 9023 5401
71 Lothian Road, Edinburgh EH3 9AZ
0870 606 5566 Fax 0870 606 5588

TSO@Blackwell and other Accredited Agents

First published 2007
Second impression with corrections 2007

ISBN 978 0 11 331045 6

Printed in the United Kingdom for The Stationery Office

N5616675 c20 09/07

Contents

List of figures

All diagrams in this publication are intended to provide an illustration of ITIL Service Management Practice concepts and guidance. They have been artistically rendered to visually reinforce key concepts and are not intended to meet a formal method or standard of technical drawing. The ITIL Service Management Practices Integrated Service Model conforms to technical drawing standards and should be referred to for complete details. Please see www.best-management-practice.com/itil for details.

List of tables

OGC's foreword

Since its creation, ITIL has grown to become the most widely accepted approach to IT Service Management in the world. However, along with this success comes the responsibility to ensure that the guidance keeps pace with a changing global business environment. Service management requirements are inevitably shaped by the development of technology, revised business models and increasing customer expectations. Our latest version of ITIL has been created in response to these developments.

This publication is one of five core publications describing the IT Service Management practices that make up ITIL. They are the result of a two-year project to review and update the guidance. The number of service management professionals around the world who have helped to develop the content of these publications is impressive. Their experience and knowledge have contributed to the content to bring you a consistent set of high-quality guidance. This is supported by the ongoing development of a comprehensive qualifications scheme, along with accredited training and consultancy.

Whether you are part of a global company, a government department or a small business, ITIL gives you access to world-class service management expertise. Essentially, it puts IT Services where they belong – at the heart of successful business operations.

Peter Fanning

Acting Chief Executive

Office of Government Commerce

Chief Architect's foreword

In 1997, Chinese manufacturers entered the motorcycle market with an unusual management strategy. Rather than preparing detailed models and drawings of subsystems, the country simply defined best-practice structures and standards. The supplier community remained free to innovate and adapt components within these rough designs and broad parameters. The results were stunning – the Chinese motorcycle industry now accounts for half of all global production and is considered a hotbed of innovation.[1]

These results are *emergent*. They are the outcomes of following low-level and practical guidance and gave rise to an industry that moves in self-organizing coordination in a variety of conditions. Instead of rigid frameworks, preventing graceful adaptation under changing conditions, there remains room for self-optimization. This is the philosophy of ITIL: good practice structures with room for self-optimization.

What is exciting about emergent behaviour and self-optimization are the surprising outcomes. When the previous version of ITIL offered its service management framework, there did not exist such solutions as federated Configuration Management Databases (CMDB), Service-oriented Architectures (SOA) or the convergence of business process, virtualization and service management. ITIL reflects the dynamics of organizations, and their need to continually adapt in a world of changing conditions.

These and other significant lessons learned have been applied to create the improved framework described in this version of the library. ITIL also looks for the first time at some business fundamentals and the relationships between all the players in modern organizations using IT. This publication on Service Strategy covers much of this new ground by examining what exactly a service is, how both the provider and the customer can mutually benefit from one supplying a service to the other, and where each side has choices.

Perhaps the strongest single idea this publication brings to ITIL is the concept of competition. Every provider faces competition. As many internal service providers have found, they will inevitably be tested against the market. The key for providers is to understand how they provide value and differentiate themselves for their target customers. For customers, it is to understand where they should best be concentrating their efforts, and where shared or external service providers can do it better. There are many factors to consider and some unfamiliar concepts may be presented, but this is an exciting journey. Take this publication as your guide.

Sharon Taylor

Chief Architect, ITIL Service Management Practices

Preface

A publication is given life by its readers. In other words, a publication is completed by its readers. This is certainly true for this publication on service management. What follows is a collection of principles, practices, and methods supporting a strategic approach to service management. The guidance is written primarily for senior managers who provide leadership and direction to organizations in the form of objectives, decisions, plans, policies, and strategies. Managers at other levels may benefit as well by understanding the underlying logic of senior management decisions. The guidance is given from the perspective of organizations in the public and private sectors tasked with providing information technology-related business services. Customers benefit from incorporating the guidance into due diligence for sourcing decisions and strategies.

This publication is the core of the ITIL framework. The creation of this version of ITIL refreshes the body of knowledge, so it continues to aid organizations seeking to develop and improve their service management capabilities. A frequently asked question is, 'Why change something that is not broken?' and a related question is, 'Does that mean what we have been following so far is wrong?' The answer to both is no. Challenges and opportunities faced by organizations change over time, requiring them to continually learn and adapt. Successful innovations gradually become best practices. Best practices quickly become good practices, which become commodities, generally accepted principles, received wisdom, or regulatory requirements. What were once distinctive characteristics of an organization become ordinary traits taken for granted by customers. This compels organizations to seek new ways to improve, and to differentiate themselves from alternatives through innovative services, operating models, systems, and processes.

ITIL is part of a large and growing body of knowledge on which service management depends. The library strengthens and extends the body of knowledge to cover new challenges and opportunities confronting the leadership of organizations. This publication is not about business strategy in general. It describes how strategic thinking is applied to service management and how service management itself is a strategic asset of an IT organization.

This publication has been reviewed by a wide group of CIOs, CTOs, senior managers, practitioners, and consultants who have applied the criteria of usefulness and relevance to the practice of service management in various organizational contexts and business environments. The findings of the OGC Public Consultation for the ITIL Refresh Project have been applied as quality criteria. This publication provides the context and basis for investing in tools and technologies allowing service management to support unprecedented levels of efficiency, scale, complexity, and uncertainty.

Contact information

Full details of the range of material published under the ITIL banner can be found at www.best-management-practice.com/itil

If you would like to inform us of any changes that may be required to this publication please log them at www.best-management-practice.com/changelog

For further information on qualifications and training accreditation, please visit www.itil-officialsite.com. Alternatively, please contact:

APMG Service Desk
Sword House
Totteridge Road
High Wycombe
Buckinghamshire
HP13 6DG
Tel: +44 (0) 1494 452450
Email: servicedesk@apmgroup.co.uk

Acknowledgements

Chief Architect and authors

Sharon Taylor   Chief Architect
(Aspect Group Inc)

Majid Iqbal (Carnegie Mellon University)   Author

Michael Nieves (Accenture)   Author

ITIL authoring team

The ITIL authoring team contributed to this guide through commenting on content and alignment across the set. So thanks are also due to the other ITIL authors, specifically Jeroen Bronkhorst (HP), David Cannon (HP), Gary Case (Pink Elephant), Ashley Hanna (HP), Shirley Lacy (ConnectSphere), Vernon Lloyd (Fox IT), Ivor Macfarlane (Guillemot Rock), Stuart Rance (HP), Colin Rudd (ITEMS), George Spalding (Pink Elephant) and David Wheeldon (HP).

Mentors

Phil Montanaro and Bill Powell.

Further contributions

A number of people generously contributed their time and expertise to this Service Strategy publication. Jim Clinch, as OGC Project Manager, is grateful to the support provided by Accenture to the authoring team on the development of this publication, particularly the contribution of Jack Bischof; and to the support of Ralph Russo (Merrill Lynch), Jenny Dugmore, Convenor of Working Group ISO/IEC 20000, Janine Eves, Carol Hulm, Aidan Lawes and Michiel van der Voort.

The authors would also like to thank D. Neil Gissler, Ran S. Mangat, Damian Harris, William McVicker, Cheryl Deitcher, William Farler, Maria Veyon, Ryan J. Thomas and Suzon Crowell of Accenture.

In order to develop ITIL Service Management Practices to reflect current best practice and produce publications of lasting value, OGC consulted widely with different stakeholders throughout the world at every stage in the process. OGC would also like to thank the following individuals and their organizations for their contributions to refreshing the ITIL guidance:

The ITIL Advisory Group

Pippa Bass, OGC; Tony Betts, Independent; Alison Cartlidge, Xansa; Diane Colbeck, DIYmonde Solutions Inc; Ivor Evans, DIYmonde Solutions Inc; Karen Ferris, ProActive; Malcolm Fry, FRY-Consultants; John Gibert, Independent; Colin Hamilton, RENARD Consulting Ltd; Lex Hendriks, EXIN; Signe-Marie

Hernes Bjerke, Det Norske Veritas; Carol Hulm, British Computer Society-ISEB; Tony Jenkins, DOMAINetc; Phil Montanaro, EDS; Alan Nance, ITPreneurs; Christian Nissen, Itilligence; Don Page, Marval Group; Bill Powell, IBM; Sergio Rubinato Filho, CA; James Siminoski, SOScorp; Robert E. Stroud, CA; Jan van Bon, Inform-IT; Ken Wendle, HP; Paul Wilkinson, Getronics PinkRoccade; Takashi Yagi, Hitachi.

Reviewers

John Adam, HP; Allan Aitchison, KPMG; Nathan Akers, Active Consulting; Oscar Almadin, IBM; Iyas Al-Sarabi, Y-consult; Uade Alukpe; Jens Jakob Andersen, Post Danmark A/S; Steve Ashing, Independent; Hartwig Bazzanella; Charles Betz, EDS; Thomas Betz, EDS; Emma Bevan, Afiniti; Michael Billimoria, ITS; Marcus Binet, Redworld; Janaki Chakravarthy, Infosys Technologies Limited; Constantinos Christofi, EMC/Accenture; Jorgen Clausen, Danfoss A/S; Luiz Antonio Comar; Jorge Luis Cordenonsi, IBM; Petrovic Dalibor, Deloitte & Touche, LLP; Graham Donoghue, Ngrid; David Favelle, Lucid IT; Maamar Ferkoun, IBM; Stephen Fritts, CTG Inc; Franco Gaggia, EDS; Mark Gillett, Alvarez and Marsal (Europe) Ltd; Leanne Gregory, IBM Australia Ltd; Geert Hahn, EDS Business Solutions GmbH; Sandra Hendriks, News Ltd; David Hinley, Gnet; Eu Jin Ho, UBS; Caspar Honee, Unisys; Young Hong, Samsung SDS; Chris Hunter, Network Rail Ltd; Peter Isbell; Rene Jacob, HP; Sharma Jitendra, Satyam; David Johnton, DAJex Ltd; Bill Ye Jun, HP; Jeyaganesh Kannan, IBM; Dwight Kayto, Sasktel; Magda Kilby, Richemont; Eddie Kilkelly, ILX Group; Andreas Knaus, Santix AG; Michael Koerfer; Michael Kresse, Serview; Aron Kumar, Accenture; Soren Laursen, Novo Nordisk A/S; Simon Learoyd, iCore Ltd; Laura Lee, Pink Elephant; Ragnar Loken, RLBR; David Lynch, GCHQ; Jan Mandrup, IBM; Edward Mangiaratti, Court Square Data Group; Jak Marion, Stavtech; Gaetan Mauguin, Bearing Point; Manoj Kumar Mauni, Maersk Global Services Centres; Patrick Mcguire; Daniel McLean, US Cellular Corporation; Chris Molloy, IBM; Michael Muenzinger, EDS; Jason Mugridge, BT; Hamid Nouri, Nouri Associates; Michael Orr, IBM; Joel Pereira, iCore Ltd; Robin Piepjohn, Icisinst; Daniel Rolles, Lend Lease; Oscar Rozalen Gaitan, Comunycarse Network Consultants; Michael Rueggeberg, EDS; Marianna Ruocco, Pink Elephant; Monalisa Sarkar, TCS; Frances Scarff, OGC; Rainer Schmidt, HTV Aalen; Karsten Smet, Microsoft; Martin Steffens, EDS Australia; Harald Steier, Ewico; Thorsten Steiling, Salzgitter Flachstahl GmbH; Mark Ross Sutherland, G2G3; Anil Tamirisa, Accenture; Roy Taylor, Northampton ac; Tikoo Vijay, Satyam; Lief Wadhvana, Canada Ontario Government; Jason Week, Microsoft; Mark Whelan, Servo Computer Services; John Windebank, Sun Microsystems Ltd; Frederieke Winkler Prins, Service Management Partners; Zachariah Wyckoff, Microsoft; John Seah Yam-Sung, Everest Innovation Pte Ltd; Rob Young, Fox IT; Steffi Zoeller, EDS.

Introduction

1 Introduction

'How do you become not optional?'
William D. Green, CEO, Accenture

1.1 OVERVIEW

In 1937, British-born economist Ronald Coase concluded that the boundaries of firms are determined by *transaction costs*.[2]

> The concept of *transaction costs* used here is not to be confused with the discrete cost of transactions such as requests, payments, trades and updates to databases. What is referred to here are the overall costs of economic exchange between two parties, including but not limited to costs incurred in finding and selecting qualified suppliers for goods or services of required specifications, negotiating an agreement, cost of consuming the goods or services, governing the relationship with suppliers, to ensuring that commitments are fulfilled as agreed.
>
> Policing and enforcement costs are the costs of making sure the other party sticks to the terms of the contract, and taking appropriate action (often through the legal system) if this turns out not to be the case.

Sometimes it makes sense for a business to own and operate assets, or conduct activities in-house. At other times, the sensible thing is to seek alternatives from the open market. As prevailing conditions change, boundaries of the firm contract or expand with decisions such as *make*, *buy*, or *rent*. Coase received the Nobel Prize in Economics for this remarkable idea.

The world is changing at a faster pace than ever before. The forces of the internet, inexpensive computing, ubiquitous connectivity, open platforms, globalization, and a fresh wave of innovation are combining in ways that dramatically alter the transaction costs in almost every business. The result is greater dynamism and flexibility in the definition of markets for services. Markets are created almost spontaneously with innovative business models and value propositions. They emerge within enterprises, defy standard industry classifications, and extend farther in geography. The digitization of commercial activities, social interactions and government has meant fewer physical constraints on new business models, strategies and relationships. Knowledge and productive capacity are more dispersed than ever before. Organizations can *rent* what they were earlier forced to *make* or *own*. Generic concepts like *rent* translate into collaborative relationships

with service providers who provide access to capabilities and resources otherwise not available to the organization.

There is similar growth in consumer services driven by various social and economic factors and technology. Among the forces driving the consumption of services are rising per capita incomes, demand for social services, size and role of the public sector, complexity of work environments, increased specialization (division of labour), and relaxation of trade barriers.[3] These trends are contributing worldwide to the growth of the service economy in a remarkable fashion.

Information technologies (IT) enable, enhance, and are embedded in a growing number of goods and services. They are connecting consumers and producers of services in ways previously not feasible, while contributing to the productivity of numerous sectors of the services industry such as financial services, communications, insurance, and retail services.[3] Government agencies, too, have experienced similar gains associated with the use of IT.

- Organizations exploit resources as and when needed without owning them, even when those resources are remotely located and simultaneously shared.
- They use self-service channels such as websites, mobile phones, and kiosks to expose business functions such as billing, order processing, reservations, and technical support to consumers. Quality of service is no longer constrained by the capacity of branches, stores, and other staffed locations.
- Entrepreneurs and individuals compose new services assembled from existing services available in the commercial and public space.
- Service-oriented architectures are allowing organizations to not only reduce complexity of their business applications and infrastructure but to further exploit such assets in new ways.

Tremendous change and growth is taking place in information-based services. Information, previously a supporting element, has become the basis for value by itself. The relaxation of physical constraints has changed our thinking about how information is produced and consumed. Recent years have seen significant increases in valuation for businesses that simply facilitate interactions or the exchange of information. Capabilities and resources in the management of IT and the management of services are no longer perceived as merely operational concern or detail. They are the basis for creating value, for competition, and distinctive performance.

The trends noted above require IT organizations to have a keener sense of the nature and dynamics of services as a means for providing value to customers. It is not surprising that growth and prosperity of a trade are accompanied by greater demands on the tools of the trade. The practice of service management grows, learns, and matures under the pressure of new challenges and opportunities.

Imagine you have been given responsibility for an IT organization. How would you decide on a strategy to serve your customers? Perhaps you would examine requirements in detail and plan appropriately. You might track ongoing demand and adjust accordingly, while maintaining operational efficiency. Surely an attentive service provider with low costs must inevitably succeed. Unfortunately, while these are all necessary factors, things are rarely so straightforward.

First, issues surrounding services are complex. Not only in their individual details but also in the dynamic complexity that comes with many moving and interrelated parts. Long-term behaviour is often different from short-term behaviour. There are many tools for dealing with details but few offer insight into how the problems we have today have developed over time. What are needed are methods to help organizations understand the likely consequences of decisions and actions.

Second, customer specifications are not always clear, certain or even correct. Much is lost in the translation from requirements document to service fulfilment. The most subtle aspect of strategic thinking lies in knowing what *needs* to happen. Customer outcomes, rather than specifications, are the genesis of services. Strategic plans, while critical for enacting change, are not enough.

A strategic perspective begins with the understanding of competition. Sooner or later, every organization faces competition. Even IT organizations with a relatively captive internal market of *owner-customers* are not entitled to a perpetual monopoly. The recent trends in outsourcing of business functions and operations have made that clear. A change in prevailing business conditions or a new business strategy pursued by the customer can suddenly expose the IT organization to competition. Even government and non-profit IT organizations have shown themselves to be subject to competitive forces. It is important for IT organizations to review their positions and know for sure how they provide *differentiated value* to their customers.

Customers perceive value in economic terms or in terms of social welfare, as is the case with pure public services offered by government agencies, or both. The differentiation can be in traditional terms such the organization's knowledge and experience with the customer's business, excellence in service quality, capabilities to reduce cost, or innovation.

The idea of *strategic assets* is important in the context of good practice in service management. It encourages IT organizations to think of investments in service management in the same way businesses think of investing in production systems, distribution networks, R&D laboratories, and various forms of intellectual property such as brands and patents. Assets such as people, processes, knowledge and infrastructure are by themselves valuable for the benefits they generate for their owners. Strategic assets are those that provide the basis for core competence, distinctive performance, durable advantage, and qualifications to participate in business opportunities. IT organizations can use the guidance provided by ITIL to transform their service management capabilities into strategic assets.

Having a cost advantage over competition is one among many options. Being the lowest-cost provider is necessary but not always sufficient to support business strategies. There is a need to develop other strengths over and above efficiency in costs. Helping customers enter new markets and quickly scale up operations, for example. An IT organization can better serve customers and outperform competition by better understanding the complexity, uncertainty, and trade-offs the customer is facing. The key is to decide on an objective or end-state that differentiates the value of what you offer, on what terms, and in what form so that it outperforms what customers consider to be alternatives. Strategy need not simply be an exercise in gathering requirements or the pursuit of operational effectiveness. It is a means to become *not optional*.

Formulating strategy has traditionally been in the hands of upper levels of management. Yet in the world of IT, where conditions change rapidly and the knowledge and expertise required for sound decisions are usually found on the front lines, IT leaders have an important role to play. From CIOs to front-line managers, each has the ability to shape and execute service strategies. The rigid 'plan and deploy' model is giving way to the dynamic 'engage and collaborate' model.

The ultimate success of service management is indicated by the strength of the relationship between customers and service providers. The publications of the core ITIL library provide the necessary guidance to achieve such success. In addition to this publication, the volumes Service Design, Service Transition, Service Operation and Continual Service Improvement define a body of knowledge and set of good practices for successful service management. They provide guidance for:

■ Converting innovative ideas and concepts into services for customers
■ Solving problems with effective and enduring solutions
■ Controlling costs and risks that can potentially destroy carefully created value
■ Learning from successes and failures to manage new challenges and opportunities.

The guidance can be applied by IT organizations in the public and private sectors; by for-profit and non-profit organizations; for internal service providers with cost-recovery objectives; and commercial outfits with profitability targets. Terms such as profitability, income, pricing, revenue and competition can be interpreted or substituted to be meaningful in the context of all service providers with rare exceptions. As such they are used throughout this publication with minimal annotation or clarification to avoid interrupting the flow of text.

Finally, the frequently cited objective of 'alignment with the business' characterizes a common problem faced by the leadership of IT organizations in general and CIOs in particular. Those who succeed in meeting this objective are those who understand the need to be business-minded. The increasing popularity of managed services and outsourcing places tremendous pressures on internal providers to adopt the structure and behaviour of a professionally managed business. A well-managed IT organization can act like a business within a business and deliver value that meets or exceeds the value proposition of commercial alternatives. For this reason, concepts such as utility, warranty, market spaces, portfolios and playing fields, are introduced.

1.2 CONTEXT

1.2.1 Information technology and services

Information technology (IT) is a commonly used term that changes meaning with context (Table 1.1). From the first perspective, IT systems, applications and infrastructure are components or sub-assemblies of a larger product. They enable or are embedded in processes and services. From the second perspective, IT is an organization with its own

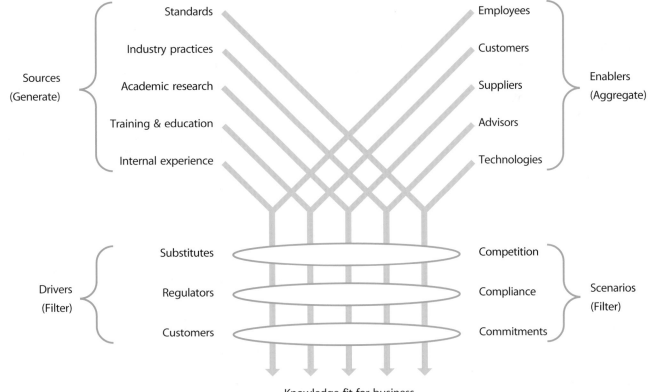

Figure 1.1 Sourcing of service management practice

set of capabilities and resources. IT organizations can be of various types such as business functions, shared services units, and enterprise-level core units.

From the third perspective, IT is a category of services utilized by business. These services are typically IT applications and infrastructure that are packaged and offered as services by internal IT organizations or external service providers. IT costs are treated as business expenses. From the fourth perspective, IT is a category of business assets that provide a stream of benefits for their owners, including but not limited to revenue, income and profit. IT costs are treated as investments. It is important to be clear what the term means in a given context. It is often used with different meanings in the same sentence or paragraph, often exacerbating problems.

1.2.2 Good practice in the public domain

Organizations operate in dynamic environments with the need to learn and adapt. There is a need to improve performance while managing trade-offs. Under similar pressure, customers seek advantage from service providers. They pursue sourcing strategies that best serve their own business interest. In many countries, government agencies and non-profit organizations have a similar propensity to outsource for the sake of operational effectiveness. This puts additional pressure on service providers to maintain a competitive advantage with respect to the alternatives that customers may have. The increase in outsourcing has exposed internal service providers in particular to unusual competition.

To cope with the pressure, organizations benchmark themselves against peers and seek to close gaps in

Table 1.1 The multiple views of IT

View	Visualization	Vernacular
IT/Component	Components of systems and processes	'Our billing system is IT-enabled.'
		'We use IT to improve interactions with our customers through self-service terminals at key locations.'
		'IT touches every part of our business. Without appropriate controls, that in itself is a risk.'
IT/Organization	Internal unit or function of the enterprise or commercial service provider	'Our IT is headed by a CIO with tremendous experience in the transportation business.'
		'Our heavily centralized IT suits our business model which more than anything requires stability and control over business operations.'
		'IT does not understand the language of our business. Much is lost in translation.'
IT/Service	Type of shared service utilized by business units	'I haven't been able to access the internet since yesterday. When do you expect the service to be restored?'
		'Our remote-access service is very secure but it is also very difficult to set up and use.'
		'We decided not to build our own enterprise applications for administrative functions. We are better off utilizing IT services provided to us under a commercial contract.'
IT/Asset	Capabilities and resources that provide a dependable stream of benefits	'IT is at the core of our business process. We use IT to create value for our customers. It is part of our core production process.'
		'Our IT investments are like Cost of Goods Sold (COGS). They are direct costs, not overheads.'
		'IT is our business.'

capabilities. One way to close such gaps is the adoption of good practices in wide industry use. There are several sources for good practices including public frameworks, standards, and the proprietary knowledge of organizations and individuals (Figure 1.1).

Public frameworks and standards are attractive when compared with proprietary knowledge:

- Proprietary knowledge is deeply embedded in organizations and therefore difficult to adopt, replicate, or transfer even with the cooperation of the owners. Such knowledge is often in the form of tacit knowledge, which is inextricable and poorly documented.
- Proprietary knowledge is customized for the local context and specific business needs to the point of being idiosyncratic. Unless the recipients of such knowledge have matching circumstances, the knowledge may not be as effective in use.
- Owners of proprietary knowledge expect to be rewarded for their long-term investments. They may make such knowledge available only under commercial terms through purchases and licensing agreements.
- Publicly available frameworks and standards such as ITIL, COBIT, CMMI, eSCM-SP, PRINCE2, ISO 9000, ISO/IEC 20000, and ISO/IEC 27001 are validated across a diverse set of environments and situations rather than the limited experience of a single organization. They are subject to broad review across multiple organizations and disciplines. They are vetted by diverse sets of partners, suppliers, and competitors.
- The knowledge of public frameworks is more likely to be widely distributed among a large community of professionals through publicly available training and certification. It is easier for organizations to acquire such knowledge through the labour market.

Ignoring public frameworks and standards can needlessly place an organization at a disadvantage. Organizations should cultivate their own proprietary knowledge on top of a body of knowledge based on public frameworks and standards. Collaboration and coordination across organizations are easier because of shared practices and standards. According to research by the UK Department of Trade and Industry (DTI), the value to the UK economy from standards is estimated to be about £2.5 billion per annum.[4]

The following public frameworks and standards are relevant to service management:

- ISO/IEC 20000
- ISO/IEC 27001

- Capability Maturity Model Integration (CMMI®)
- Control Objectives for Information and related Technology (COBIT®)
- Projects in Controlled Environments (PRINCE2®)
- Project Management Body of Knowledge (PMBOK®)
- Management of Risk (M_o_R®)
- eSourcing Capability Model for Service Providers (eSCM-SP™)
- Telecom Operations Map (eTOM®)
- Six Sigma™.

Organizations find the need to integrate guidance from multiple frameworks and standards. Expectations on the effectiveness of such integration efforts should be reasonably set as suggested by the following expert on standards:

> 'Frameworks like standards invariably form part of larger complex business systems and as such relating them to each other rigorously requires a systems discipline. Without this you are left with a few cross-references, some guidance notes, and a lot of "tacit knowledge" gluing them together.'
>
> Paul McNeillis, head of professional services at the British Standards Institution[4]

1.2.3 ITIL and good practice in service management

The context of this publication is the ITIL framework as a source of good practice in service management. ITIL is used by organizations worldwide to establish and improve capabilities in service management. ISO/IEC 20000 provides a formal and universal standard for organizations seeking to have their service management capabilities audited and certified. While ISO/IEC 20000 is a standard to be achieved and maintained, ITIL offers a body of knowledge useful for achieving the standard.

The ITIL Library has the following components:

- The ITIL Core: best practice guidance applicable to all types of organizations who provide services to a business.
- The ITIL Complementary Guidance: a complementary set of publications with guidance specific to industry sectors, organization types, operating models, and technology architectures.

The ITIL Core consists of five publications (Figure 1.2). Each provides the guidance necessary for an integrated approach as required by the ISO/IEC 20000 standard specification:

- Service Strategy

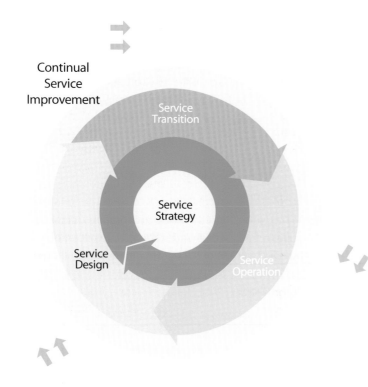

Figure 1.2 The ITIL Core

- Service Design
- Service Transition
- Service Operation
- Continual Service Improvement.

Each publication addresses capabilities having direct impact on a service provider's performance. The structure of the core is in the form of a lifecycle. It is iterative and multidimensional. It ensures that organizations are set up to leverage capabilities in one area for learning and improvements in others. The core is expected to provide structure, stability and strength to service management capabilities with durable principles, methods and tools. This serves to protect investments and provide the necessary basis for measurement, learning and improvement.

The guidance in ITIL can be adapted for use in various business environments and organizational strategies. The Complementary Guidance provides flexibility to implement the Core in a diverse range of environments. Practitioners can select Complementary Guidance as needed to provide traction for the Core in a given business context, much like tyres are selected based on the type of automobile, purpose, and road conditions. This is to increase the durability and portability of knowledge assets and to protect investments in service management capabilities.

1.2.3.1 Service Strategy

The Service Strategy volume provides guidance on how to design, develop, and implement service management not only as an organizational capability but also as a *strategic asset*. Guidance is provided on the principles underpinning the practice of service management that are useful for developing service management policies, guidelines and processes across the ITIL Service Lifecycle. Service Strategy guidance is useful in the context of Service Design, Service Transition, Service Operation, and Continual Service Improvement. Topics covered in Service Strategy include the development of markets, internal and external, service assets, Service Catalogue, and implementation of strategy through the Service Lifecycle. Financial Management, Service Portfolio Management, Organizational Development, and Strategic Risks are among other major topics.

Organizations use the guidance to set objectives and expectations of performance towards serving customers and market spaces, and to identify, select, and prioritize opportunities. *Service Strategy* is about ensuring that organizations are in a position to handle the costs and risks associated with their Service Portfolios, and are set up not just for operational effectiveness but also for distinctive performance. Decisions made with respect to Service Strategy have far-reaching consequences including those with delayed effect.

Organizations already practising ITIL may use this publication to guide a strategic review of their ITIL-based service management capabilities and to improve the alignment between those capabilities and their business strategies. This volume of ITIL encourages readers to stop and think about *why* something is to be done before thinking of *how*. Answers to the first type of questions are closer to the customer's business. Service Strategy expands the scope of the ITIL framework beyond the traditional audience of IT Service Management professionals.

1.2.3.2 Service Design

The Service Design volume provides guidance for the design and development of services and service management processes. It covers design principles and methods for converting strategic objectives into portfolios of services and service assets. The scope of Service Design is not limited to new services. It includes the changes and improvements necessary to increase or maintain value to customers over the lifecycle of services, the continuity of services, achievement of service levels, and conformance to standards and regulations. It guides organizations on how to develop design capabilities for service management.

1.2.3.3 Service Transition

The Service Transition volume provides guidance for the development and improvement of capabilities for transitioning new and changed services into operations. This publication provides guidance on how the requirements of Service Strategy encoded in Service Design are effectively realized in Service Operation while controlling the risks of failure and disruption. The publication combines practices in Release Management, Programme Management, and Risk Management and places them in the practical context of service management. It provides guidance on managing the complexity related to changes to services and service management processes, preventing undesired consequences while allowing for innovation. Guidance is provided on transferring the control of services between customers and service providers.

1.2.3.4 Service Operation

This volume embodies practices in the management of service operations. It includes guidance on achieving effectiveness and efficiency in the delivery and support of services so as to ensure value for the customer and the service provider. Strategic objectives are ultimately realized through service operations, therefore making it a critical capability. Guidance is provided on ways to maintain stability in service operations, allowing for changes in design, scale, scope and service levels. Organizations are provided with detailed process guidelines, methods and tools for use in two major control perspectives: reactive and proactive. Managers and practitioners are provided with knowledge allowing them to make better decisions in areas such as managing the availability of services, controlling demand, optimizing capacity utilization, scheduling of operations and fixing problems. Guidance is provided on supporting operations through new models and architectures such as shared services, utility computing, web services and mobile commerce.

1.2.3.5 Continual Service Improvement

This volume provides instrumental guidance in creating and maintaining value for customers through better design, introduction, and operation of services. It combines principles, practices, and methods from quality management, Change Management and capability improvement. Organizations learn to realize incremental and large-scale improvements in service quality, operational efficiency and business continuity. Guidance is provided for linking improvement efforts and outcomes with service strategy, design, and transition. A closed-loop feedback system, based on the Plan–Do–Check–Act (PDCA) model specified in ISO/IEC 20000, is established and capable of receiving inputs for change from any planning perspective.

1.3 PURPOSE

To operate and grow successfully in the long-term, service providers must have the ability to think and act in a strategic manner. The purpose of this publication is to help organizations develop such abilities. The achievement of strategic goals or objectives requires the use of strategic assets. The guidance shows how to transform service management into a strategic asset. Readers benefit from seeing the relationships between various services, systems or processes they manage and the business models, strategies or objectives they support. The guidance answers questions of the following kind:

- What services should we offer and to whom?
- How do we differentiate ourselves from competing alternatives?
- How do we truly create value for our customers?
- How do we capture value for our stakeholders?
- How can we make a case for strategic investments?
- How can Financial Management provide visibility and control over value creation?
- How should we define service quality?

- How do we choose between different paths for improving service quality?
- How do we efficiently allocate resources across a portfolio of services?
- How do we resolve conflicting demands for shared resources?

A multi-disciplinary approach is required to answer such questions. Technical knowledge of IT is necessary but not sufficient. The guidance is pollinated with knowledge from the disciplines such as operations management, marketing, finance, information systems, organizational development, systems dynamics, and industrial engineering. The result is a body of knowledge robust enough to be effective across a wide range of business environments. Some organizations are putting in place the foundational elements of service management. Others are further up the adoption curve, ready to tackle challenges and opportunities with higher levels of complexity and uncertainty.

1.4   EXPECTED USE

The Service Strategy volume is expected to be useful for IT organizations in developing capabilities in service management that set up and maintain a strategic advantage in their goals of being valuable service providers. Service Strategy covers several aspects of service management. It provides guidance useful in defining strategic objectives, providing direction for growth, prioritizing investments, and defining outcomes against which the effectiveness of service management may be measured. It is useful for influencing organizational attitudes and culture towards the creation of value for customers through services. The publication identifies objectives for effective communication, coordination, and control among various parts of a service organization having contact with customers, partners and suppliers. The knowledge in this publication is useful in determining and controlling the consequences of pursuing a particular service strategy with a given set of capabilities and resources. IT organizations are able to innovate and operate under constraints such as contractual commitments, service level requirements, and government regulations. Contracts include both formal legally binding agreements as well as informal internal agreements between parts of an organization. Strategic decisions and policies are made clear enough to every agent in the organization with a role in delivering service. High-level perspectives and positions defining service strategy are broken down into plans and actions assigned to specific roles and responsibilities in service management.

It is common practice to develop capabilities and resources that achieve strategic objectives. It is also true that strategic options considered are often constrained by capabilities at hand. Improvements and innovations can extend the range of capabilities and resources, allowing organizations to pursue new or modified objectives, in turn placing new demands on capabilities and resources. These are the dynamics of business, and service management plays an active role. Service management creates viable options for strategy and helps exercise those options through a portfolio of services. It is therefore important to understand the dependencies between strategy and service management processes.

1.4.1 Some warnings

Many problems and situations in IT resist improvement and lack predictability. At times a solution is conceived and deployed, only to present as many unintended consequences as intended ones. The long-term performance of a service or process may be frustratingly different from its short-term performance. Obvious solutions fail or worsen the situation (Figure 1.3).

Organizations find it difficult to maintain the benefits from initially successful process improvement programmes. Worse, despite the demonstrated benefits, many process improvement programmes end in failure.[5] In some puzzling instances, successful programmes worsen business performance and decrease morale. This is phenomenon is referred to as the 'Improvement Paradox'.[6]

The phrase 'People, Process, and Technology' is a useful teaching tool. A closer examination, however, reveals complexities such as time delays, dependencies, constraints and compensating feedback effects. The following are observations in the real world:

- A process improvement programme reduces the time the staff have for existing service duties, causing a decrease in service quality – exactly the opposite of intended programme goals. As quality falls, pressure to work harder increases. Pressured staff then cut back on improvement efforts.
- Funding cuts affect service quality, which in turn diminishes demand for services. The reduced demand prompts yet more funding cuts.
- Increase in service demand generates increases in operations staff. The ratio of experienced staff to new staff decreases. Less mentoring and coaching opportunities are available for the newcomers; quality of service suffers; demand for services slows; morale and productivity decrease, and staff are let go.

'Many of our service management programmes suffered from The Golden Pony. We would introduce a programme and a small number of people would immediately commit and achieve good results. Others would notice, get committed, and off goes the pony. Management would notice the results and support the program.'

'As more resources were allocated, the scope of the programme grew. It was used to do things not related to the programme. It was applied to things for which it was not designed. The programme was so popular that our training resources were overwhelmed and training became diluted. Effectiveness of the tools inevitably declined.'

'As the scope grew, the programme got more visibility. The need for direction rose in the bureaucracy. The direction soon came from such a high level that the manager in charge had no idea what the programme was really about. The quality of decision-making fell, which hurt results. So, that is what happens to the pony: it gets loaded down with stuff it was not designed to carry, the rider doesn't know what he or she is doing, and it wanders aimlessly until it dies.'

Figure 1.3 The Golden Pony (inspired by Nelson P. Repenning, MIT Sloan School of Management)

Apart from driving change through continual improvement, organizations must be prepared for rapid transitions and transformations driven by changes in an organization's environment or internal situation. Changes may be driven by mergers, acquisitions, legislation, spin-offs, sourcing decisions, actions of competitors, technology innovations and shifts in customer preferences. Service management should respond effectively and efficiently. The approach to service management provided is useful for understanding the combined effects of management decisions, dependencies, actions and their consequences.

Service management as a practice 2

2 Service management as a practice

2.1 WHAT IS SERVICE MANAGEMENT?

Service management is a set of specialized organizational capabilities for providing value to customers in the form of services. The capabilities take the form of functions and processes for managing services over a lifecycle, with specializations in strategy, design, transition, operation, and continual improvement. The capabilities represent a service organization's capacity, competency, and confidence for action. The act of transforming resources into valuable services is at the core of service management. Without these capabilities, a service organization is merely a bundle of resources that by itself has relatively low intrinsic value for customers.

> **Service management**
>
> Service management is a set of specialized organizational capabilities for providing value to customers in the form of services.

Service management capabilities are influenced by the following challenges that distinguish services from other systems of value creation such as manufacturing, mining and agriculture:

■ Intangible nature of the output and intermediate products of service processes: difficult to measure, control, and validate (or prove).

■ Demand is tightly coupled with customer's assets: users and other *customer assets* such as processes, applications, documents and transactions arrive with demand and stimulate service production.

■ High-level of contact for *producers* and *consumers* of services: little or no buffer between the customer, the front-office and back-office.

■ The perishable nature of service output and service capacity: there is value for the customer in receiving assurance that the service will continue to be supplied with consistent quality. Providers need to secure a steady supply of demand from customers.

Case study

Organizational capabilities are shaped by the challenges they are expected to overcome. An example of this is how in the 1950s Toyota developed unique capabilities to overcome the challenge of smaller scale and financial capital compared to its American rivals. Toyota developed new capabilities in production engineering, operations management and supply-chain management to compensate for limits on the size of inventories it could afford, the number of components it could make on its own, or being able to own the companies that produced them. The need for financial austerity, tight coordination, and greater dependency on suppliers led to the development of the most copied production system in the world.[7]

The characteristics described above are not universal constraints.[8] Innovative business models and technological innovation have relaxed the constraining effects of these characteristics. What matters is the need to recognize these characteristics when they do appear, and identify them as challenges in service management.

Service management is also a professional practice supported by an extensive body of knowledge, experience, and skills. A global community of individuals and organizations in the public and private sectors fosters its growth and maturity. Formal schemes that exist for the education, training and certification of practising organizations and individuals influence its quality. Industry best practices, academic research and formal standards contribute to its intellectual capital and draw from it.

The origins of service management are in traditional service businesses such as airlines, banks, hotels and telephone companies. Its practice has grown with the adoption by IT organizations of a service-oriented approach to managing IT applications, infrastructure and processes. Solutions to business problems and support for business models, strategies and operations are increasingly in the form of services. The popularity of shared services and outsourcing has contributed to the increase in the number of organizations who are service providers, including internal organizational units. This in turn has strengthened the practice of service management, at the same time imposing greater challenges on it.

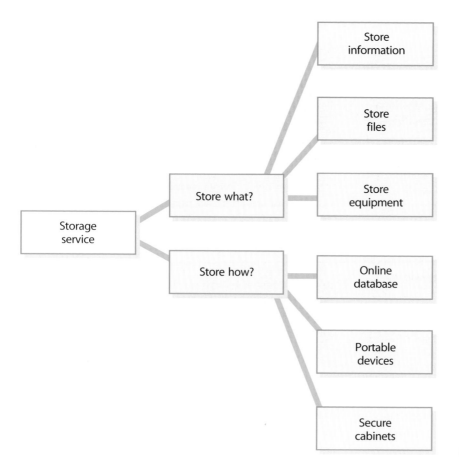

Figure 2.1 Generalized patterns and specialized instances[9]

2.2 WHAT ARE SERVICES?

2.2.1 The value proposition

Service

A service is a means of delivering value to customers by facilitating outcomes customers want to achieve without the ownership of specific costs and risks.

Services are a means of delivering value to customers by facilitating outcomes customers want to achieve without the ownership of specific costs and risks. Outcomes are possible from the performance of tasks and are limited by the presence of certain constraints. Broadly speaking, services facilitate outcomes by enhancing the performance and by reducing the grip of constraints. The result is an increase in the possibility of desired outcomes. While some services enhance performance of tasks, others have a more direct impact. They perform the task itself.

The preceding paragraph is not just a definition, as it is a recurring pattern found in a wide range of services. Patterns are useful for managing complexity, costs, flexibility and variety. They are generic structures useful to make an idea work in a wide range of environments and situations. In each instance the pattern is applied with variations that make the idea effective, economical, or simply useful in that particular case.

Take, for example, the generalized pattern of a storage system. Storage is useful for holding, organizing or securing assets within the context of some activity, task or performance. Storage also creates useful conditions such as ease of access, efficient organization or security from threats. This simple pattern is inherent in many types of storage services, each specialized to support a particular type of outcome for customers (Figure 2.1).

For various reasons, customers seek outcomes but do not wish to have accountability or ownership of all the associated costs and risks. For example, a business unit needs a terabyte of secure storage to support its online shopping system. From a strategic perspective, it wants the staff, equipment, facilities and infrastructure for a terabyte of storage to remain within its span of control. It does *not* want, however, to be accountable for all the associated costs and risks, real or nominal, actual or perceived. Fortunately, there is a group within the business with specialized knowledge and experience in

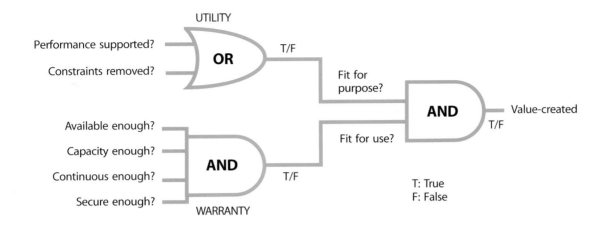

Figure 2.2 Logic of value creation through services

large-scale storage systems, and the confidence to control the associated costs and risks. The business unit agrees to pay for the storage service provided by the group under specific terms and conditions.

The business unit remains responsible for the fulfilment of online purchase orders. It is not responsible for the operation and maintenance of fault-tolerant configurations of storage devices, dedicated and redundant power supplies, qualified personnel, or the security of the building perimeter, administrative expenses, insurance, compliance with safety regulations, contingency measures, or the optimization problem of idle capacity for unexpected surges in demand. The design complexity, operational uncertainties, and technical trade-offs associated with maintaining reliable high-performance storage systems lead to costs and risks the business unit is simply not willing to own. The service provider assumes ownership and allocates those costs and risks to every unit of storage utilized by the business and any other customers of the storage service.

2.2.2 Value composition

From the customer's perspective, value consists of two primary elements: *utility* or fitness for purpose and *warranty* or fitness for use.

Utility is perceived by the customer from the attributes of the service that have a positive effect on the performance of tasks associated with desired outcomes. Removal or relaxation of constraints on performance is also perceived as a positive effect.

Warranty is derived from the positive effect being available when needed, in sufficient capacity or magnitude, and dependably in terms of continuity and security.

Utility is *what* the customer gets, and warranty is *how* it is delivered.

Customers cannot benefit from something that is fit for purpose but not fit for use, and vice versa. It is useful to separate the logic of utility from the logic of warranty for the purpose of design, development and improvement (Figure 2.2). Considering all the separate controllable inputs allows for a wider range of solutions to the problem of creating, maintaining and increasing value.

Take the case of the business unit utilizing the high-performance online storage service. For them the value is not just from the functionality of online storage but also from easy access to no less than one terabyte of fault-tolerant storage, as and when needed, with confidentiality, integrity, and availability of data. Chapter 3 of Service Strategy provides further detail on the concepts of utility and warranty.

An outcome-based definition of service moves IT organizations beyond Business-IT alignment towards Business-IT integration. Internal dialogue and discussion on the meaning of services is an elementary step towards alignment and integration with a customer's business (Figure 2.3). Customer outcomes become the ultimate concern of Product Managers instead of the gathering of requirements, which is necessary but not sufficient. Requirements are generated for internal coordination and control only after customer outcomes are well understood. Chapter 4 of Service Strategy provides detail on the practical use of outcome-based definitions.

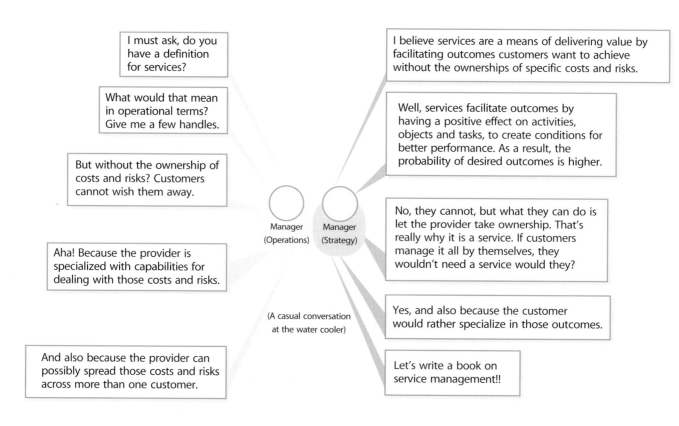

Figure 2.3 A conversation about the definition and meaning of services

Figure 2.4 Business processes apply experience, know-how and resources

2.3 THE BUSINESS PROCESS

Business outcomes are produced by business processes governed by objectives, policies and constraints. The processes are supported by resources including people, knowledge, applications and infrastructure. Workflow coordinates the execution of tasks and flow of control between resources, and intervening action to ensure adequate performance and desired outcomes. Business processes are particularly important from a service management perspective. They apply the organization's cumulative knowledge and experience to the achievement of a particular outcome (Figure 2.4).

Processes are strategic assets when they create competitive advantage and market differentiation. As a result, business processes define many of the challenges faced by service management. The nature and dynamics of the relationship between business processes and IT best explains this.

The workflow of business processes is a factor of business productivity. Business processes can span organizational and geographic boundaries, often in complex variants

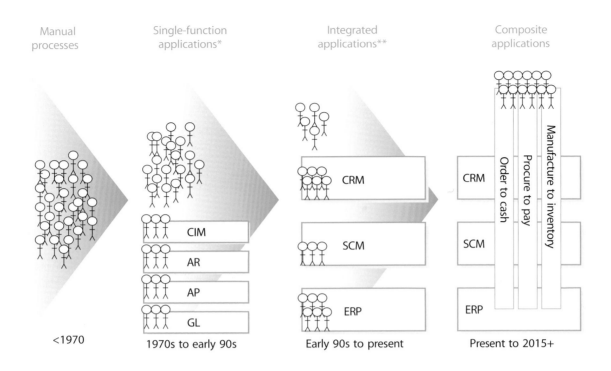

*CIM = Customer Inventory Management, AR = Accounts Receivable, AP = Accounts Payable, GL = General Ledger
**CRM = Customer Relationship Management, SCM = Supply Chain Management, ERP = Enterprise Resource Planning

Figure 2.5 The end points of a business process are often defined by enterprise applications

creating unique designs and patterns of execution (Figure 2.5). As the importance of business process has emerged, businesses have realized they must consider not only internal practices, but also their interactions with suppliers and customers. These fundamental needs form the basic motivation for the management of business processes as valuable assets.

Business managers demand IT systems that make processes more transparent, dynamically serving and expediting business process flows. End-to-end business processes have come to depend on distributed systems. Business managers challenge IT organizations to engage with them at the level of business processes. They want assurance that applications and infrastructure will support new business initiatives. However, there are coordination and cooperation problems between the two sides. Business managers may not understand the complexity and detail of creating the business process within the realm of information, applications, and infrastructure. IT managers may not have a clear understanding of exactly what business managers are trying to accomplish. The problem gets worse with complexity, duplication, and the absence of clear models for coordination and control. The following section shows how the principles of service

management are useful in solving many of these problems between the business and IT.

Process[10]

A process is a set of coordinated activities combining and implementing resources and capabilities in order to produce an outcome, which, directly or indirectly, creates value for an external customer or stakeholder.

2.4 PRINCIPLES OF SERVICE MANAGEMENT

Service management has a set of principles to be used for analysis, inference, and action in various situations involving services. These principles complement the functions and processes described elsewhere in the ITIL Core Library. When functions and processes are to be changed, these principles provide the necessary guidance and reference. When solving problems related to services, these principles are to be used to resolve ambiguity and conflict.

2.4.1 Specialization and coordination

The aim of service management is to make available capabilities and resources useful to the customer in the highly usable form of services at acceptable levels of

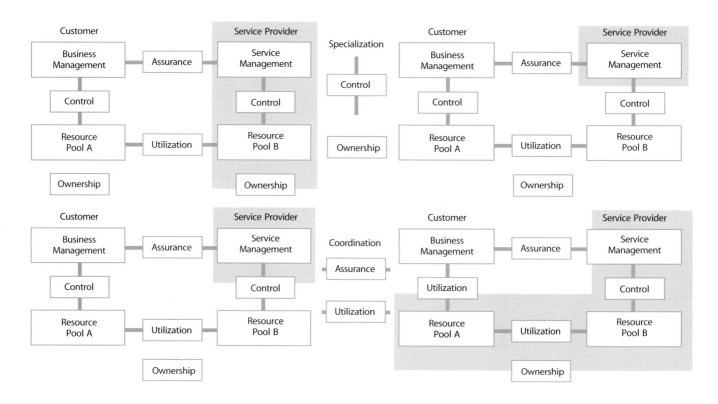

Figure 2.6 Relationships defined by the dynamics of ownership, control and utilization

quality, cost, and risks. Service providers help relax the constraints on customers of ownership and control of specific resources. In addition to the value from utilizing such resources now offered as services, customers are freed to focus on what they consider to be their core competence. The relationship between customers and service providers varies by specialization in ownership and control of resources and the coordination of dependencies between different pools of resources (Figure 2.6).

Customers specialize in business management to achieve one set of outcomes using a set of resources (Pool A). Similarly, service providers specialize in service management with another set (Pool B). Service management coordinates the dependencies between the two sides through assurances and utilization. Customers are content with utilization of certain resources (Pool B) unless ownership is a prerequisite for strategic advantage.

Specialization is a necessary condition for developing organizational capabilities. Management potential accumulates from specialized knowledge and experience with a set of resources.[11] Specialization drives the grouping of capabilities and resources under the same span of control to achieve focus, expertise, and excellence. Coordination of capabilities and resources is easier when they are under the same span of control because of accountability, authority and managerial attention. Capabilities and resources with high degree of dependency and interaction are grouped together to reduce the need for coordination.[11] Where coordination is easy through well-defined interfaces, protocols and agreements, they are placed under the control of the group most capable of managing them.[11] The strength of specialized capabilities on one side relative to the other creates the difference in potential, which justifies the transfer of resources from Pool A to Pool B and makes the case for a new or changed service.

It is important to note in this context that scale and scope of the customer and service provider organizations vary, from large enterprises to small businesses, autonomous business units and sub-divisions to small internal groups and teams who provide services. The principles remain the same. What may change are the values of variables such as the transaction costs, strategic industry factors, economies of scale and regulatory environments.

Transaction costs, the nature of resources to manage, the feasibility of encapsulating them into services, and confidence in service management drive decisions on specialization and coordination. While outsourcing is a noticeable trend, there are many instances of customers deciding to retain certain capabilities in-house or even bring them back in.

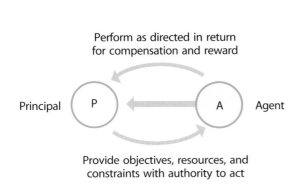

Figure 2.7 The agency model in service management

2.4.2 The agency principle

Principals employ or hire agents to act on their behalf towards some specific objectives. Agents may be employees, consultants, advisors or service providers. Agents act on behalf of principals who provide objectives, resources (or funds), and constraints for agents to act on. They provide adequate sponsorship and support for agents to succeed on their behalf. Agents act in the interest of their principals, for which they receive compensation and reward, and in their own self-interest (Figure 2.7). Written or implied contracts record this agreement between principals and agents. Employment contracts, service agreements and performance incentive plans are examples.

Within the context of service management, customers are principals who have two types of agents working for them – service providers contracted to provide services, and users of those services employed by the customer. Users need not be on the payroll of the customer. Service agents act as intermediary agents who facilitate the exchange between service providers and customers in conjunction with users. Service agents are typically the employees of the service provider but they can also be systems and processes that users interact with in self-service situations. Value for customers is created and delivered through these interlocking relationships between principals and agents. The agency model is also applied in client/server models widely used in software design and enterprise architecture. Software agents interact with users on behalf of back-end functions, processes, and systems to which they provide access.

2.4.3 Encapsulation

Customers care about affordable and reliable access to the utility of assets. They are not concerned with structural complexity, technical details, or low-level operations. They prefer simple and secure interfaces to complex configurations of resources such as applications, data, facilities, and infrastructure. Encapsulation hides what is not the customer's concern and exposes as a service what is useful and usable to them. Customers are concerned only with utilization.

Encapsulation follows three separate but closely related principles: separation of concerns, modularity, and loose coupling.

2.4.3.1 Separation of concerns

Complex issues or problems can be resolved or separated into distinct parts or concerns. Specialized capabilities and resources address each concern leading to better outcomes overall. This improves focus and allows optimization of systems and processes at a manageable scale and scope. Challenges and opportunities are suited with appropriate knowledge, skills, and experience.

It is necessary to identify persistent and recurring patterns, to separate fixed elements from those that vary, and to distinguish what from how (Figure 2.1). These separations are important for a service-oriented approach to IT management or simply service orientation. For example, it is useful to identify and consolidate demand with common characteristics but different sources and serve it with shared services.

2.4.3.2 Modularity

Modularity is a structural principle used to manage complexity in a system.[12] Functionally similar items are grouped together to form modules that are self-contained and viable. The functionality is available to other systems or modules through interfaces. Modularity contributes to efficiency and economy by reducing duplication, complexity, administrative overheads, and the cost of changes. It has a similar impact through the reuse of modules.

Encapsulation is possible at several levels of granularity, from software and hardware components to business processes and organizational design. Figure 2.8 illustrates the role of service management in encapsulating business processes and IT applications into business services and IT Services.

2.4.3.3 Loose coupling

Separation of concerns and modularity facilitate loose coupling between resources and their users. With loose coupling, it is easier to make changes internal to the resource without adversely affecting utilization. It also avoids forcing changes on the customer's side, which can add unexpected costs to the customer. Loose coupling also allows the same set of resources to be dynamically assigned to different uses. This has several advantages, including shared services, Demand Management, redundancy, and investment protection for the customer

and the service provider from reduced lock-in. Loose coupling requires good design, particularly of service interfaces, without which there will be more problems than benefits.

2.4.4 Principles of systems

System

A system is a group of interacting, interrelated, or interdependent components that form a unified whole, operating together for a common purpose.

2.4.4.1 Open-loop and closed-loop control processes

There are two types of control processes: open-loop and closed-loop. Control processes in which the value of the outcome has no influence on the process input are open-loop. Control processes in which the value of the outcome has influence (with or without some delay) on the process input in such a manner as to maintain the desired value are closed-loop. Open-loop systems take controlling action based simply on inputs. Changes in inputs result in changes in action. Effectiveness of open-loop systems depends excessively on foresight in design of all possible conditions associated with outcomes. When there are exceptions, open-loop systems are unable to cope. Control action in closed loop systems is goal driven and sensitive to disturbances or deviations.

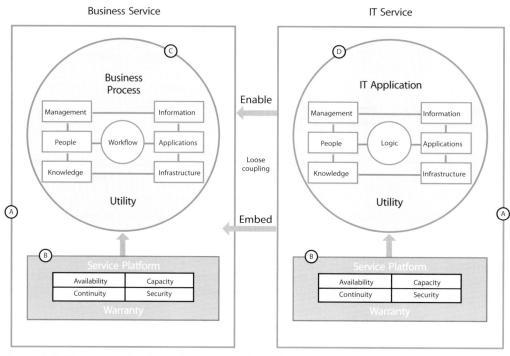

Figure 2.8 Encapsulation based on separation of concerns and modularity

Open-loop solutions attempt to solve the problem by good design, to make sure it does not occur in the first place. Once a design is implemented, mid-course corrections are not made. Closed-loop solutions, however, are based on compensating feedback. A well-designed household air-conditioner or furnace leaves the home too cool or too warm – unless regulated by the feedback of a thermostat. It is an outcome-based mindset.

Conventional brakes in automobiles apply stopping action or friction against the rotating wheels as long as the brake pedal is pressed down by the driver. Serious accidents happen when the brakes lock and cause the vehicle to lose control. To avoid this undesired situation drivers are taught not to slam the brakes, rather apply them in pumping action while constantly monitoring the braking outcome. This open-loop design expects too much of the driver's braking skills and composure by ignoring the possibility of conditioned reflexes, not taking into account the human limits of information processing, and other complicating factors such as road condition, weather, and vehicle load. Anti-lock brakes (ABS) use electronic sensors to detect the locking of brakes and loss of traction under the wheels and immediately adjust the input, cutting off and applying the braking action in rapid succession until the optimal pressure is applied on the wheels. They can override the driver's input by taking into account other factors that the driver may not be able to quickly apply. In that sense, the outcome is maintained even in the presence of rogue input.

2.4.4.2 Feedback and learning

Learning and growth are essential aspects of the way successful organizations function. Learning occurs from the presence of feedback as an input to a process in one cycle based on performance or outcome in the previous cycle. The feedback can be positive or self-reinforcing, leading to exponential growth or decline (Figure 2.9). It can be negative or self-correcting leading to balance or equilibrium. Goal-seeking behaviour is a widely observed pattern of control possible because of self-correcting feedback.

Functions, processes, and organizations can have more than one feedback loop of each type. The interaction of the feedback loops drives the behaviour of the process as it functions as a dynamic system. It is possible to visualize IT organizations as dynamic systems with functions and processes, with specialization and coordination, providing each other feedback towards the goal of meeting customer objectives. Interaction can be between processes, lifecycle phases, and functions. It is important to note that delays in negative feedback lead to oscillations or swings in the system due to intervening corrections. Improved measurement and reporting can reduce this destabilizing effect. The changes in output are not always linear or proportional to changes in input. This means that non-linearity is a widely observed characteristic of real-world systems such as service organizations. Understanding these principles helps managers correctly identify the nature of challenges and opportunities by

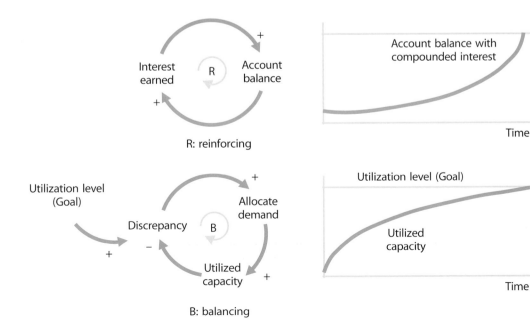

Figure 2.9 Types of feedback

observing patterns in performances and outcomes of functions and processes.

2.5 THE SERVICE LIFECYCLE

Case example 1: *Telecommunication Services*

Some time during the 1990s, a large internet service provider switched its internet service offerings from variable pricing to all-you-can-use fixed pricing. The strategic intent was to differentiate from competitor services through superior pricing plans. The service strategy worked exceedingly well – customers flocked to sign up. The outcomes, however, included large numbers of customers facing congestion or the inability to log on.

Why was there such a disconnection between the strategy and operations?

(Answer at the end of the chapter)

The Lifecycle

The architecture of the ITIL Core is based on a Service Lifecycle. Each volume of the core is represented in the Service Lifecycle (Figure 2.10). Service Design, Service Transition and Service Operation are progressive phases of the Lifecycle that represent change and transformation. Service Strategy represents policies and objectives. Continual Service Improvement represents learning and improvement.

Service Strategy (SS) is the axis around which the lifecycle rotates. Service Design (SD), Service Transition (ST), and Service Operation (SO) implement strategy. Continual Service Improvement (CSI) helps place and prioritize improvement programmes and projects based on strategic objectives.

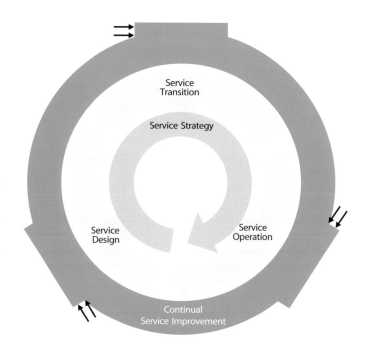

Figure 2.10 The Service Lifecycle

2.5.1 Lifecycle and systems thinking

While feedback samples output to influence future action, structure is essential for organizing unrelated information. Without structure, our service management knowledge is merely a collection of observations, practices and conflicting goals. The structure of the Service Lifecycle is an organizing framework. Processes describe how things change, whereas structure describes how they are connected. Structure determines behaviour. Altering the structure of service management can be more effective than simply controlling discrete events (Figure 2.11). Without structure, it is difficult to learn from experience. It is difficult to use the past to educate for the future. We believe we can learn from experience but we never directly confront many of the most important consequences of our actions.

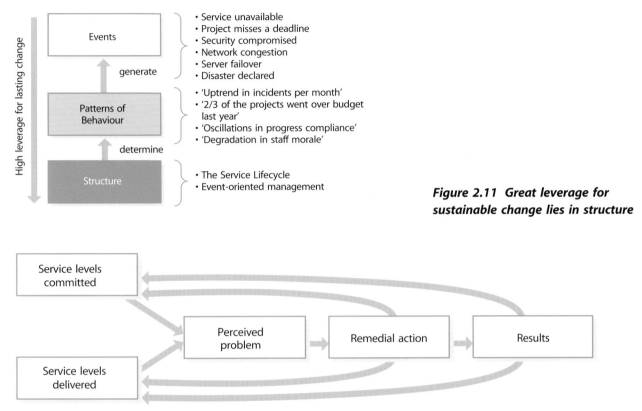

Figure 2.11 **Great leverage for sustainable change lies in structure**

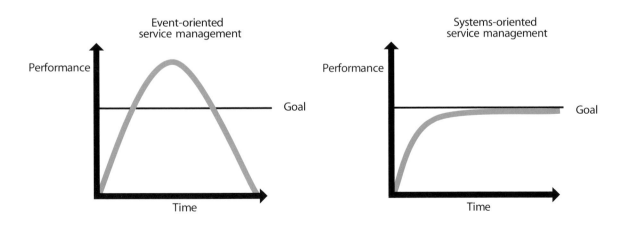

Figure 2.12 **Today's problem is often created by yesterday's solution**[13]

The Service Lifecycle is a comprehensive approach to service management: seeking to understand its structure, the interconnections between all its components, and how changes in any area will affect the whole system and its constituent parts over time (Figure 2.12). It is an organizing framework designed for sustainable performance.

A systems approach to service management ensures learning and improvement through a big-picture view of services and service management. It extends the management horizon and provides a sustainable long-term approach (Figure 2.13).

Figure 2.13 **Performance over time for differing service management structures**

2.6 FUNCTIONS AND PROCESSES ACROSS THE LIFECYCLE

2.6.1 Functions

Functions are units of organizations specialized to perform certain types of work and be responsible for specific outcomes. They are self-contained with capabilities and resources necessary for their performance and outcomes. Capabilities include work methods internal to the functions. Functions have their own body of knowledge, which accumulates from experience. They provide structure and stability to organizations.

Functions are a way of structuring organizations to implement the specialization principle. Functions typically define roles and the associated authority and responsibility for a specific performance and outcomes. Coordination between functions through shared processes is a common pattern in organization design. Functions tend to optimize their work methods locally to focus on assigned outcomes. Poor coordination between functions combined with an inward focus lead to functional silos that hinder alignment and feedback critical to the success of the organization as a whole. Process models help avoid this problem with functional hierarchies by improving cross-functional coordination and control. Well-defined processes can improve productivity within and across functions.

2.6.2 Processes

Processes that provide transformation towards a goal, and utilize feedback for self-reinforcing and self-corrective action, function as closed-loop systems (Figure 2.14). It is important to consider the entire process or how one process fits into another.

Process definitions describe actions, dependencies and sequence. Processes have the following characteristics:

- Processes are measurable – we are able to measure the process in a relevant manner. It is performance driven. Managers want to measure cost, quality and other variables while practitioners are concerned with duration and productivity.
- They have specific results – the reason a process exists is to deliver a specific result. This result must be individually identifiable and countable. While we can count changes, it is impossible to count how many Service Desks were completed. So change is a process and Service Desk is not: it is a function.
- Processes have customers – every process delivers its primary results to a customer or stakeholder. They may be internal or external to the organization but the process must meet their expectations.
- They respond to specific events – while a process may be ongoing or iterative, it should be traceable to a specific trigger.

Functions are often mistaken for processes. For example, there are misconceptions about Capacity Management being a service management process. First, Capacity Management is an organizational capability with specialized processes and work methods. Whether or not it is a function or a process depends entirely on organization design. It is a mistake to assume that Capacity Management can only be a process. It is possible to measure and control capacity and to determine

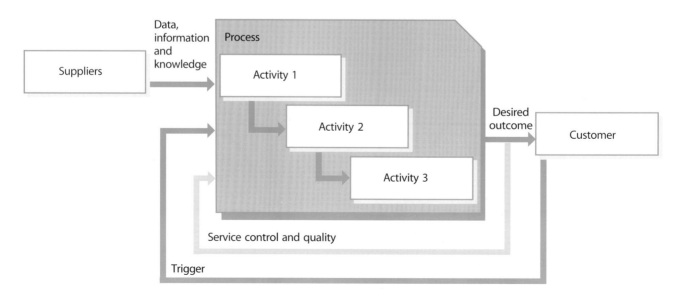

Figure 2.14 A basic process

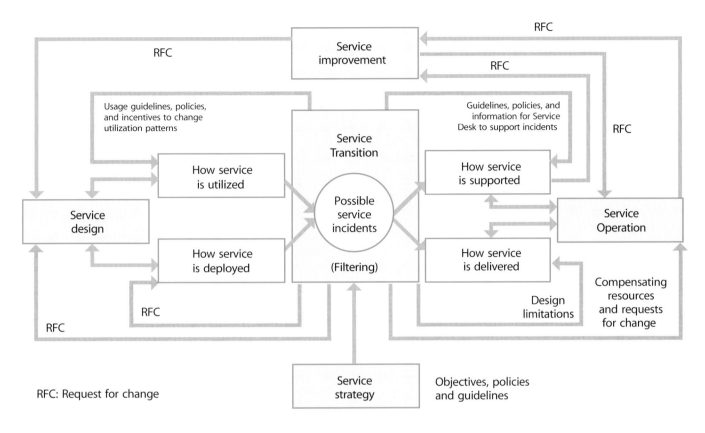

Figure 2.15 Service management processes are applied across the Service Lifecycle

whether it is adequate for a given purpose. Assuming that it is always a process with discrete countable outcomes can be an error.

2.6.3 Specialization and coordination across the lifecycle

Specialization and coordination are necessary in the lifecycle approach. Feedback and control between the functions and processes within and across the elements of the lifecycle make this possible (Figure 2.15). The dominant pattern in the lifecycle is the sequential progress starting from SS through SD-ST-SO and back to SS through CSI. That, however, is not the only pattern of action. Every element of the lifecycle provides points for feedback and control.

The combination of multiple perspectives allows greater flexibility and control across environments and situations. The lifecycle approach mimics the reality of most organizations where effective management requires the use of multiple control perspectives. Those responsible for the design, development and improvement of processes for service management can adopt a process-based control perspective. Those responsible for managing agreements, contracts, and services may be better served by a lifecycle-based control perspective with distinct

phases. Both these control perspectives benefit from systems thinking. Each control perspective can reveal patterns that may not be apparent from the other.

Case example 1 (solution): *The lack of a Service Lifecycle*

The decision to adopt the pricing strategy did not appear to be coordinated with service design, service transition or service operations, indicating a lack of holistic or systems thinking in crafting the service pricing strategy. Though strategically sound, the pricing strategy did not consider the many interrelated parts of the entire system.

Among the unintended consequences is a service strategy that appeared in the front pages of world newspapers as a colossal blunder in service management.

Service strategy principles

3

3 Service strategy principles

'People do not want quarter-inch drills. They want quarter-inch holes.'

Professor Emeritus Theodore Levitt, Harvard Business School

Case example 2: *Mobile communication services*

A well-known provider of mobile communication services has the advertising slogan, 'Can you hear me now?' Another provider has the slogan, 'Fair and Flexible'.

What dimensions of value does each slogan promote?

(Answer at the end of Section 3.1)

3.1 VALUE CREATION

3.1.1 Mind the gap

Calculating the economic value of a service can sometimes be straightforward in financial terms. In other instances, however, it is harder to quantify the value although it may still be possible to qualify it. Value is defined not only strictly in terms of the customer's business outcomes: it is also highly dependent on customer's perceptions (Figure 3.1). Perceptions are influenced by attributes of a service that are indications of value, present or prior experiences with similar attributes, and relative endowment of competitors and other peers. Perceptions are also influenced by the customer's self-image or actual position in the market, such as those of being an innovator, market leader, and risk-taker. The value of a service takes on many forms, and customers have preferences influenced by their perceptions. Definition and differentiation of value is in the customer's mind.

The more intangible the value, the more important the definitions and differentiation become. Customers are reluctant to buy when there is ambiguity in the cause-and-effect relationship between the utilization of a service and the realization of benefits. It is incumbent on providers to demonstrate value, influence perceptions, and respond to preferences.

Perceptions of value are influenced by expectations. Customers have reference values on which they base their perceptions of added value from a service. The reference value may be vaguely defined or based on hard facts. An example of reference value is the baseline that customers maintain on the cost of in-house functions or services. What matters is that it is important for the service provider to understand and get a sense of what this reference value is. This may be obtained through extensive dialogue with the customer, prior experience with the same or a similar customer, or through research and analysis available in the market. The economic value of the service is the sum of this reference value and the net difference in value the customer associates with the offered service (Figure 3.2). Positive difference comes from the utility and warranty of the service. Negative difference comes from losses suffered by the customer from utilizing the service due to poor quality or hidden costs. As stated earlier, value is defined strictly in the context of business outcomes.

Focus on business outcomes over everything else is a critical advance in outlook for many service providers. It represents a shift of emphasis from efficient utilization of resources to the effective realization of outcomes. Efficiency in operations is driven by the need for effectiveness in helping customers realize outcomes. Customers do not buy services; they buy the fulfilment of particular needs. This distinction explains the frequent disconnection between IT organizations and the businesses they serve. What the customer values is frequently different from what the IT organization believes it provides. Mind the gap.

3.1.2 Marketing mindset

What are the outcomes that matter? How are they identified and ranked in terms of customer perceptions and preferences? Effectiveness in answering such

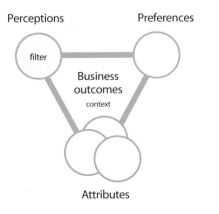

Figure 3.1 Attributes, perceptions and preferences

questions requires a marketing mindset, which is quite different from engineering and operations mindsets. Rather than focusing inward on the production of services, there is a need to look from the outside in, from the customer's perspective. A marketing mindset begins with simple questions:

■ What is our business?

■ Who is our customer?

■ What does the customer value?

■ Who depends on our services?

■ How do they use our services?

■ Why are they valuable to them?

Value can be added at different levels. What matters is the net difference (Figure 3.2). For example, service providers differentiate themselves from equipment vendors purely through added value even while using the equipment from those same vendors as assets. Differentiation can arise from the provision of communication services instead of routers and switchboards. Further differentiation may be gained from the provision of collaboration services instead of simply operating email and voice mail services. The focus shifts from attributes to the fulfilment of outcomes. With a marketing mindset it is possible to understand the components of value from the customer's perspective. As described in Section 2.2.2, value consists of two components: *utility* or fitness for purpose and *warranty* or fitness for use.

Fitness for purpose comes from the attributes of the service that have a positive effect on the performance of activities, objects, and tasks associated with desired outcomes. Removal or relaxation of constraints on performance is also perceived as a positive effect.

Fitness for use comes from the positive effect being available when needed, in sufficient capacity or magnitude, and dependably in terms of continuity and security.

It is useful to separate the logic of utility from the logic of warranty for the purpose of design, development, and improvement (Figure 2.2). Using the marketing mindset in service management provides deep insight into the challenges and opportunities related to the customer's business. Such insight is necessary for success in strategy. It is therefore critical, first and foremost, to understand the positive effect that customers perceive a service can have on their business outcomes. For customers, the positive effect is the utility of a service. The assurance of the positive effect is the warranty.

3.1.3 Framing the value of services

There is scepticism about the value realized from services when there is uncertainty in the service output. It is not good for the customer that there is certainty in costs and uncertainty in utility from one unit of output to another. When the utility of a service is not backed up by warranty, customers worry about possible losses due to poor service quality more than the possible gains from receiving the promised utility. To allay such concerns and influence customer perceptions of possible gains and losses, it is important that the value of a service is fully described in terms of utility and warranty.

The utility effect of a service is explained as the increase in possible gains from the performance of customer assets, leading to an increase in the probability of achieving outcomes (Figure 3.3). Warranty of services is explained as the decrease in possible losses for the customer from variation in performance (Figure 3.4). Customers feel more certain that every unit of demand for service will be fulfilled with the same level of utility with little variation.

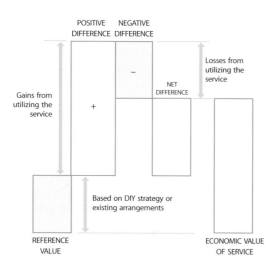

Figure 3.2 Economic value of a service[14]

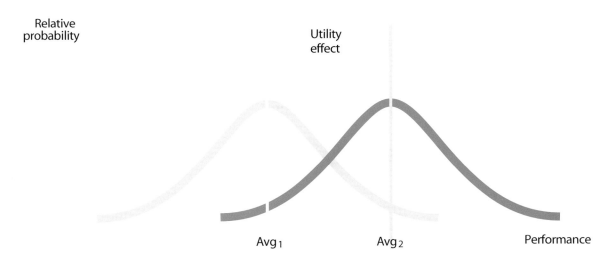

Figure 3.3 Utility increases the performance average

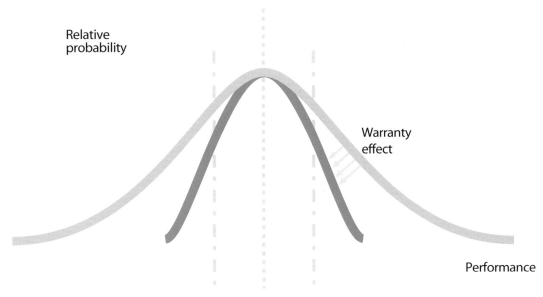

Figure 3.4 Warranty reduces the performance variation

This approach can change customer perceptions of uncertainty in the promised benefits of a service. Customers expect to see a strong link between the utilization of a service and the positive effect on the performance of their own assets, leading to higher return on assets (Figure 3.5).

A mere graphic is, however, not sufficient to convince customers. They must be assured of the actual mental mapping made by groups engaged in different parts of the Service Lifecycle. Customers may also expect evidence that policies, procedures, and guidelines are in place to uncover all costs and risks associated with service delivery and support. In the absence of such institutionalized practice, the promise of a service can just as easily turn to

peril during the course of carrying out the terms of the contract or service agreement.

3.1.4 Communicating utility

3.1.4.1 In terms of outcomes supported

Take the example of a bank that earns profit from lending money to credit-worthy customers who pay fees and interest on loans. The bank would like to disburse as many good loans as possible within a time period (desired outcome). The bank has a lending process that includes the activity of determining the credit rating of loan applicants. The bank uses a commercial credit reporting service, which is available over the phone and internet.

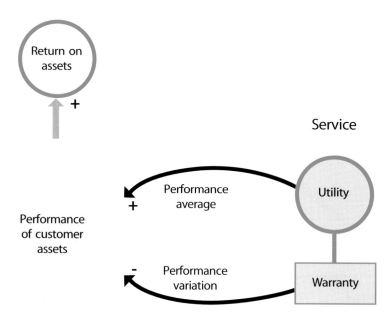

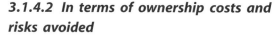

Figure 3.5 Value of a service in terms of return on assets for the customer

The service provider undertakes to supply accurate, comprehensive, and current information on loan applicants in under a minute. The lending process is the consumer of the credit report, the loan officer being the user. The utility of a credit reporting service is from the high quality of information it provides to the lending process (customer asset) to determine the credit-worthiness of borrowers, so that loan applications may be approved in a timely manner after calculating all the risks for the applicant (Figure 3.6). By reducing the time it takes to obtain good quality of information, the bank is able to have a high-performance asset in the lending process.

3.1.4.2 In terms of ownership costs and risks avoided

Value of the credit-reporting service also comes from the lending division being able to avoid certain costs and risks it would incur from operating a credit inquiry system on its own instead of using the reporting service. For example, the costs of maintaining capabilities and resources required to operate a credit reporting system would be borne entirely by the lending division. The cost per credit report would become prohibitive within the scope of the loan approval process, and would have to be passed on to the cost of the loan or be absorbed

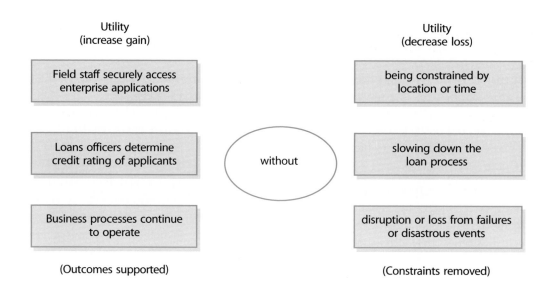

Figure 3.6 Utility framed in terms of outcomes supported and constraints removed

elsewhere within the banking system. Under prevailing conditions, buying the service turns out to be a good decision for the bank. It increases gains and reduces losses.

> An alternative strategy is for the lending division to convince other divisions within the same bank, financial services group, or industry to use its credit reporting system. This may be a viable option in which the lending division would now offer a credit reporting service to lenders along with its core service to borrowers. This is a strategic choice that has to be made by the senior managers of the lending division and their leadership at the bank. The risks of such a choice include the lending division straying from its core capabilities, inability to convince others of its competence, and attracting too little demand to make the credit reporting service economically viable.

By *using* a credit reporting service rather than *operating* a credit reporting system, the lending division is deliberately *avoiding* specific risks and costs. In effect, the lending division frees itself from certain business constraints. Sets of constraints are often traded for others provided the overall performance of the business is not lessened. Such trade-offs are made by the senior leadership of customers who are in the best position to decide. The senior leadership of service providers become business partners when they are able to support their counterparts in managing constraints on business strategies.

From the business perspective in the example above, service providers support the business strategies of their customers by removing or relaxing certain types of constraints on business models and strategies. The constraints are of the type that imposes specific costs and risks that customers wish to avoid, as follows:

- Maintaining non-core and under-utilized assets: customers would like to avoid ownership and control of assets which drain financial resources from core assets, and those used rarely or sporadically. In such cases the return on assets is typically low or uncertain, making the investments risky.
- Opportunity costs due to limited capacity and overloaded assets: assets that are overloaded are unable to serve additional units of demand or accommodate unexpected surges in demand. Insufficient capacity also means that new opportunities cannot be pursued with high probability of success.

3.1.5 Communicating warranty

Warranty ensures the utility of the service is available as needed with sufficient capacity, continuity and security.

Customers cannot realize the promised value of a service that is fit for purpose when it is not fit for use.

Warranties in general are part of the value proposition that influences customers to buy. For customers to realize the expected benefits of manufactured goods utility is necessary but not sufficient. Defects and malfunctions make a product either unavailable for use or diminish its functional capacity. Warranties assure the products will retain form and function for a specified period under certain specified conditions of use and maintenance. Warranties are void outside such conditions. Normal wear and tear is not covered. Most importantly, customers are owners and operators of purchased goods.

In the case of services, the customers are neither the owners nor the operators of service assets that provide utility. That responsibility is with service providers along with maintenance and improvements. Customers simply utilize the service. There is no wear and tear, misuse, neglect, and damage of service assets limiting the validity of warranty.

Service providers communicate the value of warranty in terms of levels of certainty. Their ability to manage service assets instils confidence in the customer about the support for business outcomes. Warranty is stated in terms of the availability, capacity, continuity and security of the utilization of services.

3.1.5.1 Availability

Availability is the most elementary aspect of assuring value to customers. It assures the customer that services will be available for use under agreed terms and conditions. The availability of a service is its most readily perceived attribute from a user's perspective. A service is available only if users can access it in an agreed manner. Perceptions and preferences vary by customer and by business context. The customer is responsible for managing the expectations and needs of its users. Within specified conditions, such as area of coverage, periods, and delivery channels, services are expected to be available to users that the customer authorizes.

Availability of a service is more subtle than a binary evaluation of available and unavailable. The customer's tolerance for graceful degradation of availability should be determined and factored into service design. For example, if a subset of users is responsible for a vital business function, service instances for these users can be hosted on dedicated resources with fault tolerance so that the customer retains some critical capability to operate.

3.1.5.2 Capacity

Capacity is an assurance that the service will support a specified level of business activity or demand at a specified level of quality. Customers drive business activity with the assurance of adequate capacity. Variations in demand are accommodated within an agreed range. Service providers undertake to maintain resources to give customers freedom from capacity shortfalls and underutilized assets. Capacity is of particular importance where the utility of the service arises from access to shared resources. Service providers help customers with shortages during periods of peak-demand.

Guaranteed capacity during particular periods or at particular locations is also valuable to customers who need to start up new or expanded operations with time-to-market as a critical success factor. Such business plans require low set-up costs and lead times. Additionally, due to the high-risks of new or expanded operations, customers may prefer not to make the investments required to own and operate business assets. Businesses that face highly uncertain demand from their own customers also find value in services on demand with little or no latency. Opportunity costs are high in terms of lost customers.

Without effective management of capacity, service providers will not be able to deliver the utility of most services. Capacity Management is a critical aspect of service management because it has a direct impact on the availability of services. The capacity available to support services also has an impact on the level of service continuity committed or delivered. Effective management of service capacity can therefore have first-order and second-order effects on service warranty.

3.1.5.3 Continuity

Continuity assures the service will continue to support the business through major failures or disruptive events. The service provider undertakes to maintain service assets that will provide a sufficient level of contingency and recovery. Specialized systems and processes will kick in to ensure that the service levels received by the customer's assets do not fall below a predefined level. Assurance also includes the restoration or normalcy in a predefined time to limit the overall impact of a failure or event. Continuity is assured primarily through redundancy and dedicated resources isolated from ripple effects.

3.1.5.4 Security

Security assures that the utilization of services by customers will be secure. This means that customer assets within the scope of service delivery and support will not be exposed to certain risks. Service providers undertake to implement general and service-level controls that will ensure that the value provided to customers is complete and not eroded by any avoidable costs and risks. Service security covers the following aspects of reducing risks:

- Authorized and accountable usage of services as specified by customer
- Protection of customers' assets from unauthorized or malicious access
- Security zones between customer assets and service assets.

Service security plays a supporting role to the other three aspects of service warranty. Effectiveness in security has a positive impact on those aspects.

Service security inherits all the general properties of the security of physical and human assets, and intangibles such as data, information, coordination, and communication. Service security has challenges imposed by the following characteristics of service management:

- Service assets are typically shared by more than one customer entity
- Value is delivered just-in-time through the orchestration of several service assets
- Customer action or inaction is a source of security risks.

3.1.6 Combined effect of utility and warranty

Value creation is the combined effect of utility and warranty. Value for customers can be increased by either of the two factors. Both are necessary: neither is sufficient by itself. Each should be considered a separate factor of value creation (Figure 3.7).

The ability to deliver a certain level of warranty to customers by itself is a basis of competitive advantage for service providers. This is particularly true where services are commoditized or standardized. In such cases, it is hard to differentiate value largely in terms of utility for customers. When customers have a choice between service providers whose services provide more or less the same utility but different levels of warranty, then they prefer the greater certainty in the support of business outcomes.

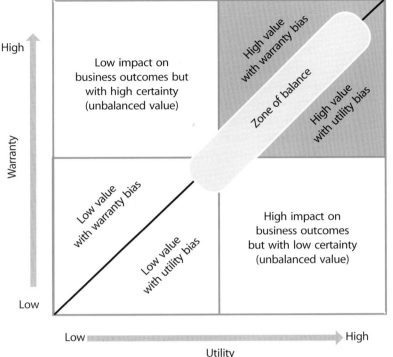

Figure 3.7 Combined effects of utility and warranty on customer assets

'Fewest calls dropped on average' is the value proposition of one major provider of mobile communication services expressed in its advertisements. An equally large competitor counteracts with the value proposition of best available coverage in the majority of urban areas. The other perpetual basis of differentiation is the number of calls made for a flat fee within peak hours of usage. This is an indirect measure of the capacity of over-subscribed service assets that service providers are assuring for the exclusive use of their customers. Of course, when competitive action leads to reduced differentiation based on warranty, service providers respond with service packages that offer additional utility, such the GPS navigation or wireless email on mobile phones.

Certain parcel delivery firms and retailers are market leaders in highly commoditized businesses simply because they offer a level of certainty unsurpassed by their peers. Their services guarantee delivery of goods on time regardless of location, time zone, or size of shipments. They are able to offer such warranties because they have developed certain service management capabilities and resources that instil a level of confidence in their operations.

Service providers should be able to develop such levels of confidence so they are able to support the business strategies of their customers. They add value to their customers by injecting this level of confidence in those strategies. Service providers emulate each other, leading to situations where providers offer similar levels of utility or

warranty. Service providers must continually improve their value propositions to break away from the pack. The improvements can drive through one or more of the service management processes.

The guidance provided in the Service Design, Service Transition, and Service Operation processes is useful in this strategic context. Service Design processes provide new and improved designs delivering better utility or better warranty. Service Transition processes ensure design improvements are directed into Service Operation while minimizing costs and risks. Service Operation processes inject the new value propositions into the customer's business by delivering higher levels of utility and warranty. The processes of Continual Service Improvement coordinate the flow of knowledge between the processes and provide feedback throughout the lifecycle.

Case example 2 (solution): *Warranty and utility*

A casual observer may quip that both provide identical services: mobile communication services. However, by adopting a marketing mindset, each provider focuses on different aspects of customer outcomes or value creation.

The slogan 'Can you hear me now?' differentiates value based on a customer's desire for warranty: service availability regardless of location.

The slogan 'Fair and Flexible' differentiates value based on a customer's desire for utility: fair pricing under a variety of service usage scenarios.

3.2 SERVICE ASSETS

'A basic code of good business behaviour is a bit like oxygen: We take an interest in its presence only when it is absent.'

Amartya Sen, Nobel Laureate in Economics

Case example 3: *Financial services*

Some time in the late 1990s, a leading financial services company launched a direct banking service. The service offered an internet-based savings and loans service.

After eight days, the company received almost 2 million website hits and over 100,000 enquiries. After five weeks, demand was so high that the company warned customers of delays of up to 28 days.

As CIO, what do you suspect is the problem?

(Answer given in Section 3.2.1)

3.2.1 Resources and capabilities

Resources and capabilities are types of assets (Figure 3.8). Organizations use them to create value in the form of goods and services. Resources are direct inputs for production. Management, organization, people, and knowledge are used to transform resources. Capabilities represent an organization's ability to coordinate, control, and deploy resources to produce value. They are typically experience-driven, knowledge-intensive, information-based, and firmly embedded within an organization's people, systems, processes and technologies. It is relatively easy to acquire resources compared to capabilities. Supplementary guidance on capabilities and resources is presented in Appendix B, Section B.1.

Case example 3 (solution): *Chokepoints in staff (overlooking customer assets)*

The constraint, it turns out, was not infrastructure capacity or availability, but a customer asset shortcoming in the form of 250 staff members. Once this chokepoint was resolved (250 hires), the company went on to win over 500,000 new customers and £5B in deposits in less than six months.

The performance or growth of services will ultimately be limited either by limits in a resource or capability, or its own potential. Attempts to push a service beyond a resource or capability limit can have strong consequences – often negating any benefits achieved.

The constraint, in this case, did not appear to be technology-related. They were account processors. The CIO missed it because he only considered service assets, overlooking the constraining effect of customer assets on the performance of his organization's services. The CIO's customer, in this case, includes the processing department.

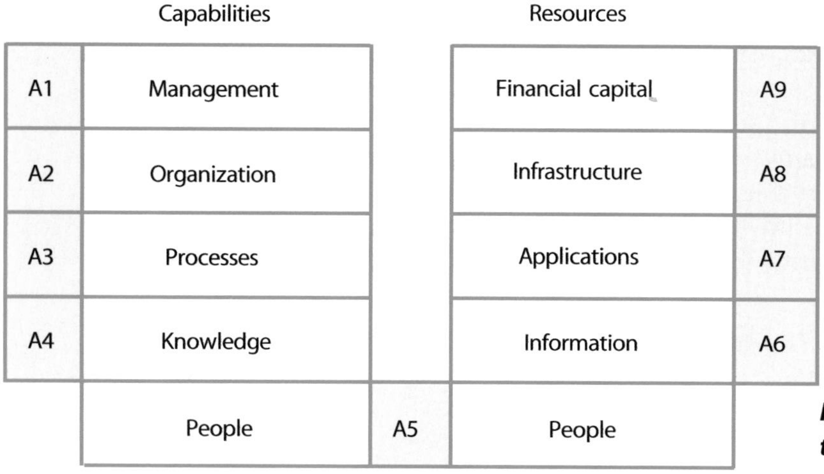

Capabilities			Resources	
A1	Management		Financial capital	A9
A2	Organization		Infrastructure	A8
A3	Processes		Applications	A7
A4	Knowledge		Information	A6
	People	A5	People	

Figure 3.8 Resources and capabilities are the basis for value creation

Capabilities are developed over time. The development of distinctive capabilities is enhanced by the breadth and depth of experience gained from the number and variety of customers, market spaces, contracts, and services. Experience is similarly enriched from solving problems, handling situations, managing risks, and analysing failures. For example, the combination of experience in a market space, reputation among customers, long-term contracts, subject matter experts, mature processes, and infrastructure in key locations, results in distinctive capabilities difficult for alternatives to offer. This assumes the organization captures knowledge and feeds it back into its management systems and processes. Investments in learning capabilities are particularly important for service providers for the development of strategic assets (See Section 4.3).

Service providers need to develop distinctive capabilities to retain customers with value propositions that are hard for competitors to duplicate. For example, two service providers may have similar resources such as applications, infrastructure, and access to finance. Their capabilities, however, differ in terms of management systems, organization structure, processes, and knowledge assets.

This difference is reflected in actual performance.

Capabilities by themselves cannot produce value without adequate and appropriate resources. The productive capacity of a service provider is dependent on the resources under its control. Capabilities are used to develop, deploy and coordinate this productive capacity. For example, capabilities such as Capacity Management and Availability Management are used to manage the performance and utilization of processes, applications and infrastructure, ensuring service levels are effectively delivered.

3.2.2 Business units and service units

3.2.2.1 The business unit

A business unit is simply a bundle of assets meant to create value for customers in the form of goods and services (Figure 3.9). Customers pay for the value they receive, which ensures that the business unit maintains an adequate return on assets. The relationship is good as long as the customer receives value and the business unit recovers costs and receives some form of compensation or profit.

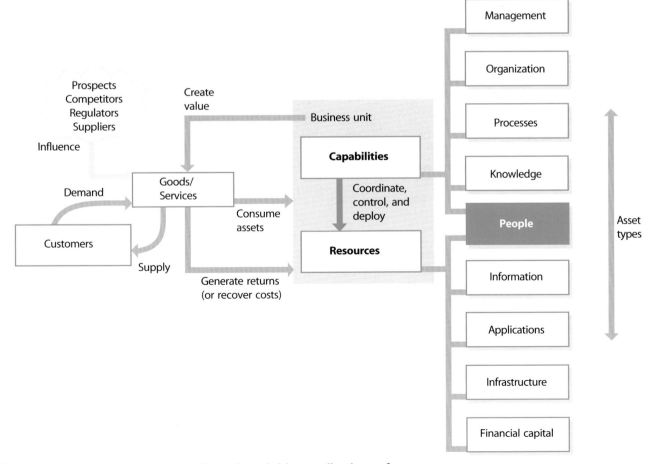

Figure 3.9 Business units are coordinated goal-driven collections of assets

The business unit's capabilities coordinate, control, and deploy its resources to create value. Value is always defined in the context of customers. Some services simply increase the resources available to the customer. For example, a storage service may assure that a customer's business systems can achieve a particular level of throughput in transaction processing with the availability of adequate, error-free and secure storage of transaction data. The storage service simply increases the capacity of the system, although one might argue that it actually enables the capability of high-volume transaction processing. Other services increase the performance of customer's management, organization, people and processes. For example, a news-feed service provides real-time market data to be used by traders to make better and quicker decisions on trades.

The relationship with customers becomes strong when there is a balance between value created and returns generated. The catalogue of goods and services amplifies the effect and strengthens the capabilities and resources of the business unit. Better returns or cost recovery allow for greater investments in capabilities and resources. The resources and capabilities complement each other.

> **Understanding the customer's business**
>
> **Back at the office**
>
> Pick a customer and carefully analyse their business to understand the ecosystem in which they operate. What conditions make the customer's business grow? How do your services create or sustain such conditions? What challenges and opportunities does their business face? How do your services help your customer address them?
>
> *Suggestion: Visualize the ecosystem diagram with the various boxes and connectors that constitute the closed-loop system for creating and sustaining value.*

The business unit could be part of an organization in the public or private sectors. Instead of revenue from sales there could be revenue from taxes collected. Instead of profits there could be surpluses. The customers of the business unit could be internal or external to the organization.

3.2.2.2 The service unit

Service units are like business units, a bundle of service assets that specializes in creating value in the form of services (Figure 3.10). Services define the relationship between business units and service units. In many instances, business units (customers) and service units are part of the same organization. In other instances service units are separate legal entities.

There are many possible relationships between business units and service units (Figure 3.11). In the example below, Service X is provided to Business Unit A by Enterprise 2. It is hosted by Service Unit 1 and Service Unit 2. Service Y is provided to Enterprise 1 by Service Unit 2. It is shared by Business Units A, B and C. Demand for Service Y is consolidated across Enterprise 1. By pooling demand across the business units, Enterprise 1 negotiates better terms and conditions for Service Y, including pricing discounts. Enterprise 2 is willing to accept those terms and conditions because consolidated demand represents a lower risk of poor return on assets for Service Unit 2 – thereby reaching the break-even point sooner.

Service Z is provided to Business Unit D by Service Unit 3, both of which exist within Enterprise 3. Service Unit 3 commercially offers Service Z to the business units of Enterprise 1. This increases the return on assets required for the service and potentially reduces the unit costs of providing the service internally to Business Unit D.

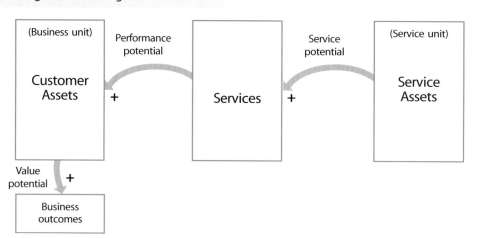

Figure 3.10 Customer assets are the basis for defining value

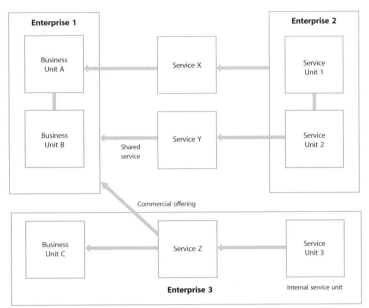

Figure 3.11 Common relationships between business units and service units

Customers and service providers are usually a part of a larger value chain or value network. Customers have their own customers to serve, and service providers are in turn served by their service providers.

3.3 SERVICE PROVIDER TYPES

'There is no such thing as a service industry. There are only industries whose service components are greater or less than those of other industries. Everybody is in service.'

Professor Emeritus Theodore Levitt, Harvard Business School

Case example 4: *Infrastructure services*

Some time in the late 1990s, the internal IT Service Provider for a global conglomerate decided to source all data centre operations to external service providers. The primary driver was lower costs. Five years and several mergers and acquisitions later, and despite having achieved its cost reductions, the internal provider is considering in-sourcing all data centre operations.

What do you suspect is the reason?

(Answer at the end of Section 3.3)

It is necessary to distinguish between different types of service providers. While most aspects of service management apply equally to all types of service providers, others such as customers, contracts, competition, market spaces, revenue and strategy take on different meanings depending on the type. There are three archetypes of business models service providers:

- Type I – internal service provider
- Type II – shared services unit
- Type III – external service provider

3.3.1 Type I (internal service provider)

Type I providers are typically business functions embedded within the business units they serve. The business units themselves may be part of a larger enterprise or parent organization. Business functions such as finance, administration, logistics, human resources, and IT provide services required by various parts of the business. They are funded by overheads and are required to operate strictly within the mandates of the business. Type I providers have the benefit of tight coupling with their owner-customers, avoiding certain costs and risks associated with conducting business with external parties.

The primary objectives of Type I providers are to achieve functional excellence and cost-effectiveness for their business units.[11] They specialize to serve a relatively narrow set of business needs. Services can be highly customized and resources are dedicated to provide relatively high service levels. The governance and administration of business functions are relatively straightforward. The decision rights are restricted in terms of strategies and operating models. The general managers of business units make all key decisions such as the portfolio of services to offer, the investments in capabilities and resources, and the metrics for measuring performance and outcomes.

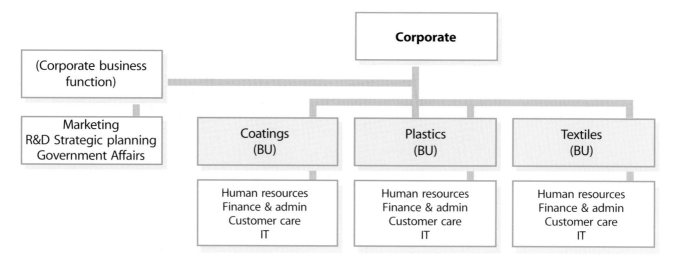

Figure 3.12 Type I providers

Type I providers operate within internal market spaces. Their growth is limited by the growth of the business unit they belong to. Each business unit (BU) may have its own Type I provider (Figure 3.12). The success of Type I providers is not measured in terms of revenues or profits because they tend to operate on a cost-recovery basis with internal funding. All costs are borne by the owning business unit or enterprise.

Competition for Type I providers is from providers outside the business unit, such as corporate business functions, who wield advantages such as scale, scope, and autonomy. In general, service providers serving more than one customer face much lower risk of market failure. With multiple sources of demand, peak demand from one source can be offset by low demand from another. There is duplication and waste when Type I providers are replicated within the enterprise.

To leverage economies of scale and scope, Type I providers are often consolidated into a corporate business function when there is a high degree of similarity in their capabilities and resources. At this level of aggregation Type I providers balance enterprise needs with those at the business unit level. The trade-offs can be complex and require a significant amount of attention and control by senior executives. As such, consolidated Type I providers are more appropriate where classes of assets such as IT, R&D, marketing or manufacturing are at the core of the organization's competitive advantage and therefore need careful control.

3.3.2 Type II (shared services unit)

Functions such as finance, IT, human resources, and logistics are not always at the core of an organization's

competitive advantage. Hence, they need not be maintained at the corporate level where they demand the attention of the chief executive's team.[11] Instead, the services of such shared functions are consolidated into an autonomous special unit called a shared services unit (SSU) (Figure 3.13). This model allows a more devolved governing structure under which SSU can focus on serving business units as direct customers. SSU can create, grow, and sustain an internal market for their services and model themselves along the lines of service providers in the open market. Like corporate business functions, they can leverage opportunities across the enterprise and spread their costs and risks across a wider base. Unlike corporate business functions, they have fewer protections under the banner of strategic value and core competence. They are subject to comparisons with external service providers whose business practices, operating models and strategies they must emulate and whose performance they should approximate if not exceed. Performance gaps are justified through benefits received through services within their domain of control.

Customers of Type II are business units under a corporate parent, common stakeholders, and an enterprise-level strategy. What may be sub-optimal for a particular business unit may be justified by advantages reaped at the corporate level for which the business unit may be compensated. Type II can offer lower prices compared to external service providers by leveraging corporate advantage, internal agreements and accounting policies. With the autonomy to function like a business unit, Type II providers can make decisions outside the constraints of business unit level policies. They can standardize their service offerings across business units and use market-based pricing to influence demand patterns.

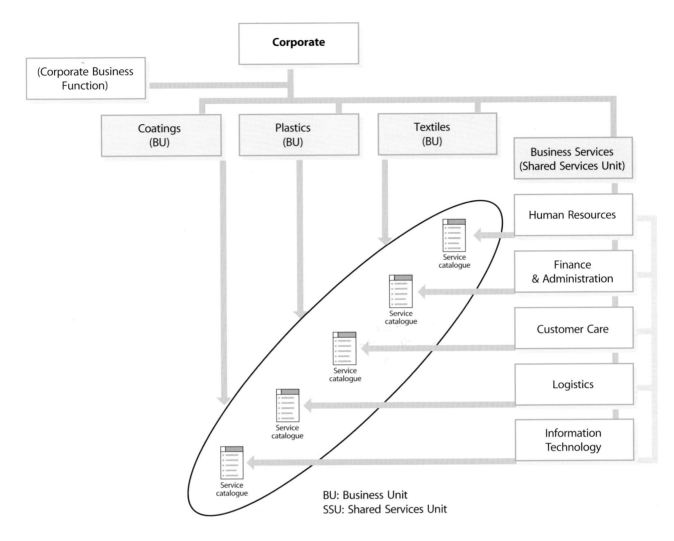

Figure 3.13 Common Type II providers

Market-based pricing

With market-based pricing there is minimal need for complex discussions and negotiations over specific requirements, technologies, resource allocations, architectures, and designs (that would be necessary with Type I arrangements) because the prices would drive adjustments, self-corrections and optimization on both sides of the value equation.

While Type II providers benefit from a relatively captive internal market for their services, their customers may still evaluate them in comparison with external service providers. This balance is crucial to the effectiveness of the shared services model. It also means that poorly performing Type II providers face the threat of substitution. This puts pressure on the leadership to adopt industry best practices, cultivate market spaces, formulate business strategies, strive for operational effectiveness, and develop

distinctive capabilities. Industry-leading shared services units have successfully been spun off by their parents as independent businesses competing in the external market. They become a source of revenues from the initial charter of simply providing a cost advantage.

3.3.3 Type III (external service provider)

The business strategies of customers sometimes require capabilities readily available from a Type III provider. The additional risks that Type III providers assume over Type I and Type II are justified by increased flexibility and freedom to pursue opportunities. Type III providers can offer competitive prices and drive down unit costs by consolidating demand. Certain business strategies are not adequately served by internal service providers such as Type I and Type II. Customers may pursue sourcing strategies requiring services from external providers. The motivation may be access to knowledge, experience, scale, scope, capabilities, and resources that are either beyond the reach of the organization or outside the scope of a carefully considered investment portfolio. Business strategies often require reductions in the asset base, fixed costs, operational risks, or the redeployment of financial assets. Competitive business environments often require customers to have flexible and lean structures. In such cases it is better to buy services rather than own and operate the assets necessary to execute certain business functions and processes. For such customers, Type III is the best choice for a given set of services (Figure 3.14). The experience of such providers is not limited to any one enterprise or market. The breadth and depth of such experience is often the single most distinctive source of value for customers. The breadth comes from serving multiple types of customers or markets. The depth comes from serving multiples of the same type.

From a certain perspective, Type III providers are operating under an extended large-scale shared services model. They assume a greater level of risk from their customers compared to Type I and Type II. But their capabilities and resources are shared by their customers – some of whom may be rivals. This means that rival customers have access to the same bundle of assets, thereby diminishing any competitive advantage those assets bestowed.

Security is always an issue in shared services environments. But when the environment is shared with competitors, security becomes a larger concern. This is a driver of additional costs for Type III providers. As a counter-balance, Type III providers mitigate a type of risk inherent to Types I and II: business functions and shared service units are subject to the same system of risks as their business unit or enterprise parent. This sets up a vicious cycle, whereby risks faced by the business units or the enterprise are transferred to the service units and then fed back with amplification through the services utilized. Customers may reduce systemic risks by transferring them

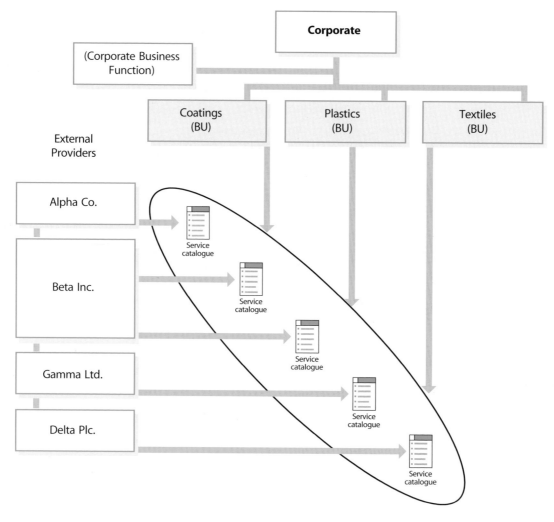

Figure 3.14 Type III providers

to external service providers who spread those risks across a larger value network.

3.3.4 How do customers choose between types?

From a customer's perspective there are merits and demerits with each type of provider. Services may be sourced from each type of service provider with decisions based on transaction costs, strategic industry factors, core competence, and the risk management capabilities of the customer. The principles of specialization and coordination costs apply.

The principle of transaction costs is useful for explaining why customers may prefer one type of provider to another. Transaction costs are overall costs of conducting a business with a service provider. Over and above the purchasing cost of services sold, they include but are not limited to the cost of finding and selecting qualified providers, defining requirements, negotiating agreements, measuring performance, managing the relationship with suppliers, cost of resolving disputes, and making changes or amends to agreements.

Additionally, whether customers keep a business activity in-house (aggregate) or decide to source it from outside (disaggregate) depends on answers to the following questions.[15]

- Does the activity require assets that are highly specialized? Will those assets be idle or obsolete if that activity is no longer performed? (If yes, then disaggregate.)
- How frequently is the activity performed within a period or business cycle? Is it infrequent or sporadic? (If yes then disaggregate.)

- How complex is the activity? Is it simple and routine? Is it stable over time with few changes? (If yes, then disaggregate.)
- Is it hard to define good performance? (If yes, then aggregate.)
- Is it hard to measure good performance? (If yes, then aggregate.)
- Is it tightly coupled with other activities or assets in the business? Would separating it increase complexity and cause problems of coordination? (If yes, then aggregate.)

Based on the answers to those questions, customers may decide to switch between types of service providers (Figure 3.15). Answers to the questions themselves may change over time depending on new economic conditions, regulations, and technological innovation. Transaction costs are discussed further under the topics of Strategy, tactics and operations (Chapter 7), Service structures (Section 3.4) and Challenges and opportunities (Chapter 9).

Customers may adopt a sourcing strategy that combines the advantages and mitigates the risks of all three types. In such cases, the value network supporting a customer cuts across the boundaries of more than one organization. As part of a carefully considered sourcing strategy, customers may allocate their needs across the different types of service providers based on whichever type best provides the business outcomes they desire. Core services are sought from Type I or Type II providers, while supplementary services enhancing core services are sought from Type II or Type III providers.

In a multi-sourced environment, the centre of gravity of a value network rests with the type of service provider

From/To	Type I	Type II	Type III
Type I	Functional reorganization	Disaggregation	Outsourcing
Type II	Aggregation	Corporate reorganization	Outsourcing
Type III	Insourcing	Insourcing	Value net reconfiguration

Figure 3.15 Customer decisions on service provider types

dominating the sourcing portfolio. Figure 3.15 shows the range of sourcing options available to customers based on the types of service providers between which controls are transferred. Outsourcing or disaggregating decisions move the centre of gravity away from the corporate core. Aggregation or in-sourcing decisions move the centre of gravity closer to the corporate core and are driven by the need to maintain firm-specific advantages unavailable to competitors. Certain decisions do not shift the centre of gravity but rather reallocate services between service units of the same type.

The sourcing structure may be altered due to changes in the business fundamentals of the customer, making one type of service provider more desirable than the other. For example, a customer merger or acquisition may dramatically alter the economics that underpin a hitherto sound sourcing strategy; see Case Example 4. The customer decides to in-source an entire portfolio of services now to be offered by a newly acquired Type I or Type II.

3.3.5 The relative advantage of incumbency

Lasting relationships with customers allow organizations to learn and improve. Fewer errors are made, investments are recovered, and the resulting cost advantage can be leveraged to increase the gap with competition (Figure 3.16).

Customers find it less attractive to turn away from well-performing incumbents because of switching costs. Experience can be used to improve assets such as processes, knowledge, and the competencies that are strategic in nature.

Service providers must therefore focus on providing the basis for a lasting relationship with customers. It requires them to exercise strategic planning and control to ensure that common objectives drive everything, knowledge is shared effectively between units, and experience is fed back into future plans and actions for a steeper learning curve.

Case example 4 (solution): *Newly acquired service provider types*

The Type II provider for the conglomerate had achieved its cost reductions through a relationship with a Type III. As a result of mergers and acquisitions activity, however, the company grew to include additional Type I providers.

When the company re-examined its service strategy, it realized it could in-source and consolidate all service providers into a single Type II – at a lower cost and with an enhanced technological distinctiveness unavailable from any Type III.

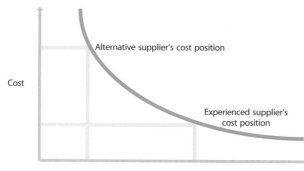

Figure 3.16 Advantage of being a well-performing incumbent

3.4 SERVICE STRUCTURES

'All models are wrong, but some of them are useful.'

George Box, statistician

Case example 5: *Commerce services*

A web-commerce company thrives despite a severe economic slowdown. The business model, based on online auctions, is profitable. However, the business model does not explain why its services succeed in creating sustainable value as other sites fail.

Process flows fail to provide insight. A value net analysis, however, reveals the distinctiveness between the auctioneer and its competitors.

What did the value net reveal about the services that a process flow could not?

(Answer in Section 3.4.1)

3.4.1 From value chains to value networks

Business executives have long described the process of creating value as links in a value chain. This model is based on the industrial age production line: a series of value-adding activities connecting an organization's supply side with its demand side. Each service provides value through a sequence of events leading to the delivery, consumption and maintenance of that particular service. By analysing each stage in the chain, senior executives presumably find opportunities for improvements.

Much of the value of service management, however, is intangible and complex. It includes knowledge and benefits such as technical expertise, strategic information, process knowledge and collaborative design. Often the value lies in how these intangibles are combined, packaged, and exchanged. Linear models have shown themselves to be inadequate for describing and understanding the complexities of value for service management, often treating information as a supporting element rather than as a source of value. Information is used to monitor and control rather than to create new value.

Case example 5 (solution): *Commerce services*

Most services focus on making a profit or performing social benefits. A value net analysis revealed the online auctioneer did both.

The value net revealed a hidden participant and their intangible exchanges: hobbyists. Hobbyists discovered they could take part in the auctioneer's micro-economy. They became professional participants with their own value capture. They created a sense of community, loyalty, feedback mechanisms and referrals.

By indirectly creating prosperity for the hobbyists, the auctioneer created prosperity for itself. The auctioneer used this insight to create a new class of services directed at hobbyists.

Value chains remain an important tool. They provide a strategy for vertically integrating and coordinating the dedicated assets required for product development. The framework focuses on a linear model but as discussed throughout this publication, linear models are seldom ideal for the complexities of service management. In this case, it is the assembly line metaphor. Upstream suppliers add value and then pass it down to the next actor downstream. This approach assumes that definitions and needs are stable and well understood. If there was a problem or delay, it was because of a weak or missing link in the chain. In this traditional service model, there are three roles: the business, the service provider and the supplier. The service provider acquires goods and services from its suppliers and assembles them to produce new services to meet the needs of the business. The business, or customer, is the last link in the chain.

The economics for linear models is based on the law of averages. If the aggregate cost of a service is competitive, then seeking a cost advantage at every link in the chain is not required or even feasible. In the day-to-day practice of manufacturing, for example, it is not practical to break down processes into independently negotiated transactions. Tight coupling is the nature of the chain.

Global sourcing and modern distribution technologies, however, have undermined this logic. A service provider no longer has the luxury of compensating for weak performance in one area with the strength of another. Further, there are often many actors performing intermediary and complementary functions who are not reflected. Also, most important in a service strategy, the focus must be on the value creating system itself, rather than the fixed set of activities along a chain.

It is important to understand the most powerful force to disrupt conventional value chains: the low cost of information. Information was the glue that held the vertical integration. Getting the necessary information to suppliers and service providers has historically been expensive, requiring dedicated assets and proprietary systems. These barriers to entry gave value chains their competitive advantage. Through the exchange of open and inexpensive information, however, businesses can now make use of resources and capabilities without owning them.

Lower transaction costs allow organizations to control and track information that would have been too costly to capture and process just years ago. Transaction costs still exist, but are increasingly more burdensome within the organization than without. This in turn has created new opportunities for collaboration between service providers and suppliers. The end result is a flexible mix of mechanisms that undermine the rigid vertical integration. New strategies are now available to service providers:

■ Marshal external talent – no single organization can organically produce all the resources and capabilities required within an industry. Most innovation occurs outside the organization.

■ Reduce costs – produce more robust services in less time and for less expense than possible through conventional value-chain approaches. If it is less expensive to perform a transaction within the organization, keep it there. If it is cheaper to source externally, take a second look. An organization should contract until the cost of an internal transaction no longer exceeds the cost of performing the transaction externally. This is a corollary to 'Coase's Law': a firm tends to expand until the costs of organizing an extra transaction within the firm become equal to the costs of carrying out the same transaction on the open market. The concept of Coase's law was first developed by Tapscott.[16]

■ Change the focal point of distinctiveness – by harnessing external talent, an organization can redeploy its own resources and capabilities to enhance services better suited to its customer or market space. Take the case of a popular North American sports league and its Type I service provider. By harnessing the capabilities of Type III infrastructure service providers, the Type I is free to redeploy its capabilities to enhance its new media services, namely, web-based services with state-of-the-art streaming video, ticket sales, statistics, fantasy leagues and promotions.

■ Increase demand for complementary services – an organization, particularly a Type I, may lack the breadth of services offered by Type II and Type III service providers. By acting as a service integrator, such organizations not only remedy the gap but boost demand through complementary offerings.

■ Collaborate – as transaction costs drop, collaboration is less optional. There are always more smart people outside an organization than inside.

Value network

A value network is a web of relationships that generates tangible and intangible value through complex dynamic exchanges through two or more organizations.

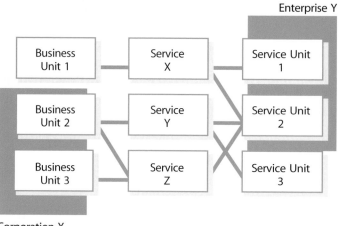

Figure 3.17 Generic value network

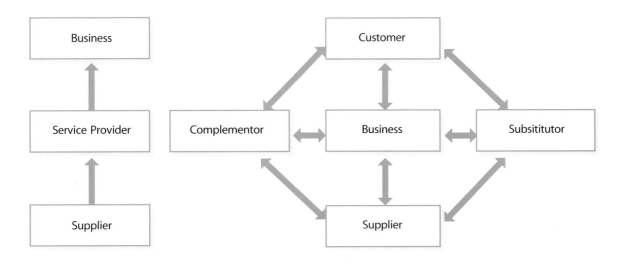

Figure 3.18 Basic value chain and value network

Once we view service management as patterns of collaborative exchanges, rather than an assembly line, it is apparent that our idea of value creation is due for revision. From a systems thinking perspective it is more useful to think of service management as a value network or net. Any group of organizations engaged in both tangible and intangible exchanges is viewed as a value network (Figures 3.17 and 3.18), whether or not they are in the same self-contained enterprise, whether private industry or public sector.

Take, for example, the financial services industry. Brokerage services leveraged IT to provide customers with market access, real-time market data and the ability to execute trades. The costs of computing, network and data were high, creating significant barriers to entry for competitors. The value proposition was based on the ability to perform these services reliably and securely.

Online brokerages, however, disaggregated these services from the proprietary systems. The same services are offered to their customers, but are now aggregated through intermediaries. The online brokerages do not own the computing, the networks or the real-time data. The value proposition is based on the services provided to the customer, not the activities performed. As a result of this strategy, the design, operations and improvement of services are performed in ways radically different from previous models.

3.4.2 Service systems

Services are often characterized by complex networks of value flows and forms of value, often involving many parties that influence each other in many ways. Value nets

serve to communicate the model in a clear and simple way. They are designed to leverage external capabilities. These sources complement the core enterprise within a business. Despite many actors, the services operate with the efficiency of a self-contained enterprise, operating on a process rather than an organizational basis. The core enterprise is the central point of execution, rather than one actor in a chain, and is responsible for the whole value network. This includes the infrastructure by which other business partners can collaborate to deliver goods and services. Intangible exchanges are not just activities that support the service; they are the service.

First consider customer expectation. Only then consider the resources and capabilities required to deliver services. This model requires high-performance information flows, not rigid supply chains. Not too long ago, business employees were the only consumers of its IT services. The pervasive examples of banking ATMs, airport kiosks, and online reservation systems illustrate this is no longer the case. Collaborative services such as Wikipedia, YouTube and Second Life suggest increasing levels of sophistication in customer interactions. As customers and suppliers become the direct users of IT Services, the expectations and requirements become more demanding – requiring a value net approach.

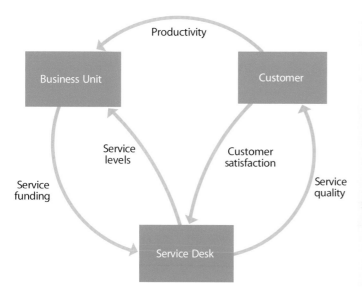

Figure 3.19 Example value network

In a value net diagram, an arrow designates a transaction. See Figure 3.19. The direction of the arrow denotes the direction of the transaction or impact on a participant: service provider or customer. Transactions can be temporary. They may include deliverables, tangible or intangible. Dotted arrows can be used to distinguish intangible transactions.

The following questions are useful in constructing and analysing the dynamics of a service model. See Figure 3.20.

■ Who are all the participants in the service?
■ What are the overall patterns of exchange or transactions?
■ What are the impacts or deliverables of each transaction on each participant?
■ What is the best way to generate value?

Case example 6: *Service Desk*

A Type I provider for a healthcare business unit performed an assessment of their Service Desk. A map of the Service Desk process was developed: Figure 3.21. This flow chart described how the Service Desk function worked. While the flow chart looked orderly, the experience of the staff did not match the documented flow. A value net analysis was subsequently performed.

The staff described informal processes used to manoeuvre around the constraints of the process model. The informal processes were needed in order to be effective. Newcomers to the staff predictably took longer to become effective as they learned these undocumented ways to do things.

The analysis moved the focus away from the linear depiction of the process. Rather, it focused on the people who were fulfilling different roles. It became apparent that simple steps on the flowchart were complex instead. They involved multiple staff members and required continuing activities throughout the entire process: Figure 3.22.

The value net appeared messy. But staff agreed that it accurately described how the Service Desk really worked. The analysis captured the intangibles for which staff were accountable but were not reflected in the flow chart.

The goal was not to replace process modelling or to map the entire organization. The method was used to describe a complex, non-linear process that had been artificially forced into the linear flow diagram.

Figure 3.20 Unit of analysis for value nets in service management

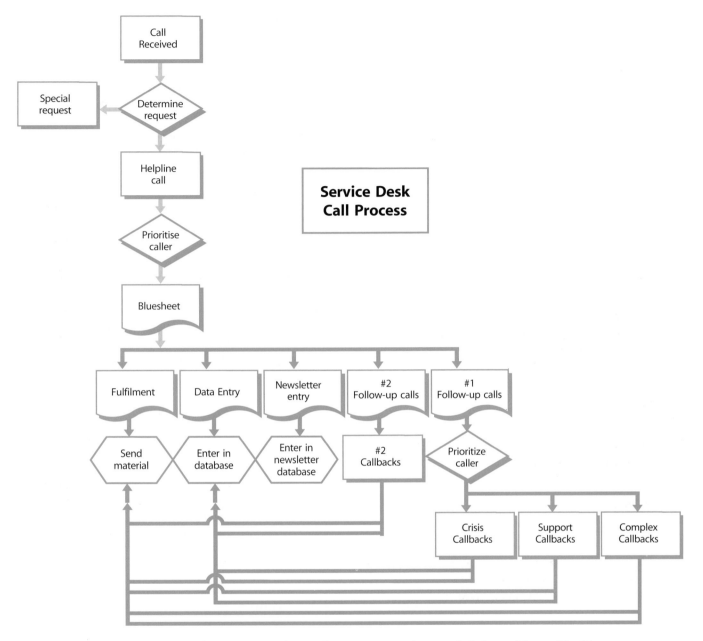

Figure 3.21 Existing flowchart of how the Service Desk was supposed to work (adapted from Allee)[17]

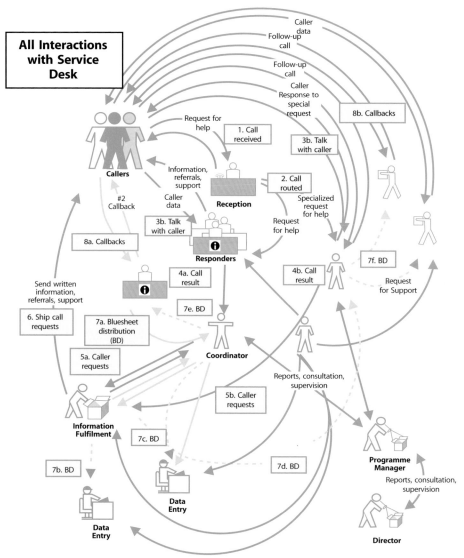

Figure 3.22 Value net exchanges showing how things really worked (adapted from Allee)[17]

Value net diagrams are tools for service analysis. They show what an organization does, how it is done and for whom. They need not be overly complex to be useful. Simple forms are used throughout the publication to illustrate service management structures and topics.

3.5 SERVICE STRATEGY FUNDAMENTALS

'The essence of strategy is choosing what not to do.'

Michael E. Porter[18]

Case example 7: *Security services*

Some time in 2001, a global network security services provider lost a major customer due to quality concerns materially affecting revenues and profits. Senior executives demanded that something be done – either cut costs or find a replacement customer.

While a replacement customer was sought, service operations dutifully reduced costs. Service quality was impacted, prompting three recently acquired customers to depart – further negatively affecting revenues and profits.

Senior executives again demanded that something be done – either cut costs of find replacement customers.

As CIO, what is your response or suggestion?

(Answer at the end of the chapter)

3.5.1 Fundamental aspects of strategy

Carl von Clausewitz remarked, 'Everything in strategy is very simple, but that does not mean that everything is very easy'. Strategic thought and action are difficult for the following reasons:

■ A level of comfort is necessary in dealing with complexity, uncertainty and conflict beyond the comfort zones of experience and codes of practice.

■ It is necessary to discern patterns, to project trends, and to estimate probabilities.

■ One must consider all factors including the interactions between them.

■ It is important to delve into underlying principles and when all else fails, it is often necessary to fall back on basic theory.

Theory is often discounted because of associations with the abstract or impractical. Theory, however, is the basis of good practice. The law of gravity, for example, is theory. Engineers use theory to solve practical problems. Investment banks use portfolio theory to validate investments. Key methods of Six Sigma are based on the theories of probability and statistics.

Managers rely on mental models that will assure them that they will indeed achieve desired outcomes. Trouble occurs when they use the wrong mental model for the problem at hand. What appears as unfixable or random often looks that way because of a misunderstanding of a process or system. Without underlying principles, it is not possible to explain why a perfectly good solution fails in one instance after tremendous success in another.

A good business model describes the means of fulfilling an organization's objectives. However, without a strategy that in some way makes a service provider uniquely valuable to the customer, there is little to prevent alternatives from displacing the organization, degrading its mission or entering its market space. A service strategy therefore defines a unique approach for delivering better value. The need for having a service strategy is not limited to service providers who are commercial enterprises. Internal service providers need just as much to have a clear perspective, positioning and plans to ensure they remain relevant to the business strategies of their enterprises.

Customers continually seek to improve their business models and strategies. They want solutions that break through performance barriers – and achieve higher quality of outcomes in business processes with little or no increase in cost, as in Figure 3.23. Such solutions are usually made available through innovative products and services. If such solutions are not available within a customer's existing span of control, service contracts, or value network, they are compelled to look elsewhere.

Service providers should not take for granted their position and role within their customer's plans even though they have the advantage of being incumbents.

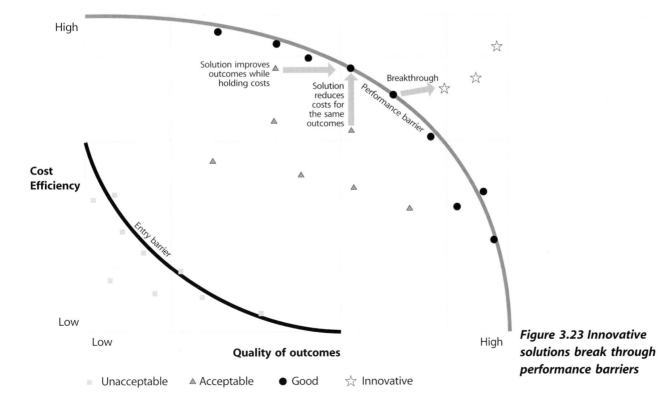

Figure 3.23 Innovative solutions break through performance barriers

The value of services from a customer's perspective may change over time due to conditions, events, and factors outside a provider's control. A strategic view of service management means a carefully considered approach to the relationships with customers and a state of readiness in dealing with the uncertainties in the value that defines that relationship.

Imagine you have been given responsibility for an IT organization. This organization could be internal or external, commercial or not-for-profit. How would you go about deciding on a strategy to serve customers? First, acknowledge that there exist other organizations whose aims are to compete with yours. Even government agencies are subject to competitive forces. While the value they create can sometimes be difficult to define and measure, these forces demand that an organization should perform its mission better than the alternatives.

Second, decide on an objective or end-state that differentiates the value of what you do, or how you do it, so that customers believe there is no true alternative. The form of value may be monetary, as in higher profits or lower expenses, or social, as in saving lives or collecting taxes. The differentiation can come in the form of barriers to entry, such as your organization's know-how of your customer's business or the broadness of your service offerings. Or it may be in the form of raising switching costs, such as lower cost structures generated through specialization or service sourcing. Either way, it is a means of doing better by being different.

The basic premise of service strategy is that service providers must meet objectives defined in terms of their customers' business outcomes while subject to a system of constraints. In a world of constrained resources and capabilities, they must hold their positions against competing alternatives. By understanding the trade-offs involved in its strategic choices, such as services to offer or markets to serve, an organization can better serve customers and outperform its competitors. The goal of a service strategy can be summed up very simply: superior performance versus competing alternatives.

Case example 8: *Internet service provider*

Some time in the mid-1990s, a line manager for a leading internet service provider (ISP) noticed a large amount of increased traffic on the bulletin board folders for two satiric stock analysts.

The ISP had adopted the strategic perspective of, 'Consumer connectivity first – any time, anywhere'.

Rather than caution the subscribers about the abnormal increase in capacity usage, the manager took an alternative path.

What do you think she did?

(Answer at the end of the chapter)

Successful strategies are based on the ability to take advantage of a set of distinct capabilities in offering superior value to customers through services. Such capabilities are viewed as strategic assets because a service provider can depend on them for success in a market space. Success comes from not only delivering value to customers but also being able to generate returns on investments. Strategic assets are carefully developed bundles of tangibles and intangibles, most notably knowledge, experience, systems, and processes. Service management is a strategic asset because it constitutes the core capabilities for service providers. Service management acts as an operating system for service assets in effectively deploying them to provide services.

A service strategy is sometimes thought of as a future course of action. When senior managers are asked to craft a strategy, the frequent response is a strategic plan detailing how the organization moves from its current state to a desired future state. But there are shortcomings with this definition of service strategy.

The first problem is conditions change. The pace of business change is quickening, no matter how large or small your organization or in what industry you compete. Opportunities arise while others disappear. The world does not hold still waiting for plans to unfold. What was good about a plan today may be rendered a liability tomorrow. A service strategy resolves big issues so that staff can get on with the small details – how best to provide services, for example, rather than debating what services to offer. But focusing on a strategic plan impedes the organization's ability to respond to changing conditions. Organizations with a high reliance on consistency and formalized procedures, for example, may lose flexibility, the ability to innovate or the ability to quickly adapt to unforeseen conditions. It turns out that a planning approach, while necessary, is insufficient – a service strategy requires more than a plan or direction.

The second problem is the constant focus on improving operational effectiveness. Operational effectiveness is absolutely necessary, but is not enough. A service strategy explains how a service provider will do better – either in what it does or how it does it – not only compared to itself but against competing alternatives. Customers hold government agencies and non-profit organizations to the same standards as service providers in the private sector. Customers must believe there are no reasonable alternatives. The form of value may be monetary, as in higher profits or lower expenses, or social, as in providing healthcare or preventing crime. If a provider's strategy focuses on operational effectiveness at the expense of distinctiveness, it will not prosper for long. Sooner or later every organization runs into competitors.

The third problem is 'value capture'. Plans are not well suited to provide the ongoing insight needed to maintain a value capture capability. Value capture is that portion of value creation that a provider gets to keep. While strategy is hard, the underlying logic is simple: there are only two ways one service provider can outperform another – either get customers to pay more for a service or provide the service at a lower cost. To accomplish either requires being different – how else to justify charging more or using fewer resources? So while a service provider may create value through distinctiveness, it may not be able to keep any of it. Moreover, the conditions for capturing value do not last indefinitely. Take the case of a labour arbitrage strategy: service providers decrease labour costs by making use of less expensive off-shore personnel. Early adopters made great gains because, for a while, the services they offered were priced lower than any competing alternative. But as more and more service providers made use of off-shore resources, the cost of services was lowered for everyone. This was great for customers but bad for providers – this distinctiveness dissipated. Value was created for customers but service providers were not able to keep any of it.

Strategic failure is often linked to contradictory issues like these. For an IT executive to be a strategist means not just holding opposing views but having the ability to synthesize them. They include the ability to react *and* predict, adapt *and* plan. In fact, high performing service providers are skilled in blending frames of reference when crafting service strategy.

Service providers must meet objectives defined in terms of their customers' business outcomes while subject to a system of constraints. By understanding the trade-offs involved in its strategic choices, such as services to offer or markets to serve, an organization can better serve customers and outperform its competitors. The goal of a service strategy can be summed up as *superior performance versus competing alternatives*.

A high-performance service strategy, therefore, is one that enables a service provider to consistently outperform competing alternatives over time, across business cycles, industry disruptions and changes in leadership. It comprises both the ability to succeed today and positioning for the future.

What distinguishes high-performing service providers is the manner in which they construct and maintain superior performance. While many providers compete on the basis of a single point of differentiation, the competitive essence is almost always achieved through the balance, alignment and renewal of three building blocks: market focus and position, distinctive capabilities and performance anatomy (Figure 3.24).

Figure 3.24 Building blocks of a high performance service strategy (based on Accenture research and analysis)

Service providers seeking to improve are most apt to encounter problems when they favour one building block to the exclusion of the others. For example, an external provider (Type III) may overemphasize the importance of scale – an over-reliance on advantage through market focus and position at the expense of distinctive capabilities. In other words, why does scale matter to the customer? Or a shared services (Type II) provider may overemphasize the importance of low cost – an over-reliance on advantage through distinctive capabilities at the expense of performance anatomy. That is, an inability to execute despite the cost advantage.

Service providers are also at risk when they fail to refresh and renew the building blocks – for example, by continuing to rely on capabilities that are no longer distinctive, or by resting on the laurels of a once successful strategy long after it has lost its relevance. For example, an internal provider (Type I) may continue to rely on customer know-how while its customer seeks lower cost structures. High-performance service providers continually balance, align and renew the building blocks.

The three building blocks of high performance service providers:

Market focus and position – The spotlight is on optimal scale within a market space. A market space is defined by a set of outcomes that customers desire, which can be supported through one or more services. This is the 'where and how to compete' aspects of a service strategy. High-performance service providers – even Type I and II providers – have remarkable clarity when it comes to setting this strategic direction. They understand the dynamics of their market space, and the customers within, better than their competing alternatives, and manage through appropriate strategies. Such strategies allow the provider to build and manage valuable Service Portfolios, achieve optimal scale, exploit positioning advantages in the value network, and identify and possibly enter alternative market spaces or serve new customers.

Distinctive capabilities – The spotlight is on creating and exploiting a set of distinctive, hard-to-replicate capabilities that deliver a promised customer experience. This is about understanding the critical interplay between resources, capabilities, value creation and value capture. To create value, a service provider develops a formula for doing business that successfully translates a big idea regarding customer needs into a distinctive and cost-effective set of connected capabilities and resources to satisfy those needs.[19] This ability is sometimes referred to as 'differentiation on the outside and simplification on the inside'.

To be a high-performance service provider, be clear about what capabilities really contribute to enhancing customer outcomes. Understand the need to build distinctive capabilities that are demonstrably better and, in the short term, difficult to replicate by competing alternatives. This includes mastering technical capabilities and excelling at innovation, as well as lower cost structures and customer know-how. Take for example, the Type I service provider who, after years of outsourcing, decided to in-source its application-hosting services. By incorporating virtualization and dynamic provisioning technologies, the provider created speed and cost structures no outsourcer could match – precisely the same distinctive capabilities that prompted the provider to outsource in the first place.

Performance anatomy – The spotlight is on creating cultural and organizational characteristics that move service providers toward their goal of out-executing competing alternatives. Performance anatomy comprises a set of organizational world views that are measurable and actionable by organizational leadership. Example views include:

■ Services are a strategic asset
■ Workforce productivity is a key execution differentiator
■ Performance measurement is highly selective in its focus and metrics
■ Continual improvement and renewal are real and permanent necessities.

3.5.1.1 Government and non-profit organizations

Government and non-profit organizations appear to operate in environments unaffected by the pressures of competition and markets. The ethics of social-sector services are about helping people, not beating them. But strategic competition is not at odds with a social-sector's sense of mission. Government and non-profit organizations must also operate under limited and constrained resources and capabilities. Stakeholders and customers demand as much social return as possible for money invested. Eventually, these constituents will consider competing alternatives.

A government or non-profit organization's strategy, much like that of its commercial counterparts, explains how its unique service approach will deliver better results for society. When the need for social-sector services are so demanding, superior performance versus competing alternatives is a compelling imperative. No commercial enterprise can succeed by attempting to be all things to all people. Similarly, governments and non-profit organizations should make choices in what they will and, just as important, will not do.

3.5.2 The Four Ps of strategy

The lifecycle has, at its core, service strategy. The entry points to service strategy are referred to as 'the Four Ps' following Mintzberg[20] (Figure 3.25). They identify the different forms a service strategy may take.

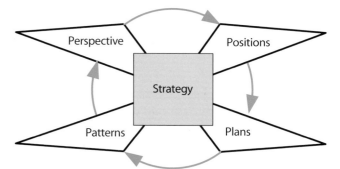

***Figure 3.25 Perspectives, positions, plans and patterns*[21]**

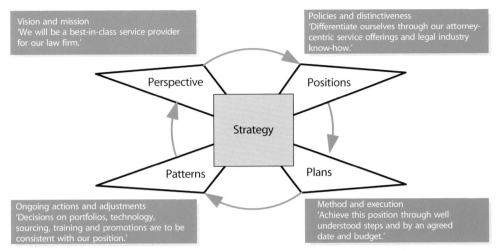

Figure 3.26 Strategic approach taken by a Type II provider for an international law firm

■ Perspective – describes a vision and direction. A strategic perspective articulates the business philosophy of interacting with the customer or the manner in which services are provided. For example, a shared service provider (Type II) for a global law firm may adopt the strategic perspective of, 'We will be a best-in-class service provider for our law firm'. The CIO determined that his business most values a certain type of service provider. By setting a perspective of competing against other industry-specific providers he not only narrows the field of competing alternatives, but also cements his own distinctiveness in the minds of his customers (Figure 3.26).

■ Position – describes the decision to adopt a well-defined stance. Should the provider compete on the basis of value or low cost? Specialized or broad sets of services? Should value be biased towards utility or warranty? An internal service provider (Type I) restricted to serving one business unit may adopt a position based on 'product know-how' or 'customer responsiveness'. The law firm CIO may adopt a needs-based position: attorney-centric offerings for knowledge, collaboration and document management services.

■ Plan – describes the means of transitioning from 'as is' to 'to be'. A plan might detail, 'How do we offer high-value or low-cost services?' Or in the case of our law firm CIO, 'How do we achieve and offer our specialized services?'

■ Pattern – describes a series of consistent decisions and actions over time. A service provider who continually offers specific services with deep expertise is adopting a 'high-value' or 'high-end' service strategy. A service provider who continually offers dependable and reliable services is adopting a 'high-warranty' strategy.

If mid-course corrections are to be made within the framework of an existing perspective and position, this is where those decisions and actions are formulated. The law firm CIO, for example, may decide to offer the same specialized services but with enhanced levels of client privacy (warranty).

Requirements and conditions are dynamic. A service provider may begin with any one form and evolve to another. For example, a service provider might begin with a perspective: a vision and direction for the organization. The service provider might then decide to adopt a position articulated through policies, capabilities and resources. This position may be achieved through the execution of a carefully crafted plan. Once achieved, the service provider may maintain its position through a series of well-understood decisions and action over time: a pattern.

The use of all the Four Ps, rather than one over the other, allows for emergent as well as intended service strategies. Best-practice service strategies mix these in some way: maintain control while fostering learning; see the big picture while deciding on details.

3.5.3 Strategy as a perspective

Strategy as a perspective defines the governing set of beliefs, values, and a sense of purpose shared by the entire organization. It sets the overall direction in which the service provider moves to fulfil its purpose and construct its performance anatomy. Some pithy real-world examples:

■ 'Focus on the user and all else will follow.'

■ 'It's all about growth, innovation and the deployment of technology, led by the greatest people anywhere.'

■ 'Consumer connectivity first – any time, anywhere.'

- '[Our] purpose is to improve the quality of life of the communities we serve.'
- 'We will be a best-in-class service provider in [our] industry.'

Despite its high-level abstraction, do not make the mistake of casually ignoring or trivializing perspective. Unlike plans or patterns, perspectives are not easily changed. Take the perspective of Swiss watchmakers, for example, when confronted with the emergence of quartz technology – a Swiss invention. Dismissing the technology as a novelty incompatible with the perspective of skill-intensive craftsmanship, the Swiss watch industry was nearly decimated by the Japanese. That is, until it adopted the technology for major market niches and reclaimed market share through a perspective centred on fashion rather than workmanship.

Or take the real-world service providers who held a perspective of:

- '… highly efficient back-office operations' during the emergence of service outsourcing
- '… low cost service provider' during the emergence of off-shore skilled labour
- '… technology-specific expertise' with the emergence of open systems and software.

Perspective is attained with the help of clarifying questions asked within the context of the service provider's stakeholders, which includes primarily its owners, its customers, and its employees. Conversely, well-defined perspective serves as a reference for subsequent positions, plans, or patterns of action the service provider may adopt and enact. Public assertions made by a service provider are usually based on strategy as a perspective and reflected in its value proposition to customers. The value proposition may be implicit in the customers it serves, the services it offers, and the particular perspective of service quality it adopts. A clear perspective helps make this value proposition explicit. This strategy is defined at the highest level of abstraction and maintains the organization's farthest planning horizon. It drives other control views of strategy (the other 'Ps') and is modified based on feedback from those views.

Once a perspective has been attained, here is a test:

- Does it capture what you intend to do for only the next three to five years, or does it capture a more timeless essence of your organization's distinctiveness?
- Is it clear and memorable?
- Does it have the ability to promote and guide action?
- Does it set boundaries within which people are free to experiment?

The distillation of an organization's strategy into a memorable and prescriptive phrase is important. A sound strategy is of little use unless people understand it well enough to apply it during unforeseen or ambiguous opportunities.

3.5.4 Strategy as a position

Strategy as a position is expressed as distinctiveness in the minds of customers. This often means competing in the same space as others but with a differentiated value proposition that is attractive to the customer. Whether it is about offering a wide range of services to a particular type of customer, or being the lowest-cost option, it is a strategic position. Three broad types of positions are variety-based positions, needs-based positions, and access-based positions.

3.5.4.1 Variety-based positioning

Variety-based positioning focuses on a particular variety of customers' needs and aims to meet them in distinctive fashion. It requires a relatively narrow catalogue of services but with depth in terms of service levels, options, and packages. Service assets are highly specialized to deliver this narrow catalogue. Service providers try to meet all the needs of any given customer segment. Success is in terms of performing exceptionally well in meeting a sub-set of needs (Figure 3.27). Capabilities are strong on leveraging economies of scale, managing similar demand from different customers, and fulfilling it with a small and stable catalogue of services. Growth is based predominantly on new opportunities for the same catalogue of services. For example, a service provider may specialize in payroll services for several groups within a business unit, several business units within an enterprise, or several enterprises within a region.

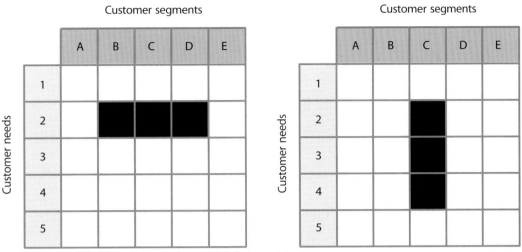

Figure 3.27 Variety-based (left) and needs-based (right) positioning

3.5.4.2 Needs-based positioning

In needs-based positioning, service providers choose to provide most or all of the needs of a particular type of customer (Figure 3.27). It requires a relatively wide catalogue of services covering various aspects of the customer's business. This is closer to the traditional approach of grouping customers in segments and then aiming to best serve the needs of one or more targeted segments. Service providers do not worry about meeting the needs of every type of customer. They distinguish themselves by performing exceptionally well in meeting most of the needs of a particular customer or segment. Capabilities are strong on leveraging economies of scope, managing different demands from the same customers, and fulfilling them with a flexible catalogue of services. Growth is based predominantly on new services in the catalogue from the same source of demand.

For example, a service provider may specialize in supporting most or all of the business needs of a group of hospitals. It may offer a catalogue of services that covers infrastructure services, application maintenance, information security, document management and disaster recovery services specialized for the healthcare industry. It maintains expertise on electronic medical records, privacy issues, medical equipment, and claims processing. Similarly, a provider focusing on the financial services industry has deep insight into the peculiar challenges and opportunities faced by investment banks, insurers, and brokerage firms.

Type I and Type II providers are often positioned to serve a customer segment of one. They have only one customer at the enterprise level even if there are several at the business unit level. Many internal IT organizations are expected to meet all the IT needs of the business that

own them. They do not worry about meeting the needs of other enterprises and can therefore organize their service assets to best serve one enterprise customer.

3.5.4.3 Access-based positioning

In access-based positioning, service providers distinguish themselves through their ability to serve customers with particular needs with respect to location, scale, or structures (Figure 3.28). Customers vary in size, location, and structure. They deploy business assets in a manner that best serves their own business models and strategies. Some operate networks of retail branches, stores, trading desks, or point-of-sale terminals that serve as access points for users of their own services. Others have business assets concentrated at a few large-scale facilities such as factories, warehouses, distribution centres, and call centres. The employees of some customers are highly mobile with extensive travel and intensive communications needs. Others may have staff mostly in offices and laboratories.

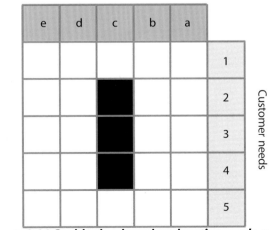

Figure 3.28 Positioning based on location, scale or structure

Positioning of any type requires service assets to be specialized and deployed in patterns that best satisfy the patterns of demand generated by business activities, cycles, and events of the target market spaces. This is mostly an opportunity to consolidate, stabilize, learn, and grow into a high-performing service provider with focus. Specialization of service assets allows service providers to deliver greater levels of utility to targeted segments. It also means risks from the high level of asset specificity when there are sudden or drastic changes in the market space from which some providers never recover.

Asset specifity

The more specialized an asset gets, the lower its usefulness for other purposes. A point-of-sale terminal has higher asset-specificity than a PC workstation or storage device that can be re-purposed. Asset specificity applies to organization and people assets as well. Type I providers who have never served more than one customer find it hard to adjust to corporate mergers and acquisitions.

When a tax collection agency decides to accept electronic filing of tax returns and electronic funds transfer (EFT), there is a significant change in its patterns of business activity. Consequently, some service providers, including the agency's own internal units, have better access-based strategies than others to serve the agency. An insurance company offers to initiate the claims process at the site of an accident. It does so by dispatching claims handling staff to the accident site with all the resources necessary for the claims process. This strategy not only provides distinctive value to its policyholders but also speeds processes and reduces administrative costs from lengthy cases. It puts an office-based clerical job out on the front-line in vehicles specially equipped with the necessary business applications. The insurance company itself adopts an access-based strategy to distinguish itself from competing insurers.

Other service providers in turn may compete to win the business of this progressive insurer by offering mobile workplace services that automate and integrate the claims processing vehicles with back-office systems. Service providers with knowledge and experience in mobile systems and applications, similar to those used by emergency medical services, would have a distinctive advantage.

Service providers may adopt one or more of these generic types of positioning (Figure 3.29). There are no universal rules for these positioning strategies, simply plans and patterns that work, or definitions to comply with. Concrete plans are required, however, to maintain strategic positions from which the mission and objectives are achieved. A sound position guides the organization in what to do and, just as important, in what not to do.

Once a position has been attained, here is a test:

- Does it guide the organization in making decisions between competing resource and capability investments?
- Does it help managers test the appropriateness of a particular course of action?
- Does it set clear boundaries within which staff should and should not operate?
- Does it allow freedom to experiment within these constraints?

3.5.5 Strategy as a plan

Strategy as a plan is a course of action from one point to another within a competitive scenario. Often referred to as an intended strategy, it is the deliberate course of action charting a path towards strategic objectives. The planning

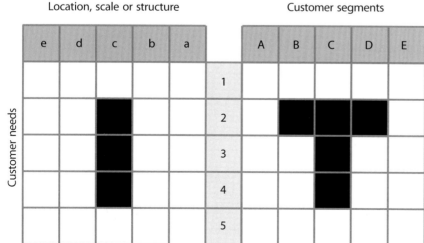

Figure 3.29 Combining variety-based, needs-based and access-based positioning

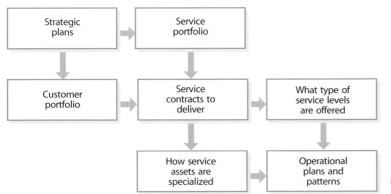

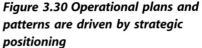

Figure 3.30 Operational plans and patterns are driven by strategic positioning

horizons are typically long term but lengths may vary across organizations, industries and strategic context. Again, plans are the direct means of achieving goals and objectives. They commonly focus on financial budgets, portfolio of services, new service development, investments in service assets, and improvement plans (Figure 3.30).

Each plan focuses on achieving well-defined outcomes or conditions in a particular context. The key inputs to a plan are frequently derived from the results of the strategic assessment, and are framed by the strategic position and perspective.

Plans are linked by the need to achieve certain strategic objectives. For example, building infrastructure capacity, consolidating staff at key locations, licensing a new set of software applications, and complying with an industry standard may all be parts of the same strategic plan to reach a distinctive position.

Service management can be viewed as a coordinated set of plans with which service providers plan and execute their service strategies. The difference between success and failure in strategic leadership and direction is largely dependent on how well this coordinated set is put together, put to work, and controlled in execution. Two service providers with equal sets of resources may achieve different degrees of success simply because of their strategic plans.

3.5.6 Strategy as a pattern

Strategy as a pattern is an organization's fundamental way of doing things. They are the basis of what are called emergent strategies, distinctive patterns in action reinforced over time by repeated success. For example, rather than pursuing a plan to cut service costs through service sourcing, the provider makes sourcing decisions one at a time – testing the validity of the idea. First it may source telecommunication services, then application

hosting, then security services, and so on, until a strategic pattern has emerged.

The patterns are embedded in a service provider's way of doing business. Management systems, organization, policies, processes, schedules, and budgets are all discernible patterns of action that are documented and controlled. They are the consequence of perspectives, positions, and plans directed by senior leadership in service of a particular customer or market space. Others exist in the form of tacit knowledge carried by those who carry them out. They may be neither documented nor discernible because they are unexpected outcomes realized in pursuit of certain goals or objectives. Nevertheless, they deliver value to customers so managers must capture and codify them into the organization's documented practices.

Consistent and controllable patterns are part of the service provider's distinctive capabilities. These patterns are valuable because they emerge inside the organization as a direct consequence of actions taken by managers and their teams. Therefore they are likely to be a signature of the organization and a source of competitive advantage. While industry practices and standards are available to all, signature processes can truly distinguish the value provided by a service provider.[22] Best practices are patterns in action for superior outcomes over the normal expected performance using prevalent practice in comparable circumstances. Organizations can set their own improvement threshold for designating a pattern as a best practice. Other criteria may include elements of innovation, efficiency gains, external recognition, and the transferability of the related knowledge.

Patterns are useful in identifying areas of opportunity. Useful patterns in performance can be codified into practice and made available as reusable assets to other parts of the organization. When patterns in action become systems and processes, they are placed under

Table 3.1 Service management patterns

Example patterns of action	Description
How-to patterns	Set the operating style of the organization. The framing of how activities are performed, for example: ■ R&D staff must rotate through operations ■ All customer questions must be answered on the first email or calls ■ Operations staff must be minimally certified
Boundary patterns	Set the focal point of the organization. The body of opportunities that should, or should not, be pursued, for example: ■ Hardware acquisitions must be done through strategic vendors ■ New technologies must conform to a certain standard ■ New projects must follow a standard methodology
Priority patterns	Set the allocation of resources. The ranking of new opportunities, for example: ■ Service stability outweighs speed of deployment ■ Speed of deployment outweighs service stability
Timing patterns	Set the rhythm of the organization. Staff are synchronized with customer and business cycles, for example: ■ End-of-quarter and end-of-year required enhanced service levels ■ When legislature is in session, no changes are allowed

Configuration Management so they may be stabilized, standardized, and improved. They are the past guidance from which to reaffirm or correct the current strategy. As business cycles continue, new patterns in action may emerge and provide feedback.

Case example 7 (solution): *Surprisingly, the solution was to suspend new sales*

The CIO understood:

1 Service operations were caught in a vicious cycle with disastrous long-term consequences.

2 Customers were leaving due to a strategic weakness. Customers differentiated the value of security services through service quality. Perspectives and positions based on cost and technology were incorrect.

3 By refocusing staff and budget on service operations, the organization repaired and rebuilt its distinctive quality capabilities for remaining customers. Customer churn was halted.

The solution, while painful in the short term, allowed the provider to break the vicious cycle and pave a long-term strategy for regaining customers. The counter-intuitive breakthrough was based on (a) a big picture view of services and (b) the precept of *superior performance versus competing alternatives*.

When managers put in renewal or improvement activities, they advance their organization to an advanced level of maturity. Strategy as patterns in action can therefore be a very powerful perspective of strategy because it engages all levels of management and rests on systematic learning. Service management can be viewed as an adaptive network of patterns through which strategic objectives are realized. Some patterns in action are shown in Table 3.1.

Case example 8 (solution): *She used service management as a strategic asset*

Rather than caution the subscribers about the marked increase in capacity usage, the manager offered the irreverent analysts the chance to create their own site. The site, now called the Motley Fool, continues to be a heavily trafficked destination for financial advice. The line manager eventually became president of programming.

The manager understood the service provider's strategic intent: deeper consumer connectivity or broader distribution.

Service strategy

4

4 Service strategy

4.1 DEFINE THE MARKET

4.1.1 Services and strategy

Organizations have an interest in strategy within the context of service management in two distinct but related perspectives. There are strategies for services and there are services for strategies (Figure 4.1). From one perspective, strategies are developed for services offered. Providers differentiate their services from competing alternatives available to customers.

From the other perspective, service management is a competence for offering services as part of a business strategy. A software vendor may decide to offer software as a service. It combines its capabilities in software development with new capabilities in service management. It also makes use of its capabilities in maintaining software applications to bundle technical support as part of the core service. By adopting a service-oriented approach supported by service management capabilities, the vendor has transformed itself into a service business. This approach has also been adopted by internal software engineering groups who have changed from being cost centres to being profit centres.

For example, the market leader in airline reservation systems originated from a successful internal computer-based reservation system of a major airline. Such transformations require strong capabilities in marketing, finance, and operations.

4.1.2 Understand the customer

Organizations strive to achieve business objectives using whatever assets they have at hand, subject to various constraints. Constraints include costs and risks attributable to complexity, uncertainty and conflicts in the business environment. The value-creating potential of the business depends on the performance of business assets. Assets must perform well at their full potential. The assets may

be owned by the business or available for use from others under various types of financial arrangements.

More often than not such arrangements are agreements or contracts for services. Business managers are given the responsibility, authority, and resources necessary to deliver certain outcomes using the best possible means. Services are a means for managers to enable or enhance the performance of business assets leading to better outcomes. The value of a service is best measured in terms of the improvement in outcomes that can be attributed to the impact of the service on the performance of business assets. Some services increase the performance of customer assets, some services maintain performance, and yet others restore performance following adverse events. A major aspect of providing value is preventing or reducing the variation in the performance of customer assets.

In a trading system, for example, it is not enough for the service to feed the trading system with real-time market data. To minimize trading losses the data feed must be available without interruption during trading hours, and at as many trading desks necessary with a contingency system in place. An investment bank is therefore willing to pay a premium for a news-feed service providing a higher level of assurance than a service used by a competitor. The difference translates into greater trading gains.

Focus on customer assets

The performance of customer assets should be a primary concern of service management professionals because without customer assets there is no basis for defining the value of a service.

4.1.3 Understand the opportunities

Customers own and operate configurations of assets to create value for their own customers. The assets are the means of achieving outcomes that enable or enhance value creation. For example, for a lending bank value is

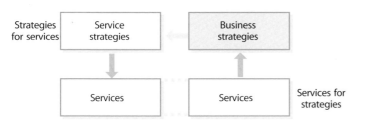

Figure 4.1 Strategies for services and services for strategies

Objective

Desired outcome

Increase the number of loan applications processed on time

Metric

Figure 4.2 Analysing an outcome[23]

created by the outcome of processing a loan application on time (Figure 4.2). Customers receiving the loan will have access to the required financial capital and the lender benefits from the onset and accrual of interest. The lending process is therefore a business asset whose performance leads to specific business outcomes.

It is important for managers to gain deep insight into the businesses they serve or target. This includes identifying all the outcomes for every customer and market space that

falls within the scope of the particular strategy. For the sake of clarity, outcomes are classified and codified with reference tags that can be used in various contexts across the Service Lifecycle (Table 4.1).

Customer outcomes that are not well supported represent opportunities for services to be offered as solutions. Some outcomes are supported by services existing in a catalogue. Other outcomes can possibly be supported by services in the pipeline but presently in the design and

Table 4.1 Example of a scheme to tag customer outcomes

Category	Tag	Outcome statement
Enhanced capabilities (EC)	EC1	Decision making and action in response to business events is faster
	EC2	Increase in knowledge, skills, and experience for business processes
	EC3	Business processes are enhanced with superior logic
	EC4	Industry best practices are available through application updates
	EC5	Supply chain is extended
	EC6	Availability of specialized knowledge and expertise
Increased performance (IP)	IP1	Increase in throughput of business processes
	IP2	Decrease in average collection period (accounts receivables)
	IP3	Increase in return on assets
	IP4	Increase in customer satisfaction
Enhanced resources (ER)	ER1	Resources are freed up for new opportunities
	ER2	Increase in productivity of staff
	ER3	Increased flexibility in operations
	ER4	Increase in available resources
Reduced costs (RC)	RC1	Decrease in fixed costs of business process
	RC2	Decrease in unit costs of employee benefits administration
	RT3	Lower start-up time for new or expanded operations
Reduced risks (RR)	RR1	Decrease in operational risks from variation in performance of assets
	RR2	Decrease in operational risks from shortage in capacity of assets
	RR3	Business continuity is assured. Passed audit.
	RR4	Business processes are compliant with regulations

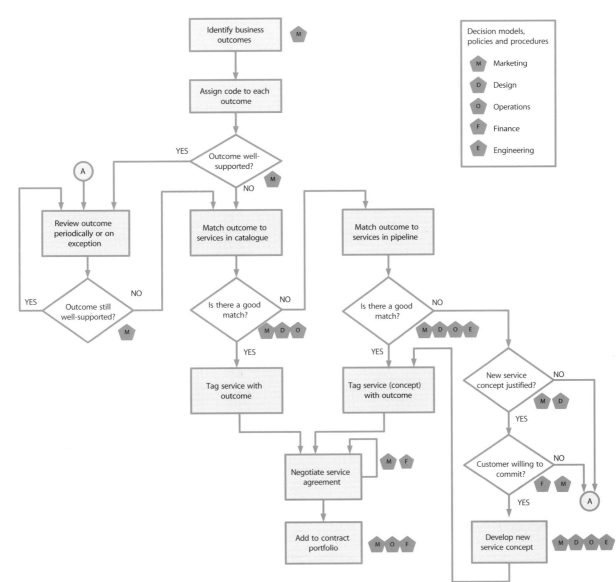

Figure 4.3 Customer outcomes are used to tag services and service assets

development phases. Outcomes that are presently well supported are periodically reviewed. New opportunities emerge when changes in the business environment cause a hitherto well-supported outcome to be poorly supported (Figure 4.3).

Services and service assets are tagged with the customer outcomes they facilitate. This is a principle similar to the idea of tagging materials, components and sub-assemblies to the final products they are embedded in. The valuation of services and service asset becomes easier when it is possible to visualize the customer outcomes they facilitate. Mapping of customer outcomes to services and service assets can be accomplished as part of a Configuration Management System (CMS).

Gaining insight into the customer's business and having good knowledge of customer outcomes is essential to developing a strong business relationship with customers.

Business Relationship Managers (BRMs) are responsible for this. They are 'customer focused' and manage opportunities through a Customer Portfolio.

In many organizations BRMs are known as Account Managers, Business Representatives, and Sales Managers. Internal IT Service Providers need this role to develop and be responsive to their internal market. They work closely with Product Managers who take responsibility for developing and managing services across the lifecycle. They are 'product-focused' and perceive the environment through a Service Portfolio.

An outcome-based definition of services ensures that managers plan and execute all aspects of service management entirely from the perspective of what is valuable to the customer. Such an approach ensures that services not only create value for customers but also capture value for the service provider.

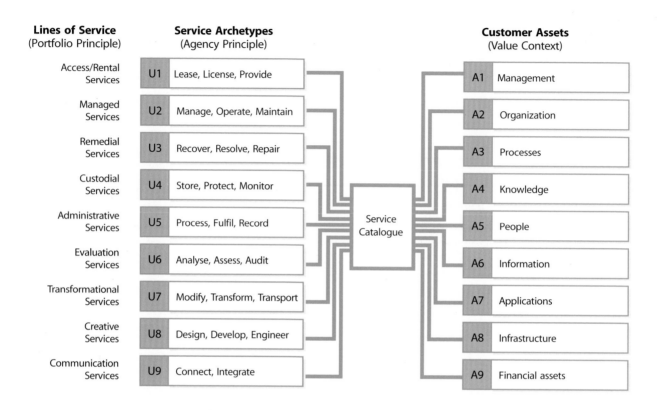

Figure 4.4 Provider business models and customer assets

4.1.4 Classify and visualize

Services differ primarily by how they create value and in what context. Service archetypes are like business models for services. They define how service providers act on behalf of customers to create value (Figure 4.4). Customer assets are the context in which value is created because they are linked to business outcomes that customers want.

Customers own and operate different types of assets (Ay) depending on several factors such as strategic industry factors, customers, competitors, business models, and strategy.

A combination of service archetype and customer assets (Ux-Ay) represents an item in the Service Catalogue. Several services in a catalogue may belong to the same

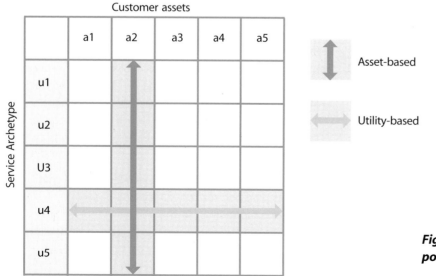

Figure 4.5 Asset-based and utility-based positioning

archetype or model (Ux). Many service archetypes may be combined with the same type of customer asset (Ay) under an asset-based service strategy. The same archetype may be used to serve different types of customer assets under a utility-based service strategy (Figure 4.5). This is a variation of need-based and access-based positioning. The strategy of the service provider will determine the contents of the Service Catalogue.

It is useful for managers to visualize services as value-creating patterns made up of customer assets and service archetypes (Figure 4.6). Some combinations have more value for customers than others even though they may be made of similar asset types and archetypes. Services with closely matching patterns indicate opportunity for consolidation or packaging as shared services. If the Applications asset type appears in many patterns, then service providers can have more investments in capabilities and resources that support services related to Applications. Similarly, if many patterns include the Security archetype, it is an indication that security has emerged as a core capability. These are just simple examples of how the Service Catalogue can be visualized as a collection of useful patterns. Service strategy can result in a particular collection of patterns (intended strategy) or a collection of patterns can make a particular service strategy attractive (emergent strategy).

This visual method can be useful in communication and coordination between functions and processes of service management. These visualizations are the basis of more formal definitions of services. Proper matching of the value-creating context (customer assets) with the value-creating concept (service archetype) can avoid shortfalls in performance. For example, the customer's business may involve reviewing and processing of application forms, requests, and account registrations. Questions of the following type can be useful:

- Do we have the capabilities to support workflow applications?
- What are the recurring patterns in processing application forms and requests?
- Do the patterns vary based on time of year, type of applicants, or around specific events?
- Do we have adequate resources to support the patterns of business activity?
- Are there potential conflicts in fulfilling service level commitments? Are there opportunities for consolidation or shared resources?
- Are the applications and requests subject to regulatory compliance? Do we have knowledge and experience of regulatory compliance?

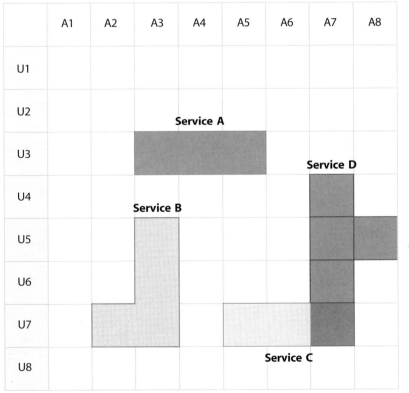

Services C and D share market space A7-U7

When services share market spaces they also tend to share capabilities, resources, costs, risks, challenges, opportunities etc.

Services with high degree of overlap could be consolidated under the same operations. Variants of services have very high degree of overlap.

Similar services can have the same core service package.

Figure 4.6   Visualization of services as value-creating patterns

Table 4.2 Probing questions to gain insight

With respect to themselves	With respect to their customers
Who are our service providers?	Who are their customers?
How do services create value for them?	How do they create value?
What assets do we deploy to provide value?	Which of their assets receive value?
Which assets should we invest in?	Which of our assets do they value most?
How should we deploy our assets?	How do they deploy their assets?

- Do we come in direct contact with the customers of the business? If yes, are there adequate controls to manage user interactions and information?

The preceding set of questions is an instance of a more generic set of probing questions that is useful to gain valuable insight into the customer's business (Table 4.2). These are not merely questions. When effectively applied, they are tools of incision used to dissect business outcomes that customers want services to support. They reveal not only challenges associated with a particular customer or business environment but also the opportunities.

4.2 DEVELOP THE OFFERINGS

4.2.1 Market space

A market space is defined by a set of business outcomes, which can be facilitated by a service. The opportunity to facilitate those outcomes defines a market space. The following are examples of business outcomes that can be the bases of one or more market spaces.

- Sales teams are productive with sales management system on wireless computers
- E-commerce website is linked to the warehouse management system
- Key business applications are monitored and secure
- Loan officers have faster access to information required on loan applicants
- Online bill payment service offers more options for shoppers to pay
- Business continuity is assured.

Each of the conditions is related to one or more categories of customer assets, such as people, infrastructure, information, accounts receivables and purchase orders, and can then be linked to the services that make them possible. Each condition can be met through multiple ways (Figure 4.7). Customers will prefer the one that means lower costs and risks. Service providers create these conditions through the services they deliver and thereby provide support for customers to achieve specific business outcomes.

A market space therefore represents a set of opportunities for service providers to deliver value to a customer's business through one or more services. This approach has definite value for service providers in building strong relationships with customers. Customers often express dissatisfaction with a service provider even when terms and conditions of service level agreements (SLAs) are fulfilled. Often it is not clear how services create value for customers. Services are often defined in the terms of resources made available for use by customers. Service definitions lack clarity on the context in which such resources are useful, and the business outcomes that justify the expense of a service from a customer's perspective. This problem leads to poor designs, ineffective operation and lacklustre performance in service contracts. Service improvements are difficult when it is not clear where improvements are truly required. Customers can understand and appreciate improvements only within the context of their own business assets, performances and outcomes. A proper definition of services takes into account the context in which customers perceive value from the services.

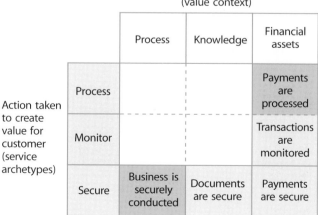

Market space defined in terms of outcomes desired by customers

Figure 4.7 Market spaces are defined by the outcomes that customers desire

4.2.2 Outcome-based definition of services

An outcome-based definition of services ensures that managers plan and execute all aspects of service management entirely from the perspective of what is valuable to the customer. Such an approach ensures that services not only create value for customers but also capture value for the service provider.

Solutions that enable or enhance the performance of the customer assets indirectly support the achievement of the outcomes generated by those assets. Such solutions and propositions hold utility for the business. When that utility is backed by a suitable warranty customers are ready to buy.

> Services are a means of delivering value to customers by facilitating outcomes customers need to achieve without owning specific costs and risks.

Well-formed service definitions lead to effective and efficient service management processes. Generic examples are given below:

■ Example 1: Collaboration services provide value to the customer when cooperative business communications are conducted without the constraints of location or device. Value is created when the provider operates for the customer store-and-forward and real-time methods of electronic messaging, so that (the customer's) employees can compose, send, store and receive communications in a manner convenient, reliable and secure, for a specified community of users.

■ Example 2: Application-hosting services provide value to the business when business function services and processes continue to operate without the need to invest capital in a non-core business capability. Value is created when the provider maintains for the business an application software platform system and assures that employees and business systems can work continuously in a manner convenient, secure and reliable, for a specified portfolio of services.

■ Example 3: Mobile workplace services provide value to the customer when business activity is conducted without the constraints of fixed location. Value is created when the provider operates for the customer a wireless messaging system and assures that (the customer's) employees and business systems can exchange voice and data messages in a manner convenient, reliable and secure, within a specified area of coverage.

■ Example 4: Order-to-cash services provide value to the business when purchase orders are converted to cash flows without the need to invest capital in a non-core business capability. Value is created when the provider licenses to the business an order fulfilment system and assures that the sales teams and online shoppers can enter or modify purchase orders in a manner convenient, fast and secure within a specified time schedule.

Service definitions are useful when they are broken down into discrete elements that can then be assigned to different groups, who will manage them in a coordinated manner to control the overall effect of delivering value to customers (Figure 4.8).

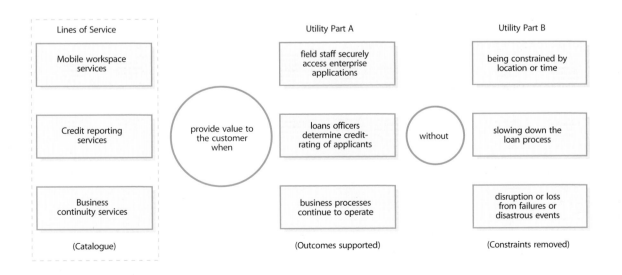

Figure 4.8 Actionable components of service definitions in terms of utility

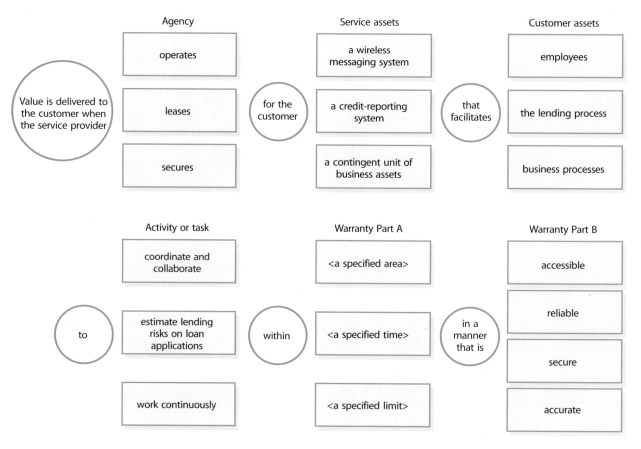

Figure 4.9 Actionable components of service definitions in terms of warranty

Being able to define services in an actionable manner has its advantages from a strategic perspective. It removes ambiguity from decision making and avoids misalignment between what customers want and what service providers are organized and capable enough to deliver.

Well-constructed definitions make it easier to visualize patterns across Service Catalogues and portfolios that earlier were hidden due to unstructured definitions (Figure 4.9). Patterns bring clarity to decisions across the Service Lifecycle. Table 4.3 shows the type of questions that can guide analysis of service definitions to make them actionable.

Table 4.3 Analysis of service definitions for action

Service type	Utility (Part A and B)
What services do we provide?	What outcomes do we support?
Who are our customers?	How do they create value for their customers?
	What constraints do our customers face?
Customer assets	**Service assets**
Which customer assets do we support?	What assets do we deploy to provide value?
Who are the users of our services?	How do we deploy our assets?
Activity or task	**Warranty**
What type of activity do we support?	How do we create value for them?
How do we track performance?	What assurances do we provide?

Without the context in which the customers use services it is difficult to completely define value. Without complete definition of value, there cannot be complete production of value. As a result, outcomes are not fulfilled to the customer's satisfaction.

However, it is not to say that a service cannot be developed without a customer in hand. It simply means that the story of a service begins either with the needs of a specific customer or a category of customers (i.e. market space). Customer needs exist and are fulfilled independent of service providers or their services. However, value for a customer rests on not only fulfilment of these needs, but also how they are fulfilled, and often at what risks and costs. Certain services create value by preventing or recovering from undesirable conditions or states. In such cases customers may desire a change in the risks to which their assets may be exposed. In either case, the second-order effect of services is that the changes they produce, or prevent, have a positive and usually measurable effect on the performance and outcomes of the customer's business.

These types of questions and others of a similar nature are crucial for an organization to consider in the implementation of a strategic approach to service management. They are applied by all types of service providers, internal and external. What changes is the context and meaning of certain ideas such as customers, contracts, competition, market spaces, revenue and strategy. In fact, these clarifying questions are particularly important for internal service providers who typically operate within the realm of an enterprise or government agency, have customers who are also owners, and whose strategic objectives may not always be clear.

4.2.3 Service Portfolio, Pipeline and Catalogue

The Service Portfolio represents the commitments and investments made by a service provider across all customers and market spaces. It represents present contractual commitments, new service development, and ongoing service improvement plans initiated by Continual Service Improvement (Figure 4.10). The portfolio also includes third-party services, which are an integral part of service offerings to customers. Some third-party services are visible to the customers while others are not. Chapter 5 provides further guidance on how to develop and manage portfolios.

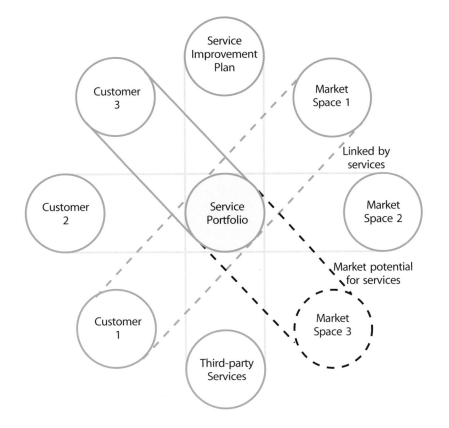

Figure 4.10 Service Portfolio

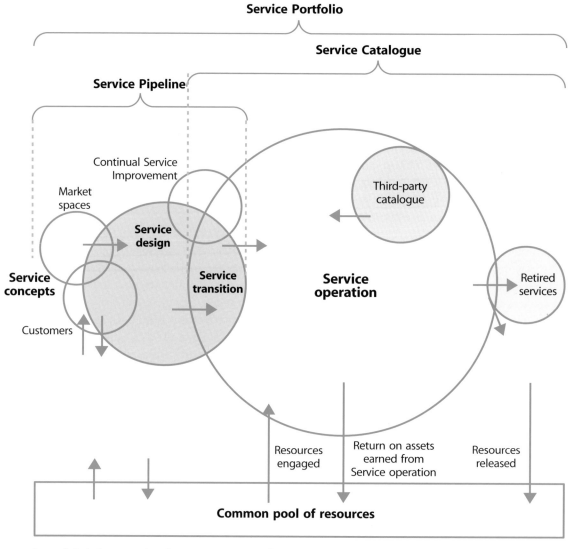

Area of circle is proportional to resources currently engaged in the lifecycle phase (Service Portfolio and Financial Management)

Figure 4.11 Service Pipeline and Service Catalogue

The portfolio management approach helps managers prioritize investments and improve the allocation of resources. Changes to portfolios are governed by policies and procedures. Portfolios instil a certain financial discipline necessary to avoid making investments that will not yield value. Service Portfolios represent the ability and readiness of a service provider to serve customers and market spaces. The Service Portfolio is divided into three phases: Service Catalogue, Service Pipeline and Retired Services (Figure 4.11).

The Service Portfolio represents all the resources presently engaged or being released in various phases of the Service Lifecycle. Each phase requires resources for completion of projects, initiatives and contracts. This is a very important governance aspect of Service Portfolio Management (SPM).

Entry, progress and exit are approved only with approved funding and a financial plan for recovering costs or showing profit as necessary. The Portfolio should have the right mix of services in the pipeline and catalogue to secure the financial viability of the service provider. The Service Catalogue is the only part of the Portfolio that recovers costs or earns profits.

In summary, SPM is about maximizing value while managing risks and costs. The value realization is derived from better service delivery and customer experiences. Through SPM, managers are better able to understand quality requirements and related delivery costs. They can then seek to reduce costs through alternative means while maintaining service quality. The SPM journey begins with documenting the organization's standardized services, and

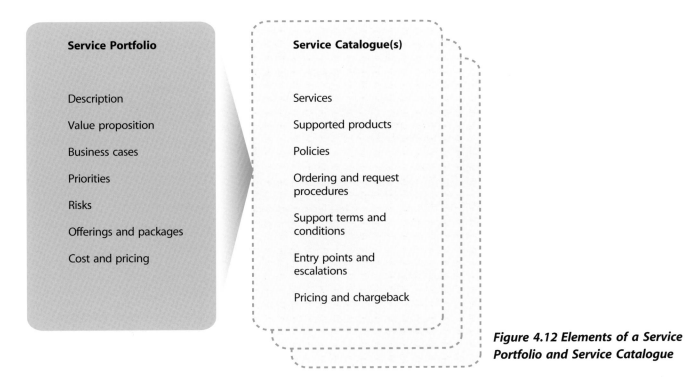

Figure 4.12 Elements of a Service Portfolio and Service Catalogue

as such has strong links to Service Level Management, particularly the Service Catalogue (Figure 4.12).

4.2.3.1 Service Catalogue

The Service Catalogue is the subset of the Service Portfolio visible to customers. It consists of services presently active in the Service Operation phase and those approved to be readily offered to current or prospective customers. Items can enter the Service Catalogue only after due diligence has been performed on related costs and risks. Resources are engaged to fully support active services.

The Catalogue is useful in developing suitable solutions for customers from one or more services. Items in the Catalogue can be configured and suitably priced to fulfil a particular need. The Service Catalogue is an important tool for Service Strategy because it is the virtual projection of the service provider's actual and present capabilities. Many customers are only interested in what the provider can commit now, rather than in future. The value of future possibilities is discounted in the present.

It serves as a service order and demand channelling mechanism. It communicates and defines the policies, guidelines and accountability required for SPM. It defines the criteria for what services fall under SPM and the objective of each service. It acts as the acquisition portal for customers, including pricing and service-level commitments, and the terms and conditions for service provisioning. It is in the Service Catalogue that services are decomposed into components; it is where assets,

processes and systems are introduced with entry points and terms for their use and provisioning. As providers may have many customers or serve many businesses, there may be multiple Service Catalogues projected from the Service Portfolio. In other words, a Service Catalogue is an expression of the provider's operational capability within the context of a customer or market space.

The Service Catalogue is also a visualization tool for SPM decisions. It is in the catalogue that demand for services comes together with the capacity to fulfil it. Customer assets attached to a business outcome are sources of demand (Figure 4.13). In particular, they have expectations of utility and warranty. If any items in the catalogue can fulfil those expectations, a connection is made resulting in a service contract or agreement. Catalogue items are clustered into Lines of Service (LOS) based on common patterns of business activity (PBA) they can support.

LOS performing well are allocated additional resources to ensure continued performance and anticipate increases in demand for those services. Items performing above a financial threshold are deemed viable services. An effort is to be made to make them popular by introducing new attributes, new service level packages (SLP), improved matching with sources of demand, or by new pricing policies. If performance drops below a threshold, then they are marked for retirement. A new Service Transition project is initiated and a Transition Plan is drafted to phase out the service.

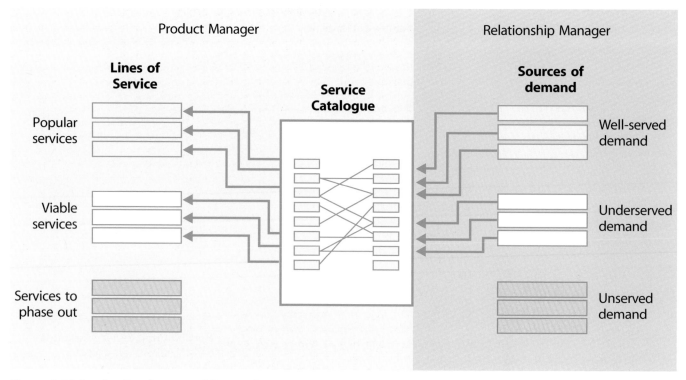

Figure 4.13 Service Catalogue and Demand Management

Services with poor financial performance may be retained in the Catalogue with adequate justification. Some catalogue services may have strategic use of such contingency for another service and contractual obligations to a few early customers. Whatever the justification, it must be approved by senior leadership who may choose to subsidize. This issue differs with Type I (internal) providers who are often required to maintain a catalogue of service, regardless of their independent financial viability.

A subset of the Service Catalogue may be third-party or outsourced services. These are services that are offered to customers with varying levels of value addition or combination with other Catalogue items. The Third-Party Catalogue may consist of core service packages (CSP) and SLP. It extends the range of the Service Catalogue in terms of customers and market spaces. Third-party services may be used to address underserved or unserved demand (Figure 4.13) until items in the Service Pipeline are phased into operation. They can also be used as a substitute for services being phased out of the Catalogue. Sourcing is not only an important strategic option but can also be an

operational necessity. Section 6.5 provides more guidance on sourcing strategy.

Candidate suppliers of the Third-Party Catalogue may be evaluated using the eSourcing Capability Model for Service Providers (eSCM-SP™) developed by Carnegie Mellon University.

4.2.3.2 Service Pipeline

The Service Pipeline consists of services under development for a given market space or customer. These services are to be phased into operation by Service Transition after completion of design, development, and testing. The pipeline represents the service provider's growth and strategic outlook for the future. The general health of the provider is reflected in the pipeline. It also reflects the extent to which new service concepts and ideas for improvement are being fed by Service Strategy, Service Design and Continual Improvement. Good Financial Management is necessary to ensure adequate funding for the pipeline.

4.2.3.3 Retired services

Some services in the Catalogue are phased out or retired. Phasing out of services is part of Service Transition. This is to ensure that all commitments made to customers are duly fulfilled and service assets are released from contracts. When services are phased out, the related knowledge and information are stored in a knowledge base for future use. Phased-out services are not available to new customers or contracts unless a special business case is made. Such services may be reactivated into operations under special conditions and SLAs that are to be approved by senior management. This is necessary because such services may cost a lot more to support and may disrupt economies of scale and scope.

4.2.3.4 The role of Service Transition

Approval from Service Transition is necessary to add or remove services from the Service Catalogue. This is necessary for the following reasons:

- Once an item enters the catalogue it must be made available to customers who demand it. Due diligence is necessary to ensure that the service is a complete product that can be fully supported. This includes technical feasibility, financial viability, and operational capability. Incomplete products offered in haste can result in significant losses for service providers and customers.
- Items in the Service Catalogue are mostly in the Service Operation phase with contractual commitments made to customers. Any changes to the catalogue have to be evaluated for impact on the ability to meet those commitments.
- Adding items to the Service Catalogue means the need to set aside capabilities and resources for present and prospective customers. This is like maintaining spares for every piece of equipment in every type of aircraft in operation in the fleet. Having more has advantages if each item is doing well. Otherwise, valuable resources are locked by catalogue items not doing well. There is a need to balance flexibility and choice for customers with the increase in complexity, uncertainty, and resource conflicts.

Standardization and reuse

> Standardization and reuse of components are critical for cost-effective delivery of services. They also reduce the costs due to complexity. Incremental units of capacity of services configured from shared and reusable components can be cheaper.

There are instances in which certain business needs cannot be fulfilled with services from a catalogue. The service provider has to decide how to respond to such cases. The options are typically along the following lines:

- Explain to the customer why the need cannot be fulfilled.
- Explain what is needed of the customer in terms of commitment, sponsorship or funding for new service development. Customers may reconsider their needs in view of service development costs they may have to bear.
  - Develop the service if the customer makes the necessary commitment
  - Decline the opportunity if the customer cannot commit.
- Consider supporting the customer in partnership with third parties.

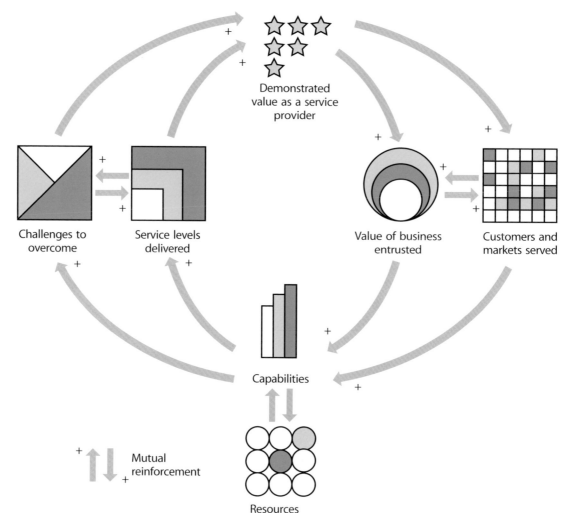

Figure 4.14 Growth and maturity of service management into a trusted asset

4.3 DEVELOP STRATEGIC ASSETS

Service providers should treat service management as a strategic asset and entrust it with challenges and opportunities in terms of customers, services, and contracts to support. Investments made in trusted assets are less risky because they have the capability to deliver consistently time and again. Service management begins with capabilities that coordinate and control resources to support a catalogue of services (Figure 4.14). Challenges are overcome in achieving progressively higher service levels. There is mutual reinforcement between the two. Capabilities and resources are adjusted until the goal is reached. Customers perceive demonstrated value from the service provider.

Customers perceive benefits in a continued relationship, and entrust the provider with the business of increasing value and also adding new customers and market spaces to the realm of possibilities. This justifies further investments in service management in terms of capabilities and resources, which have a tendency to reinforce each other.

Stakeholders may initially trust the provider with low-value contracts or non-critical services. Service management responds by delivering the performance expected of a strategic asset. The performance is rewarded with contract renewals, new services, and customers, which together represent a larger value of business. To handle this increase in value, service management must invest further in assets such as process, knowledge, people, applications and infrastructure. Successful learning and growth enables commitments of higher service levels as service management gets conditioned to handle bigger challenges.

Over time, this virtuous cycle results in higher capability levels and maturity in service management leading to a higher return on assets for the service provider. Services play the role of a belt that engages service assets with customer assets (Figure 4.15). Service agreements or contracts define the rules of engagement. Unless properly

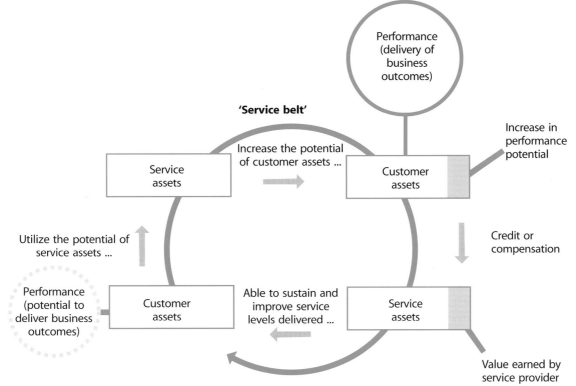

Figure 4.15 Mutual welfare when service assets are engaged in supporting customer outcomes

defined the cost of service assets spent in support of customers' assets may be difficult to account for and recover. This leads to situations where there is adequate creation of value for the customer but inadequate value capture for the provider.

Value capture is an important notion for all types of service providers, internal and external. Good business sense discourages stakeholders from making major investments in any organizational capability unless it demonstrates value capture. Internal providers are encouraged to adopt this strategic perspective to continue as viable concerns within a business. Cost recovery is necessary but not sufficient. Profits or surpluses allow continued investments in service assets that have a direct impact on capabilities.

Linking value creation to value capture is a difficult but worthwhile endeavour. In simplest terms customers buy services as part of plans for achieving certain business outcomes. Say, for example, the use of a wireless messaging service allows the customer's sales staff to connect securely to the sales force automation system and complete critical tasks in the sales cycle. This has a positive impact on cash flows from payments brought forward in time. By linking purchase orders and invoices expedited from use of the wireless service it is possible to sense the impact of the service on business outcomes. They can be measured in terms such as Days Sales Outstanding (DSO)

and average time of the Order-to-Cash cycle. The total cost of utilizing the service can then be weighed against the impact on business outcomes.

It is difficult to establish the cause-and-effect relationship between the use of the service and the changes in cash flows. Quite often, there are several degrees of separation between the utilization of the service and the benefits customers ultimately realize. While absolute certainty is difficult to achieve, decision making nevertheless improves.

4.3.1 Service management as a closed-loop control system

As defined earlier, service management is a set of organizational capabilities specialized in providing value to customers in the form of services. The capabilities interact with each other to function as a system for creating value. Service assets are the source of value and customer assets are the recipients (Figure 4.16). Services have the potential to increase the performance of customer assets and create value to the customer organization. Improvements in the design, transition and operation of the service increase this customer performance potential and reduce the risks of variations on customer assets. This requires a clear and complete understanding of customer assets and desired outcomes.

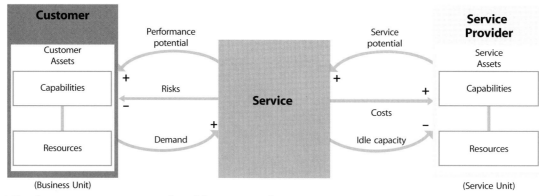
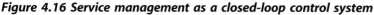

Figure 4.16 Service management as a closed-loop control system

Services derive their potential from service assets. Service potential is converted into performance potential of customer assets. Increasing the performance potential frequently stimulates additional demand for the service in terms of scale or scope. This demand translates into greater use of service assets and justification for their ongoing maintenance and upgrades. Unused capacity is reduced. Costs incurred in fulfilling the demand are recovered from the customer based on agreed terms and conditions.

From this perspective, service management is a closed-loop control system with the following functions, to:

■ Develop and maintain service assets
■ Understand the performance potential of customer assets
■ Map service assets to customer assets through services
■ Design, develop, and operate suitable services
■ Extract service potential from service assets
■ Convert service potential into performance potential
■ Convert demand from customer assets into workload for service assets
■ Reduce risks for the customer
■ Control the cost of providing services.

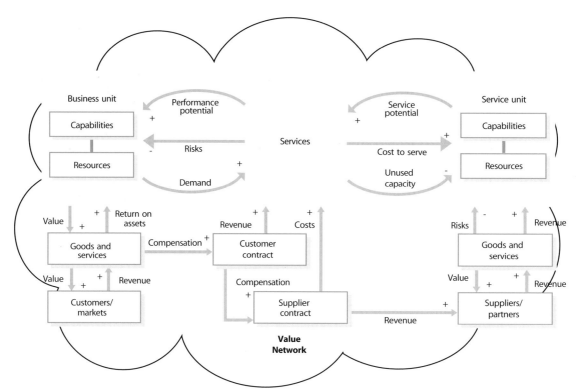

Figure 4.17 Service management as a strategic asset and a closed-loop system

4.3.2 Service management as a strategic asset

To develop service management as a strategic asset, define the value network within which service providers operate in support of their customers. This network may exist entirely within a business enterprise, as is often the case for Type I and Type II providers (Figure 4.17). More often the value network extends across organizational boundaries to include external customers, suppliers, and partners. By identifying the key relationships and interactions in the network, managers have better visibility and control over the systems and processes they operate. This allows managers to manage the complexity that exists in their business environments as customers pursue their own business models and strategies. It also helps account for all the costs and risks involved in providing a service or supporting a customer.

Strategic assets are dynamic in nature. They are expected to continue to perform well under changing business conditions and objectives of their organization. That requires strategic assets to have learning capabilities. Performance in the immediate future should benefit from knowledge and experience gained from the past. This requires service management to operate as a closed-loop system that systematically creates value for the customer and captures value for the service provider. An important aspect of service management is controlling the interactions between customer assets and service assets.

4.3.2.1 Increasing the service potential

The capabilities and resources (service assets) of a service provider represent the service potential or the productive capacity available to customers through a set of services (Figure 4.17). Projects that develop or improve capabilities and resources increase the service potential. For example, implementation of a Configuration Management System leads to improved visibility and control over the productive capacity of service assets such as networks, storage, and servers. It also helps quickly to restore such capacity in the event of failures or outages. There is greater efficiency in the utilization of those assets and therefore service potential because of capability improvements in Configuration Management. Similar examples are given below in Table 4.4. One of the key objectives of service management is to improve the service potential of its capabilities and resources.

Table 4.4 Examples of how service potential is increased

Service management initiative	Increasing service potential from capabilities	Increasing service potential from resources
Data centre rationalization	Better control over service operations	Increases the capacity of assets
	Lower complexity in infrastructure	Increases economies of scale and scope
	Development of infrastructure and technology assets	Capacity building in service assets
Training and certification	Knowledgeable staff in control of Service Lifecycle	Staffing of key competencies
	Improved analysis and decisions	Extension of Service Desk hours
Implement incident management process	Better response to service incidents	Reducing losses in resource utilization
	Prioritization of recovery activities	
Develop service design process	Systematic design of services	Reuse of service components
	Enrichment of design portfolio	Fewer service failures through design
Thin client computing	Increased flexibility in work locations	Standardization and control of configurations
	Enhanced service continuity capabilities	Centralization of admin functions

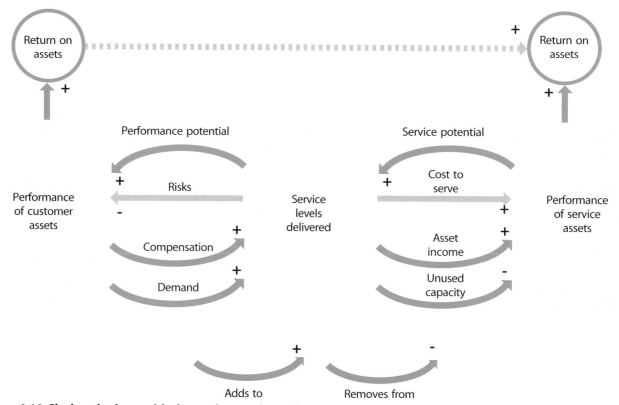

Figure 4.18 Closing the loop with demand, capacity and cost to serve

Through Configuration Management, all service assets should be tagged with the name of the services to which they add service potential. This helps decisions related to service improvement and Asset Management. Clear relationships make it easier to ascertain the impact of changes, make business cases for investments in service assets, and identify opportunities for scale and scope economies. It identifies critical service assets across the Service Portfolio for a given customer or market space.

4.3.2.2 Increasing performance potential

The services offered by a service provider represent the potential to increase the performance of customer assets (Figure 4.18). Without this potential there is no justification for customers to procure the services. Visualize and define the performance potential of services so that all decisions made by managers are rooted in the creation of value for customers. This approach avoids many of the problems of service businesses where value for customers is created in intangible forms and therefore harder to define and control. Working backwards from the performance potential of customers ensures that service providers are always aligned with business needs regardless of how often those needs change.

The performance potential of services is increased primarily by having the right mix of services to offer to

customers, and designing those services to have an impact on the customer's business. The key questions to be asked are:

- What is our market space?
- What does that market space want?
- Can we offer anything unique in that space?
- Is the space already saturated with good solutions?
- Do we have the right portfolio of services developed for a given market space?
- Do we have the right catalogue of services offered to a given customer?
- Is every service designed to support the required outcomes?
- Is every service operated to support the required outcomes?
- ·Do we have the right models and structures to be a service provider?

The productive capacity of service assets is transformed into the productive capacity of customer assets. An important aspect of delivering value for customers through services is the reduction of risks for customers. By deciding to utilize a service, customers are often seeking to avoid owning certain risks and costs. Therefore the performance potential of services also arises from the removal of costs and risks from the customer's businesses.

For example, a service that securely processes payments or transfer of funds for the customer reduces the risks of financial losses through error and fraud and at the same time reduces the cost per transaction by leveraging economies of scale and scope on behalf of the customer. The service provider can deploy the same set of service assets to process a large volume of transactions and free the customer from having to own and operate such assets. For certain business functions such as payroll, finance, and administration, the customer may face the financial risk of under-utilized or over-utilized assets and may therefore prefer a service offered by a Type I, Type II or a Type III service provider.

4.3.2.3 Demand, capacity and cost

When services are effective in increasing the performance potential of customer assets there is an increase in the demand for the services. This acts as a positive feedback to the system to be taken into account. An increase in the performance potential leads to an increase in customer demand (Figure 4.18). The demand for services is accompanied by compensation from customers for the service levels received. The form of compensation received depends on the type of agreement between the service

unit and business unit. The higher the service levels, the greater the compensation that services providers can expect to achieve. All decisions in service management should be directed towards increasing this positive feedback. The compensation earned by the service contributes to the incomes earned by the service assets deployed by the service unit to deliver and support the service. The returns depend on the asset income and the cost to serve. The model is used by managers for managing the finances of every service. In general, the cost to serve increases with the service levels delivered. However, the actual nature of this relationship varies across service delivery systems.

As the maturity of service management increases, it is possible to deliver higher levels of utility and warranty without a proportional increase in costs. Due to the effect of fixed costs and overheads, the costs of providing additional units of service output can decrease with an increase in the demand for services. Service assets are in a productive state when they are engaged in supporting customer assets. In every demand cycle of the customer, value is created by a corresponding delivery cycle. Value creation for the customer is matched by value capture for the service provider.

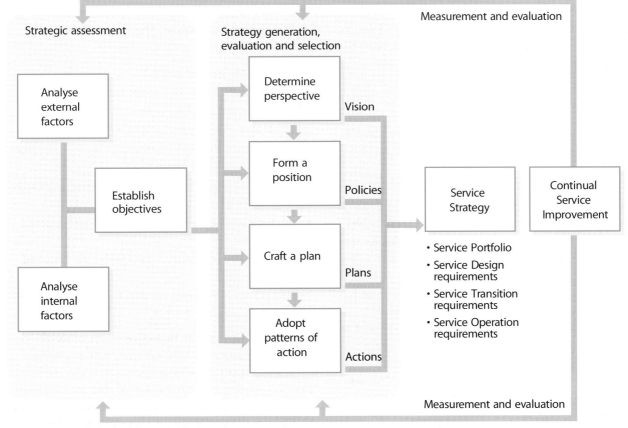

Figure 4.19 Forming and formulating a service strategy

4.4 PREPARE FOR EXECUTION

Every model represents a kind of process. This model represents a clear and practical approach for formulating service strategies. It does not, however, guarantee success. What is needed is, through reflection and examination, to make a strategy suitable in an organization's context or situation. Strategy involves thinking as well as doing. See Figure 4.19. For senior managers accountable for investment decisions, financial- and personnel-related, the stakes are high. Strategy is critical to the performance of the organization. Service strategies must be formed and be formulated. Broad outlines are deliberate while details are allowed to emerge and adapt en route.

4.4.1 Strategic assessment

In crafting a service strategy, a provider should first take a careful look at what it does already. It is likely there already exists a core of differentiation. An established service provider frequently lacks an understanding of its own unique differentiators. The following questions can help elucidate a service provider's distinctive capabilities:

Which of our services or service varieties are the most distinctive?

Are there services that the business or customer cannot easily substitute? The differentiation can come in the form of barriers to entry, such as the organization's know-how of the customer's business or the broadness of service offerings. Or it may be in the form of raised switching costs, due to lower cost structures generated through specialization or service sourcing. It may be a particular attribute not readily found elsewhere, such as product knowledge, regulatory compliance, provisioning speeds, technical capabilities or global support structures.

Which of our services or service varieties are the most profitable?

The form of value may be monetary, as in higher profits or lower expenses, or social, as in saving lives or collecting taxes. For non-profit organizations, are there services that allow the organization to perform its mission better? Substitute 'profit' with 'benefits realized'.

Which of our customers and stakeholders are the most satisfied?

Which customers, channels or purchase occasions are the most profitable?

Again, the form of value can be monetary, social or other.

Which of our activities in our value chain or value network are the most different and effective?

The answers to these questions will likely reveal patterns that lend insight to future strategic decisions. These decisions, and related objectives, form the basis of a strategic assessment. See Table 4.5.

Table 4.5 Internal and external factors for a strategic assessment

Factor	Description
Strength and weaknesses	The attributes of the organization. For example, resources and capabilities, service quality, operating leverage, experience, skills, cost structures, customer service, global reach, product knowledge, customer relationships and so on.
Distinctive competencies	As discussed throughout the chapter, 'What makes the service provider special to its business or customers?'
Business strategy	The perspective, position, plans and patterns received from a business strategy. For example, a Type I and II may be directed, as part of a new business model, to expose services to external partners or over the internet.
	This is also where the discussion on customer outcomes begins and is carried forward into objectives setting.
Critical success factors	How will the service provider know when it is successful? When must those factors be achieved?
Threats and opportunities	Includes competitive thinking. For example, 'Is the service provider vulnerable to substitution?'
	Or, 'Is there a means to outperform competing alternatives?'

4.4.2 Setting objectives

Objectives represent the results expected from pursuing strategies, while strategies represent the actions to be taken to accomplish objectives. Clear objectives provide for consistent decision making, minimizing later conflicts. They set forth priorities and serve as standards. Organizations should avoid the following means of 'not managing by objectives'.

- Managing by crisis – the belief that the measure of an organization is its problem solving ability. It is the approach of allowing events to dictate management decisions.
- Managing by extrapolation – continuing the same activities in the same manner because things are going well.
- Managing by hope – making decisions on the belief they will ultimately work out.
- Managing by subjective – doing the best you can to accomplish what should be done. There is no general plan.

To craft its objectives, an organization must understand what outcomes customers desire to achieve and determine how best to satisfy the important outcomes currently underserved. This is how metrics are determined for measuring how well a service is performing. The objectives for a service include three distinct types of data. These data sources are the primary means by which a service provider creates value. See Table 4.6.

There are four common categories of information frequently gathered and presented as objectives. Senior managers should understand the risk that comes with each category, if not altogether avoided:[23]

- Solutions – customers present their requirements in the form of a solution to a problem. Customers may lack the technical expertise to be able to arrive at the best possible solution. Customers may be ultimately disappointed by the very solution they present. To

mitigate this risk, rather than looking to customer ideas about the service itself, look for the criteria they use to measure the value of a service.

- Specifications – customers present their requirements in the form of specifications – vendor, product, architectural style, computing platform, etc. By accepting specifications, a provider needlessly prevents its own organization from devising optimal services.
- Needs – customers present their requirements as high-level descriptions of the overall quality of the service. By their nature, high-level descriptions do not include a specific benefit to the customer. For example, '…service will be available 99.9% of the time'. These inputs are frequently ambiguous and imprecise. They leave the provider wondering what customers really mean: '99.9% of business hours? 99.9% of a calendar year? Does this include maintenance windows? Can the 0.1% be used all at once?' By leaving room for interpretation, the provider leaves too much to chance. Be sure all input is measurable and actionable (Figure 4.20).
- Benefits – customers present their requirements in the form of benefit statements. Again, the risk is in the ambiguity or imprecision of the statements. 'Highly reliable', 'Faster response' and 'Better security' take on many meanings and present different implications for the organization.

When service providers solicit requirements, customers respond in a manner and language meaningful and convenient to them. This customer-driven approach fails because it inevitably solicits the wrong inputs – the type that cannot be used to predictably ensure success. This explains the frequent disconnection between IT organizations and the businesses they serve. What the customer values is frequently different from what the organization believes it provides. Service providers should think very differently. A clear understanding of what the customer values is called a marketing mindset, compared to a manufacturing mindset. Rather than focusing inward

Table 4.6 Customer tasks, outcomes and constraints

Type of Objective Data	Description
Customer tasks	What task or activity is the service to carry out? What job is the customer seeking to execute?
Customer outcomes	What outcomes is the customer attempting to obtain? What is the desired outcome?
Customer constraints	What constraints may prevent the customer from achieving the desired outcome? How can the provider remove these constraints?

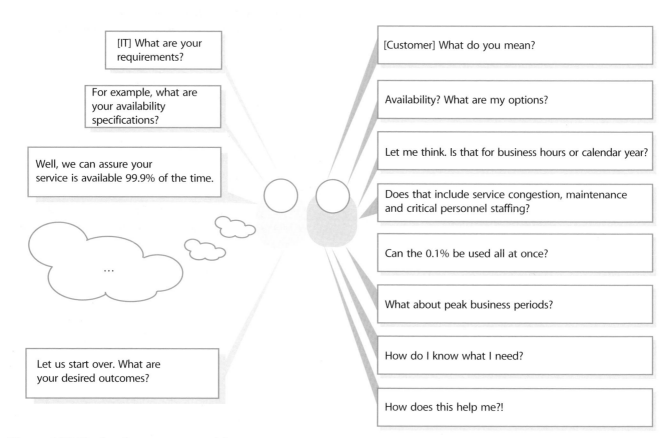

Figure 4.20 Moving from customer-driven to customer-outcomes

on the production of services, look from the outside in, from the customer's view. Rather than lagging indicators, begin with the leading indicators of Table 4.6, Common business objectives. These indicators lead to a clearer understanding of service utility and service warranty, which in turn lead to defining better requirements. Customers do not buy services; they buy the satisfaction of a particular need.

4.4.3 Aligning service assets with customer outcomes

Service providers must manage assets much in the same manner as their customers. Service assets are coordinated, controlled, and deployed in a manner that maximizes the value to customers while minimizing risks and costs for the provider. For example, a messaging service such as wireless email increases the performance of one of the most critical and expensive type of customer assets: managers and staff. The customer deploys these assets in a manner that gets the most out of their productive capacities.

This means, for example, that sales managers spend more time on-site with clients, technicians are quickly dispatched to cover equipment failures in the field, and

administrative staff are consolidated at strategic locations to improve operational effectiveness. To support the customer, the service provider configures and deploys its assets in a manner that effectively supports the customer's own deployments. It may require the design, deployment, operation, and maintenance of highly available and secure messaging on wireless phones or computers. What matters is that the customer's employees are able to coordinate business activities, access business applications and control business processes.

4.4.4 Defining critical success factors

For every market space there are critical success factors that determine the success or failure of a service strategy. These factors are influenced by customer needs, business trends, competition, regulatory environment, suppliers, standards, industry best practices and technologies. Critical success factors are also referred to in business literature as strategic industry factors (SIF) and have the following general characteristics:[24]

- They are defined in terms of capabilities and resources
- They are proven to be key determinants of success by industry leaders

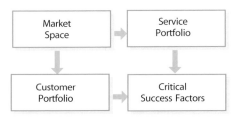

Figure 4.21 Critical success factors

- They are defined by market space levels, not peculiar to any one firm
- They are the basis for competition among rivals
- They change over time, so they are dynamic not static
- They usually require significant investments and time to develop
- Their value is extracted by combination with other factors.

Critical success factors by themselves are altered or influenced by one or more of the following factors:

- Customers
- Competitors
- Suppliers
- Regulators.

Identifying critical success factors for a market space is an essential aspect of strategic planning and development. In each market space service providers require a core set of assets in order to support a Customer Portfolio through a Service Portfolio (Figure 4.21). For example, in the market space for high-volume real-time data processing, such as those required by the financial services industry, service providers must have large-scale computer systems, highly reliable network infrastructure, secure facilities, knowledge

of industry regulations, and a very high level of contingency. Without these assets, it would not be possible for such service units to provide the utility and warranty demanded by customers in that market space.

The dynamic nature of markets, business strategies, and organizations requires critical success factors to be reviewed periodically or at significant events such as changes to Customer Portfolios, expansion into new market spaces, changes in the regulatory environment and disruptive technologies. For example, new legislation for the healthcare industry on the portability and privacy of patient data would alter the set of critical success factors for all service providers operating in market spaces related to healthcare.

The dominating success of a new market leader in search engines and online advertising may add a new critical success factor through a combination of innovative business model and technological capability. Most critical success factors are a combination of several service assets such as financial assets, experience, competencies, intellectual property, processes, infrastructure, and scale of operations.

Critical success factors determine the service assets required to implement a service strategy successfully. For example, if a strategy requires services to be made available across a large network of locations or a wide area of coverage, the service provider must not only build capacity at key locations. The provider must also operate the network as a system of nodes so that the cost of serving all customers is roughly identical to and within a price point consistent with a strategic position in a market space. Not all critical success factors need favour large organizations or economy of scale in operations. Some strategies favour organizations small in size but highly competitive through the knowledge they have of customers and related market spaces. Managers must

Customer assets

Service belt	S	A1	A2	A3
Service archetypes	U1		X, Y, S	
	U2	Y, Z, B	X, Y, Z	Y, Z, A
	U3		X, Y, W	

X, Y, R, A, B, S, W Service assets are critical success factors. Of these, X and Y are common across market spaces so they are highly leveraged assets.

Figure 4.22 Critical success factors leveraged across market spaces

therefore conduct evaluation exercises to ascertain the critical success factors in force.

One way to define critical success factors is by customer assets and the service archetypes (Figure 4.22). For example, in healthcare, IT Service Providers have extensive knowledge of hospital procedures, medical equipment, interactions between physicians, clinicians and pharmacists, insurance policies and privacy regulations. Service providers present in market spaces related to the quality of outcomes in healthcare typically have physicians and clinicians on their payroll. Service strategies for the healthcare market spaces take into account the need to deal with users with highly specialized skills, special-purpose equipment, low tolerance for error, and the need to balance security with usability of services. These are critical success factors for a cluster of market spaces related to healthcare. A subset of these critical success factors is shared by other market spaces such as military applications. Critical success factors can therefore span more than one market space. They represent opportunities for leveraging economies of scale and scope.

4.4.5 Critical success factors and competitive analysis

CSFs are determinants of success in a market space. They are also useful in evaluating a service provider's strategic position in a market space and driving changes to such positions. This requires CSFs to be further refined in terms of some distinct value proposition to customers. For example, being competitive in a market space may require very high levels of availability, fail-safe operation of IT infrastructure, and adequate capacity to support business

continuity of services. In many market spaces cost-effectiveness is a common CSF, while in others it may be specialized domain knowledge or reliability of infrastructure. Customer satisfaction, richness of service offerings, compliance with standards and global presence are also common CSFs. Type I and Type II providers tend to score well on familiarity with the customer's business.

Conduct a strategic analysis for every market space, major customer and Service Portfolio to determine current strategic positions and desired strategic positions for success. This analysis requires service providers to gather data from customer surveys, service level reviews, industry benchmarks, and competitive analysis conducted by third parties or internal research teams. Each critical success factor is measured on a meaningful index or scale. It is best to adopt indices and scales that are commonly used within a market space or industry to facilitate benchmarking and comparative analysis. Critical success factors are used to define playing fields, which serve as reference frameworks for evaluation of strategic positions and competitive scenarios (Figure 4.23).

Playing fields have the following benchmarks that determine the various zones in which a service provider is currently positioned or plans to be.

■ Entry level: performance below this level is not acceptable to customers (grey in Figure 4.23)

■ Industry average: performance below this level is not competitive (white in Figure 4.23)

■ Industry best: performance above this level signifies leadership (green in Figure 4.23).

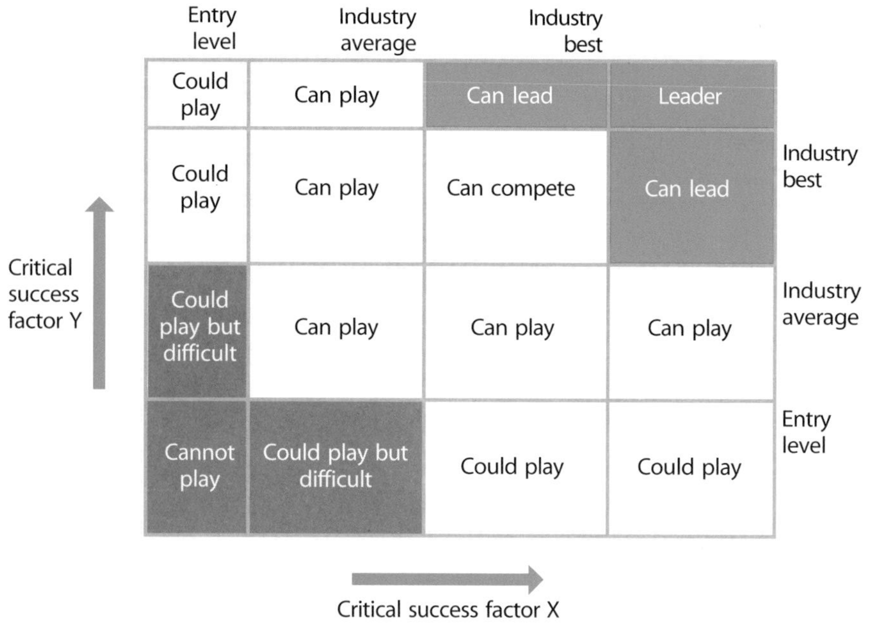

Figure 4.23 Critical success factors and competitive positions in playing fields

These benchmarks are relative (not absolute) and their values on an index may vary over time. For example, the initial entry-level benchmark for cost as a CSF may be quite easy to cross in a new market space with low levels of competition. The benchmark may become higher (lower costs) because of competitive action combined with technology innovations or other factors, such as excessive supply of resources in the market space (as happened a few years ago with telecommunications bandwidth). Strategic analysis should take into account not only the current benchmarks for a playing field but also the direction in which they are expected to move (higher or lower), the magnitude of change, and the related probabilities.

This analysis is necessary for service providers to avoid being surprised by changes in the market space that can completely destroy their value proposition. Type I service providers may be particularly vulnerable to such blind spots if they are not accustomed to the business analysis found in Type II and Type III providers. Type I providers

also face competition even if they have captive customers within their enterprise. The playing field is used to conduct strategic analysis of Market Spaces, Customer Portfolios (Figure 4.24), Service Portfolios, and Contract Portfolios. Managers decide the required scenarios to construct using applicable CSFs, scales and indices.

4.4.6 Prioritizing investments

One common problem service providers have is prioritizing investments and managerial attention on the right set of opportunities. There is a hierarchy in customer needs analogous to Maslow's Hierarchy of Needs for individuals. At any one time, the business needs of customers are fulfilled to varying levels of satisfaction. The combination of hierarchy or importance of a need and its current level of satisfaction determines the priority in the customer's mind for purchases. The best opportunities for service providers lie in areas where an important customer need remains poorly satisfied (Figure 4.25).

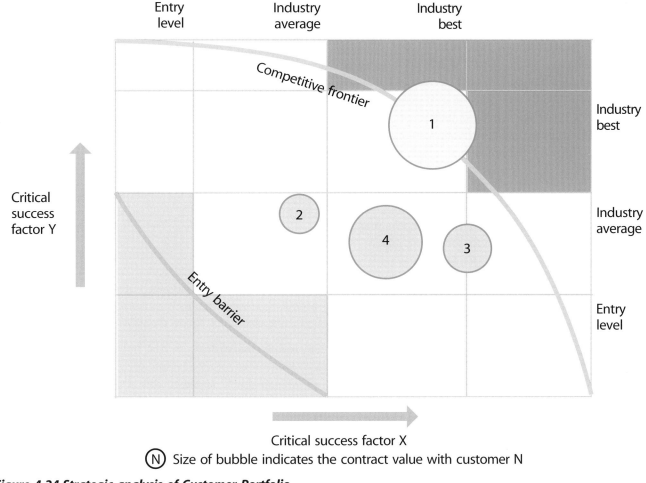

Figure 4.24 Strategic analysis of Customer Portfolio

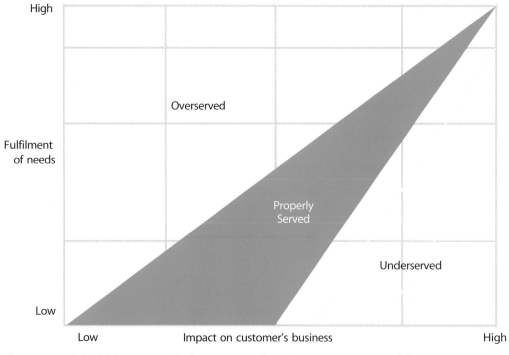

Figure 4.25 Prioritizing strategic investments based on customer needs[23]

Service Portfolios should be extended to support such areas of opportunity. This typically means there is a need for services to provide certain levels of utility and warranty. However, managers should not overlook the costs and risks in such areas. There are usually strong reasons why certain needs of customers remain unfulfilled. Breakthrough performance and innovation are usually required to successfully deliver value in underserved areas of opportunity.

4.4.7 Exploring business potential

Service providers can be present in more than one market space. As part of strategic planning, service providers should analyse their presence across various market spaces. Strategic reviews include the analysis of strengths, weaknesses, opportunities and threats in each market space. Service providers also analyse their business potential based on unserved or underserved market spaces. This is an important aspect of leadership and direction provided by the senior management of service providers. The long-term vitality of the service provider rests on supporting customer needs as they change or grow as well exploiting new opportunities that emerge. This analysis identifies opportunities with current and prospective customers. It also prioritizes investments in service assets based on their potential to serve market spaces of interest. For example, if a service provider has strong capabilities and resources in service recovery, it explores all those market spaces where such assets can deliver value for customers.

Begin with a broad set of outcomes such as business asset productivity. This defines a broad market space. Lost business asset productivity is linked with how it is recovered through services. Unserved and underserved customer needs are identified within this context and focus is applied based on existing strengths and opportunities. This defines narrower market spaces with specialization based on the categories of business assets and the manner in which they are supported by services (service archetypes).

Providers decide which customer needs are effectively and efficiently served through services, while choosing to serve certain market spaces and avoid others. This essential aspect of service strategy is broken down into the following decisions. Firstly, identify:

■ Market spaces that are best served by existing service assets
■ Market spaces to avoid with existing service assets.

Then for each market space to be served (Figure 4.26), decisions are made with respect to:

■ Services to offer (Service Portfolio)
■ Customers to serve (Customer Portfolio)
■ Critical success factors
■ Underserved market spaces

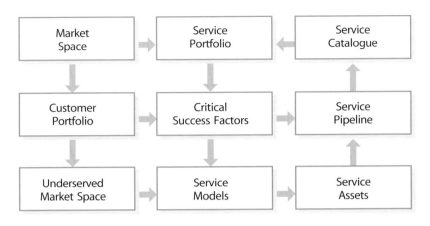

Figure 4.26 New service development

- Service models and service assets
- Service Pipeline and Service Catalogue.

Market space analysis for Type I and Type II providers follows similar principles to those for Type III. Differences are in terms of the extent to which decisions are influenced by:

- Priority and strategic value
- Investments required
- Financial objectives (including profit motive)
- Risks involved
- Policy constraints.

4.4.8 Alignment with customer needs

Understand the mutual relationship between customers and market spaces. Customers can contain one or more market spaces. Market spaces can contain one or more customers (Figure 4.27).

- The market spaces of Type I service providers are internal to the organizational unit within which they are embedded.
- The market spaces of Type II providers are internal to the enterprise but distributed across the constituent business units and the corporate functions.
- The market spaces of Type III providers are typically distributed across more than one enterprise customer.

The business strategy of a service provider usually determines the placement of market spaces. However, the placement of market spaces also influences the type of strategies to be pursued. This mutual influence will lead to adjustments and changes over any given planning horizon

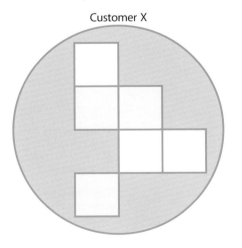

Customer X

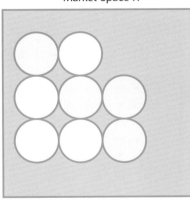

Market Space X

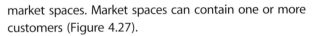

☐ Served market space

☐ Unserved market space

◯ Served customer

◯ Unserved customer

Figure 4.27 Customers and market spaces

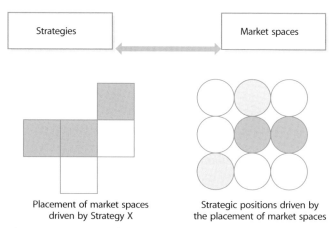

Placement of market spaces driven by Strategy X

Strategic positions driven by the placement of market spaces

Figure 4.28 Strategies and market spaces

(Figure 4.28). Since market spaces are defined based on outcomes desired by customers, the changes and adjustments are ultimately based on the dynamics of the customer's business environment. Over time there will be cohesiveness between strategies and market spaces from mutual alignment and reinforcement.

Since market spaces are defined in terms of the business needs of customers, service provider strategies are therefore aligned to customers. This is the most important reason why service providers must think in terms of market spaces and not simply industry sectors, geographies, or technology platforms. This is intuitive to the senior leadership of Type I providers because they are accustomed to being driven more by the outcomes

expected by their business units than by the traditional segmentation of markets.

4.4.9 Expansion and growth

Once service strategies are linked to market spaces, it is easier to make decisions on Service Portfolios, designs, operations, and long-term improvements. Investments in service assets such as skills sets, knowledge, processes, and infrastructure are driven by the critical success factors for a given market space. The growth and expansion of any business is less risky when anchored by core capabilities and demonstrated performance. Successful expansion strategies are often based on leveraging existing service assets (Figure 4.29) and Customer Portfolios to drive new growth and profitability.

The resultant exposure to costs and risks is far lower in this approach compared to ad hoc expansions, which are purely opportunistic in nature. This is because expanding into adjacent market spaces leverages service assets that are common across market spaces. This means that additional investments are hedged across new and existing market spaces. If for any reason the expansion fails or business opportunities do not materialize, there will be a greater salvage value for the new investments made. To further reduce the risks of expansion strategies, it is best to leverage the presence in market spaces that have achieved sufficient growth. Growth and maturity could mean either improving results in existing market

	A1	A2	A3	A4	A5	A6	A7	A8
U1								
U2						▓		▓
U3					▓			
U4								
U5					▓		▓	
U6								
U7								
U8								

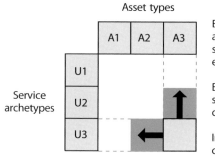

Asset types

Service archetypes

Expansion into an adjacent market space by leveraging existing assets.

Based on proven service management capabilities.

Increase share of customer's wallet.

Figure 4.29 Expansion into adjacent market spaces

spaces or expanding the portfolio to other market spaces with a high potential for success.

Contracts represent combinations of customers and services. Contracts exist where there are commitments to a customer with respect to a service. Service agreements are types of contracts. It follows that Contract Portfolios are based on the interaction of the Customer Portfolio and the Service Portfolio. Changes to the Contract Portfolio are driven by changes to either the Customer Portfolio or the Service Portfolio (Figure 4.30). Growth in a market space is achieved by:

- Extensions to existing contracts (same service/same customer)
- Increases in demand (greater share of customer's wallet)
- Providing complementary services.

Strategic planning and review includes examining opportunities for growth within current customers and services. Growth in a market space is dependent on demonstrated ability to deliver value and a strong record with existing customers. Chapter 5 provides further guidance to senior managers on how to prioritize investments and allocate resources in a manner that reduces risks of failure.

4.4.10 Differentiation in market spaces

In a given market space, services provide utility to customers by delivering benefit with a level of certainty (i.e. warranty). Market spaces can be defined anywhere an opportunity exists to improve the performance of customer assets. Service strategy is about how to provide distinctive value in each market space. Service providers should analyse every market space they support and determine their position with respect to the options that customers have with other service providers.

In any given market space there are critical success factors that determine whether or not a service provider is competitive in offering services. These factors are defined in terms of the relative importance of a set of outcomes or benefits as perceived by customers. Examples are affordability, number of service channels or delivery platforms, lead times to activate new accounts, and the availability of services in areas where customers have business operations (Figure 4.31).

Appropriate indices or scales are necessary. A value curve can then be plotted by linking the performance on each scale or index corresponding to a critical success factor.[25] Market research can determine the value curve that represents the average industry performance or one that represents key competitors. Feedback obtained from customers through periodic reviews or satisfaction surveys

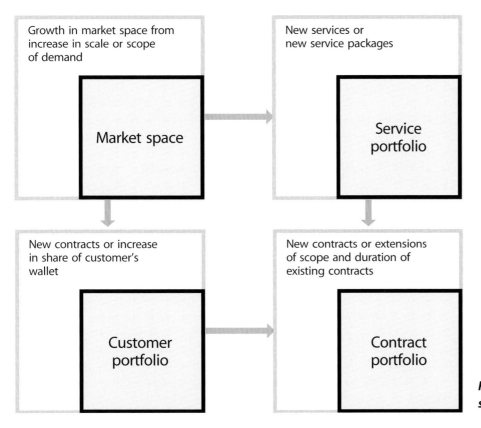

Figure 4.30 Growth in a market space

are used to plot your own value curve in a given market space or for your Customer Portfolio.

Service strategies should then seek to create a separation between the value curves, which are nothing but differentiation in the market space. The greater the differentiation, the more distinctive the value proposition offered in your services as perceived by customers. The differentiation is normally created through better a better mix of services, superior service designs, and operational effectiveness that allows for efficiency and effectiveness in the delivery and support of services. Through various combinations of factors there are many ways in which to create differentiation. service management is about making decisions on the service design, transition, operation, and improvement that lead to differentiation in every supported market space.

Again, this is just as applicable to Type I providers. It is a good practice to periodically review the competitive position of every service in the corresponding market space. This is particularly important in relation to shifts in business trends or major changes in the business environment that may alter the economics behind the customer's decision to source a service.

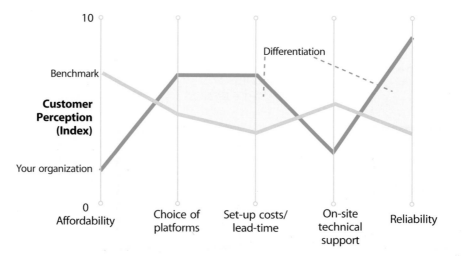

Benchmark may be based on industry averages, closest rival or most attractive alternative for the customer. Customer perception may be measured on some suitable scale or index accepted within the industry or region.

Figure 4.31 Differentiation in the market space

Service economics

5

5 Service economics

'Economy does not lie in sparing money, but in spending it wisely.'

Thomas Henry Huxley

5.1 FINANCIAL MANAGEMENT

Operational visibility, insight and superior decision making are the core capabilities brought to the enterprise through the rigorous application of Financial Management. Just as business units accrue benefits through the analysis of product mix and margin data, or customer profiles and product behaviour, a similar utility of financial data continues to increase the importance of Financial Management for IT and the business as well.

Financial Management as a strategic tool is equally applicable to all three service provider types. Internal service providers are increasingly asked to operate with the same levels of financial visibility and accountability as their business unit and external counterparts. Moreover, technology and innovation have become the core revenue-generating capabilities of many companies.

Financial Management provides the business and IT with the quantification, in financial terms, of the value of IT Services, the value of the assets underlying the provisioning of those services, and the qualification of operational forecasting. Talking about IT in terms of

services is the crux of changing the perception of IT and its value to the business. Therefore, a significant portion of Financial Management is working in tandem with IT and the business to help identify, document and agree on the value of the services being received, and the enablement of service demand modelling and management.

5.1.1 Enterprise value and benefits of Financial Management

The landscape of IT is changing as strategic business and delivery models evolve rapidly, product development cycles shrink, and disposable designer products become ubiquitous. These dynamics create what often appears to IT professionals as a dichotomy of priorities: increasing demands on performance and strategic business alignment, combined with greater demand for superior operational visibility and control. Much like their business counterparts, IT organizations are increasingly incorporating Financial Management in the pursuit of:

- Enhanced decision making
- Speed of change
- Service Portfolio Management
- Financial compliance and control
- Operational control
- Value capture and creation.

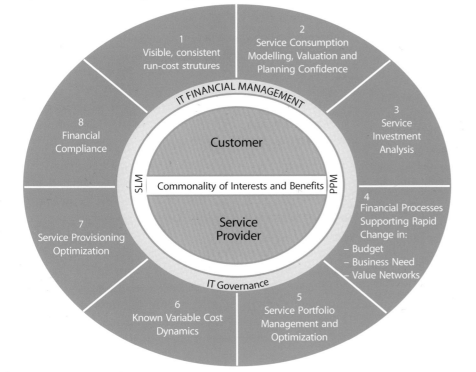

Figure 5.1 Shared imperatives framework: business and IT

IT organizations are conceding they are quite similar to market-facing companies. They share the need to analyse, package, market and deliver services just as any other business. They also share a common and increasing need to understand and control factors of demand and supply, and to provision services as cost-effectively as possible while maximizing visibility into related cost structures. This commonality is of great value to the business as IT seeks to drive down cost while improving its service offerings. The framework below illustrates the commonality of interests and benefits between the business and IT (Figure 5.1).

Service and strategy design both benefit greatly from the operational decision-making data that Financial Management aggregates, refines and distributes as part of the Financial Management process. Rigorously applied, Financial Management generates meaningful critical performance data used to answer important questions for an organization:

- Is our differentiation strategy resulting in higher profits or revenues, lower costs, or greater service adoption?
- Which services cost us the most, and why?
- What are our volumes and types of consumed services, and what is the correlating budget requirement?
- How efficient are our service provisioning models in relation to alternatives?
- Does our strategic approach to service design result in services that can be offered at a competitive 'market price', substantially reduce risk or offer superior value?
- Where are our greatest service inefficiencies?
- Which functional areas represent the highest priority opportunities for us to focus on as we generate a Continual Service Improvement strategy?

Without meaningful operational financial information, it is not possible to answer these questions correctly, and strategic decisions become little more than instinctive responses to flawed or limited observations and information, often from a single organizational unit. Such methods can often incorrectly steer strategy, service design, and tactical operational decisions.

Whereas Financial Management provides a common language in which to converse with the business, Service Valuation provides the storyline from which the business can comprehend what is actually delivered to them from IT. Combined with Service Level Management, Service Valuation is the means to a mutual agreement with the business regarding what a service is, what its components are, and its actual cost or worth.

Additionally, the application of Service Valuation discussed in this chapter transforms the discussion and interaction between IT and the business customer, and the way customers plan for and consume IT services. The use of Financial Management to provide services with cost transparency (such as via a Service Catalogue) that can then be clearly understood by the business and rolled into planning processes for demand modelling and funding, is a powerful benefit. Such maturity in an IT operation can generate enormous cost savings and Demand Management capabilities.

5.1.2 Concepts, inputs and outputs

Like its business equivalent, IT Financial Management responsibilities and activities do not exist solely within the IT finance and accounting domain. Rather, many parts of the enterprise interact to generate and consume IT financial information, including operations and support units, project management organizations, application development, infrastructure, Change Management, business units, end users etc. These entities aggregate, share and maintain the financial data they need. The Financial Management data used by an IT organization may reside in, and be owned by the accounting and finance domain, but responsibility for generating and utilizing it extends to other areas. Financial Management aggregates data inputs from across the enterprise and assists in generating and disseminating information as an output to feed critical decisions and activities such as those discussed below.

5.1.2.1 Service Valuation

Service Valuation quantifies, in financial terms, the funding sought by the business and IT for services delivered, based on the agreed value of those services. FM calculates and assigns a monetary value to a service or service component so that they may be disseminated across the enterprise once the business customer and IT identify what services are actually desired.

The pricing of a service is the cost-to-value translation necessary to achieve clarity and influence the demand and consumption of services. The activity involves identifying the cost baseline for services and then quantifying the perceived value added by a provider's service assets in order to conclude a final service value. The primary goal of Service Valuation is to produce a value for services that the business perceives as fair, and fulfils the needs of the provider in terms of supporting it as an ongoing concern. A secondary objective is the improved management of demand and consumption behaviour. It is helpful to restate what constitutes service value so that the translation to price can be more easily dissected:

> 'Value is created when service providers are able to deploy their capabilities and resources (i.e. service assets), and with a certain level of assurance, deliver to the customer a greater utility of their services. As established earlier, this utility is in the form of enhancing or enabling the performance of customer assets, and contributing to the realization of business outcomes.'

Within this definition, the service value elements of warranty and utility require translation of their value to an actual monetary figure. Therefore service valuation focuses primarily on two key valuation concepts:

Provisioning Value is the actual underlying cost to IT related to provisioning a service, including all fulfilment elements, both tangible and intangible. Input comes from financial systems, and consists of payment for actual resources consumed by IT in the provisioning of a service. These cost elements include items such as:

- Hardware and software licence costs
- Annual maintenance fees for hardware and software
- Personnel resources used in the support or maintenance of a service
- Utilities, data centre or other facilities charges
- Taxes, capital or interest charges
- Compliance costs.

The sum of these actual service costs typically represents the baseline from which the minimum value of a service is calculated since providers are seldom willing to offer a service where they are unable to recover the provisioning cost. Of course there are exceptions to this, especially related to Type I providers in situations where alternatives for provisioning of a specific service are limited or non-existent.

Service Value Potential is the value-added component based on the customer's perception of value from the service or expected marginal utility and warranty from using the service, in comparison with what is possible using the customer's own assets (Figure 5.2). Provisioning Value elements add up first to establish a baseline. The value-added components of the service are then monetized individually according to their perceived value to estimate the true value of the service package. All of these components would then be summed along with the baseline costs to determine the ultimate value of the service. The interrelated concepts of provisioning value and perceived service value potential are illustrated in Figure 5.2.

Provisioning Value elements are typically easier to quantify due to availability of purchasing and human resources (HR) information. However, a number of techniques are available to assist with the identification of service value potential, and are addressed elsewhere in this publication and the Service Design publication. The evolution of traditional accounting methods toward a service-oriented approach that supports the decomposition and valuation of value potential components is discussed later in this section.

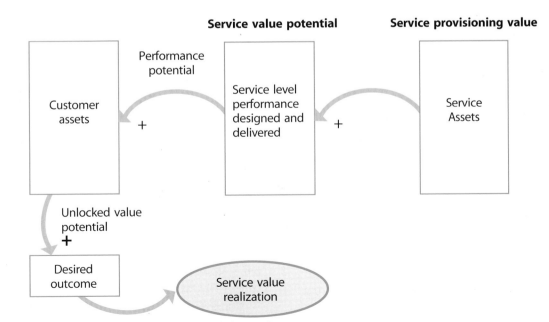

Figure 5.2 Customer assets are the basis for defining value

5.1.2.2 Demand modelling

Poorly managed service demand is a source of cost and risk. The tight coupling of service demand and capacity (consumption and production) requires Financial Management to quantify funding variations resulting from changes in service demand. Financial demand modelling focuses on identifying the total cost of utilization (TCU) to the customer, and predicting the financial implications of future service demand. The Service Catalogue provides critical information on service demand for modelling, decision making, and control.

Demand modelling uses service-oriented financial information with factors of demand and supply in order to model anticipated usage by the business, and provisioning requirements by IT. This is for identifying funding requirements, variations and drivers of those variations, and to assist in the management of service demand. In this context, inputs for managing service demand include pricing and incentive adjustments that are intended to alter customer consumption patterns. Without critical demand data from Capacity Management and the Service Catalogue, translated into financial requirements, this is not possible.

Mature service organizations are able to apply the practice of Service Valuation to their Service Catalogue to establish a value for each service, service component, and service level package. This enables the capability to generate demand plans and related financial requirements for expected service consumption. This service demand planning is translated to financial funding requirements for the entire enterprise at a business unit level or lower, and consumption of both services and budgets can be viewed in real time through an extension of the Service Catalogue.

Through the application of Financial Management, the Service Catalogue is able to provide customers with the capability to regulate their demand and prepare budgets. This partly addresses the problem of over-consumption by business and subsequent dissonance with the value of the service. Capacity planning also provides important information related to service demand by providing usage data and trend reporting largely from a technical component perspective (think bandwidth, resources, processing capacity etc. that carry a financial impact), and by tracking significant expected variances in demand related to strategic events such as product launches, entry into new markets, and acquisitions or divestitures. Demand modelling can leverage data from capacity management because of the tight coupling.

5.1.2.3 Service Portfolio Management

Financial Management is a key input to Service Portfolio Management. By understanding cost structures applied in the provisioning of a service, a company can benchmark that service cost against other providers. In this way, companies can use IT financial information, together with service demand and internal capability information, discussed previously, to make beneficial decisions regarding whether a certain service should be provisioned internally. For instance, if a company identifies its internal cost of providing 'Service A' to be £50 per month per user, and then finds a provider with the economics of scale and the focused skill set required to offer the identical service for £33 per month, the company may decide that it would rather focus its resources on other services where it possesses a greater ability to offer lower cost and/or higher quality, and to outsource Service A to the other provider.

Case example 9: *Service Portfolio optimization*

One of the world's largest financial companies invests in opening its own OEM-certified desktop repair centres. Due diligence reveals that its scale enables it to offer these services at a lower cost than the market.

The firm regularly benchmarks its internal costs of providing desktop support, desktop repair and desktop provisioning, and compares these with the prices of Type II and Type III providers. On discovering a service that can no longer be offered at a cost 'below market', or a new service that can be provisioned internally because of benefits from the scale advantage, the firm adjusts accordingly.

The recurring financial approach to Service Portfolio results in the continual improvement of service cost structures, and measurably enhances the competitive position of the company.

This concept is no different from that of traditional businesses aligning their market-facing service and product portfolios to their core capabilities. It is a prudent strategy to exit a business (service) line that is not as profitable or cost-effective, or does not deliver the requisite combination of quality and value relative to alternatives. Many IT organizations, however, refrain from identifying service-oriented costs and making them visible to the enterprise. The result over time is a portfolio of services with ineffective cost structures and decrease in the customer's perception of value and satisfaction. Service Portfolio Management is further elaborated in Section 5.3.

5.1.2.4 Service provisioning optimization

Financial Management provides key inputs for Service Provisioning Optimization (SPO). SPO examines the financial inputs and constraints of service components or delivery models to determine if alternatives should be explored relating to how a service can be provisioned differently to make it more competitive in terms of cost or quality.

A typical candidate for this type of examination includes services that have been identified for removal from the Service Portfolio because they can no longer be provisioned efficiently relative to other providers or service alternatives, or because they experience declining usage due to factors such as obsolescence. In this example, Financial Management would provide critical input to the enterprise regarding existing service cost structures, and assist with the financial analysis of alternative delivery methods, service mix, financing structures and so on. It would also serve to determine or validate whether a service provisioning alternative would reduce an organization's service cost structure or enhance service value. It is this financial analysis of service components, constraints and value that is at the heart of Financial Management's interaction with Service Provisioning Optimization.

5.1.2.5 Planning confidence

One goal of Financial Management is to ensure proper funding for the delivery and consumption of services. Planning provides financial translation and qualification of expected future demand for IT services. Financial Management Planning departs from historical IT planning by focusing on demand and supply variances resulting from business strategy, capacity inputs and forecasting, rather than traditional individual line item expenditures or business cost accounts. As with planning for any other business organization, input should be collected from all areas of the IT organization and the business.

Planning can be categorized into three main areas, each representing financial results that are required for continued visibility and service valuation:

■ Operating and Capital (general and fixed asset ledgers)

■ Demand (need and use of IT services – discussed earlier in this chapter)

■ Regulatory and Environmental (compliance).

Operating and Capital planning processes are common and fairly standardized, and involve the translation of IT expenditures into corporate financial systems as part of the corporate planning cycle. Beyond this, the importance of this process is in communicating expected changes in the funding of IT services for consideration by other business domains. The impact of IT services on capital planning is largely underestimated, but is of interest to tax and fixed asset departments if the status of an IT asset changes.

Regulatory and Environmental-related planning should get its triggers from within the business. However, FM should apply the proper financial inputs to the related services value, whether cost based or value based. For example:

> **Case example 10:** *Regulatory and Environmental planning impacts*
>
> At a consumer products corporation, it was determined that all servers older than three years should be replaced. Plans were properly communicated and, when the time came, a business case was prepared. Adequate justification was provided to substantiate the replacement need, and the related ROI based on the required expenditure barely fitted within acceptable corporate thresholds.
>
> Towards the end of the implementation, it was realized that local governmental regulations and the company's desired practice of environmental stewardship required special disposal of the old equipment since the casings contained measurable amounts of lead. The cost to remove and properly dispose of the equipment was substantial enough to negatively impact the ROI calculation of the project, and pushed it beyond acceptable tolerance. If the project team had correctly recognized the true costs of replacement, requisite funding would have been identified and included in the planning mechanism.

In this example, ignoring the impact of equipment disposal when building the business case resulted in an overstatement of the benefits of replacement and consequently required adjustments to the funding model.

Confidence is the notion that financial inputs and models for service demand and supply represent statistically significant measures of accuracy. Data confidence is important for two reasons: 1) the critical role data plays in achieving the objectives of Financial Management, and 2) the possibility of erroneous data undermining decision making.

Since Financial Management performs unique financial translation and qualification functions, there is an obligation to ensure that the confidence level of planning data and information is high. Questions about its accuracy will undermine its perceived value. It is therefore important to follow good security practices for access and rights management so that information quality is not compromised. Planning confidence is ultimately a combination of service-oriented demand modelling translated into measurable financial requirements with a high degree of statistical accuracy. The financial requirements act as inputs to critical business decision making.

5.1.2.6 Service investment analysis

Financial Management provides the shared analytical models and knowledge used throughout an enterprise in order to assess the expected value and/or return of a given initiative, solution, programme or project in a standardized fashion. It sets the thresholds that guide the organization in determining what level of analytical sophistication is to be applied to various projects based on size, scope, resources, cost and related parameters.

The objective of service investment analysis is to derive a value indication for the total lifecycle of a service based on 1) the value received, and 2) costs incurred during the lifecycle of the service. Section 5.1.3, on 'Methods, models, activities and techniques', discusses a number of concepts and methods for exploiting IT investment analysis to improve capital expenditure and IT operations processes.

Assumptions about the service are a key component of analysing investments. The granularity of assumptions used in investment analysis can have significant impact on the outcome of the analysis. For example, a service obtained via an instantly self-deployable packaged software solution residing on a single desktop and requiring little user support will have a different investment profile than a service obtained through custom development, global customer interaction and other resources that go into creating, deploying and supporting an enterprise solution with multiple language users. In Service Investment Analysis, it is best to lean toward the use of an exhaustive inventory of assumptions rather than a limited set of high-level inputs, in order to generate a more realistic and accurate view of the investment being made.

5.1.2.7 Accounting

Accounting within Financial Management differs from traditional accounting in that additional category and characteristics must be defined that enable the identification and tracking of service-oriented expense or capital items.

Financial Management plays a translational role between corporate financial systems and service management. The result of a service-oriented accounting function is that far greater detail and understanding is achieved regarding

service provisioning and consumption, and the generation of data that feeds directly into the planning process. The functions and accounting characteristics that come into play are discussed below:

- Service recording – the assignment of a cost entry to the appropriate service. Depending on how services are defined, and the granularity of the definitions, there may be additional sub-service components.
- Cost Types – these are higher level expenses categories such as hardware, software, labour, administration, etc. These attributes assist with reporting and analysing demand and usage of services and their components in commonly used financial terms.
- Cost classifications – there are also classifications within services that designate the end purpose of the cost. These include classifications such as:
  - Capital/operational – this classification addresses different accounting methodologies that are required by the business and regulatory agencies.
  - Direct/indirect – this designation determines whether a cost will be assigned directly or indirectly to a consumer or service.
    - Direct costs are charged directly to a service since it is the only consumer of the expense.
    - Indirect or 'shared' costs are allocated across multiple services since each service may consume a portion of the expense.
  - Fixed/variable – this segregation of costs is based on contractual commitments of time or price. The strategic issue around this classification is that the business should seek to optimize fixed service costs and minimize the variable in order to maximize predictability and stability.
  - Cost Units – A Cost Unit is the identified unit of consumption that is accounted for a particular service or service asset.

As accounting processes and practices mature toward a service orientation, more evidence is created that substantiates the existence and performance of the IT organization. The information available by translating cost account data into service account information dramatically changes the dynamics and visibility of service management, enabling a higher level of service strategy development and execution.

5.1.2.8 Compliance

Compliance relates to the ability to demonstrate that proper and consistent accounting methods and/or practices are being employed. This relates to financial asset valuation, capitalization practices, revenue recognition, access and security controls etc. If proper practices are documented and known, compliance can be easily addressed. It becomes imperative then to address responsibility for being aware of regulatory and environmental risks that can affect the service operation and the customer's business.

Over the past decade a number of important regulatory and standards-related issues and opportunities have been introduced that impact Financial Management. Certain legislation has had enormous impact on financial audit and compliance activities. The public demand for accurate, meaningful data regarding the value of a company's transactions and assets places greater pressure on Financial Management. There are wide variations in the impact of such legislation that should be considered. Public frameworks such as COBIT and the advice and consent of public accountants and auditors are valuable to service management.

The implementation of public frameworks and standards such as COBIT, ISO/IEC 20000, Basel II, and other industry specific regulation may appear to be pure costs with no tangible benefits. However, regulatory compliance tends to improve data security and quality processes, creating a greater need for understanding the costs of compliance. Services provisioned to one industry at a certain price may not necessarily be provisioned at the same price to a different industry segment. There are instances where the cost of compliance has been large enough to have an impact on the pricing of a service.

5.1.2.9 Variable Cost Dynamics

Variable Cost Dynamics (VCD) focuses on analysing and understanding the multitude of variables that impact service cost, how sensitive those elements are to variability, and the related incremental value changes that result. Among other benefits, VCD analysis can be used to identify a marginal change in unit cost resulting from adding or subtracting one or more incremental units of a service. Such an analysis is helpful when applied toward the analysis of expected impacts from events such as acquisitions, divestitures, changes to the Service Portfolio or service provisioning alternatives etc.

This element of service value can be daunting since the number and type of variable elements can range dramatically depending on the type of service being analysed. The sensitivity analytics component of Variable Cost Dynamics is also a complex analytical tool because of the number and types of assumptions and scenarios that are often made around variable cost components. Below is

a very brief list of possible variable service cost components that could be included in such an analysis:

- Number and type of users
- Number of software licences
- Cost/operating footprint of data centre
- Delivery mechanisms
- Number and type of resources
- The cost of adding one more storage device
- The cost of adding one more end-user licence.

The analysis of Variable Cost Dynamics often follows a line of thinking similar to market spaces, covered elsewhere in this publication. The key value derived from this body of knowledge focuses on more precisely determining what fixed and variable cost structures are linked to a service, and how they alter based on change (either incremental or monumental), what the service landscape should look like as a result, how a service should be designed and provisioned, and what value should be placed on a service.

5.1.3 Methods, models, activities and techniques

This section of the chapter is intended to provide guidance in the form of sample models, methods, activities and techniques for key areas. The guidance provided in this section is not intended to include all possibilities or alternatives, but to provide a sampling of best practice.

5.1.3.1 Service valuation

During the activities of service valuation, regardless of the lifecycle, time horizon or service chosen, decisions will need to be made regarding various issues. This section discusses the more common points of contention that all IT centres will need to address.

Direct versus indirect costs are those that are either: 1) clearly directly attributable to a specific service, versus 2) indirect costs that are shared among multiple services. These costs should be approached logically to first determine which line items are sensible to maintain, given the data available and the level of effort required. For example, hardware maintenance service components can be numerous and detailed, and it may not be of value to decompose them all for the purpose of assigning each to a line item cost element.

Once the depth and breadth of cost components are appropriately identified, rules or policy to guide how costs are to be spread among multiple services may be required. In the hardware maintenance example, rules can be created so that a percentage of the maintenance is allocated to any related services equally, or allocation rules could be based on some logical unit of consumption. Perceived equality of consumption often drives such decisions.

Labour costs are another key expenditure requiring a decision to be made. This decision is similar to that of 'direct versus indirect' above, compounded by the complexity and accuracy of time tracking systems. If the capability to account for resources allocated across services is not available, then rules and assumptions must be created for allocation of these costs. In its simplest form, organizing personnel costs across financial centres based on a service orientation is a viable method for aligning personnel costs to services. Similarly, administration costs for all IT services can be collected at a macro level within a financial centre, and rules created for allocation of this cost amongst multiple services.

Variable cost elements include expenditures that are not fixed, but which vary depending on things such as the number of users or the number of running instances. Decisions need to be made based on the ability to pinpoint services or service components that cause increases in variability, since this variability can be a major source of price sensitivity. Pricing variability over time can cause the need for rules to allow for predictability. Associating a cost with a highly variable service requires the ability to track specific consumption of that service over time in order to establish ranges. Predictability of that cost can be addressed through:

■ Tiers – identifying price breaks where plateaus occur within a provider so that customers are encouraged to obtain scale efficiencies familiar to the provider.

■ Maximum cost – prescribing the cost of the service based on the maximum level of variability. This would then most likely cause overcharging, but the business may prefer 'rebates' versus additional costs.

■ Average cost – this involves setting the cost of the service based on historical averaging of the variability. It would leave some amount of over- or under-charge to be addressed at the end of the planning cycle.

Translation from cost account data to service value is only possible once costs are attributed to services rather than, or in addition to, traditional cost accounts. The example shown in Figure 5.3 illustrates the FM translation of traditional cost account data into service account information, and ultimately into the valuation of the service. This metamorphosis provides a powerful layer of visibility to the cost structures of services.

In this example, detailed service-oriented cost entries are captured and applied in order to establish the underlying cost baseline for the service (the first component of service valuation). Once this baseline has been established, monetary conversion of the value of any anticipated marginal enhancement to the utility and warranty of a customer's existing service assets occurs in order for the total potential value of the service to be determined.

After determining the fixed and variable costs for each service, steps should be taken to determine the variable cost drivers and range of variability for a service. This drives any additional amount that should be added to the calculation of potential service value in order to allow for absorption of consumption variability. Determining the perceived or requisite value to add to the calculation is also dependent on the operating model chosen since this takes into account culture, organization, and strategic direction.

Pricing the perceived value portion of a service involves resolving a grey area between historical costs, perceived value-added, and planned demand variances. Through this exercise, depending on the level of cost visibility present, even if actual costs are not recovered, the goal of providing cost visibility and value is demonstrated.

5.1.3.2 Service provisioning models and analysis

As companies analyse their current methods for providing services there are some basic alternatives to be considered that assist in framing the discussion and the analysis. There are distinct advantages to the various provisioning service models available, and while there are non-financial aspects to consider, such as service quality and transition readiness, this section will only address the financial analysis of the presented models.

The **Managed Services** provisioning model is the more traditional variant commonly known in the industry. In its simplest form, it is where a business unit requiring a service funds the provision of that service for itself. The service provider attempts to calculate the cost of the service in terms of development, infrastructure, manpower etc. so that the business and the service provider can plan for funding accordingly. In this simple example, the service is managed through the customer-specific application of service-related hardware, software and manpower, and the business unit pays for the entire service.

This is typically the most expensive service provisioning model because the resources used to provide the service are completely dedicated to the service of a single entity. If the consumer does not utilize the service and related resources to the fullest extent technically possible, then

Traditional Chart of Accounts

Applying Invoice to Chart of Accounts

Salary	60,000
Server Maintenance	25,000
Hardware Depreciation	15,000
TOTAL	**100,000**

Service-Oriented Accounting for IT

Service Oriented Cost Accounting and Identification

Service Maintenance Invoice   25,000
* Service: Collaboration Service A
* Cost Type: Hardware
* Classifications:
  - [>] Operational   vs.   Capital
  -     Direct   vs. [>] Indirect
  - [>] Fixed   vs.   Variable
* Unit Basis for Charging serial number

Hardware Depreciation   15,000
* Service: Financial Reporting
* Cost Type: Hardware
* Classifications:
  - Operational   vs. [>] Capital
  - Direct   vs. [>] Indirect
  - [>] Fixed   vs.   Variable
* Unit Basis for Charging user extension

Salary   60,000
* Service: Service Enhancement Project ABC
* Cost Type: Labour
* Classifications:
  - Operational   vs. [>] Capital
  - [>] Direct   vs.   Indirect
  -     Fixed   vs. [>] Variable
* Unit Basis for Charging personnel ID

Total Service-Oriented Accounting Entries 100,000
(Same 100,000, but service-oriented accounting treatment)

Service Cost Subset:
Collaboration Service

Total Costs for Collaboration Service   25,000

Service Cost #1-	50,000	
Service, Collaboration Service		
Annual Maintenance		
Service Cost #2-	125,000	
Collaboration Service		
Software		
Service Cost #3-	25,000	
Collaboration Service		
Other Characteristics, etc.		

200,000

Total Service Expenditure   **225,000**

Server maintenance invoice is aggregated with other service specific invoices

Valuing the Collaboration Service

Sample Breakdown of Service Cost by Accounting Characteristic

Collaboration Service Total Cost Breakdown by Characteristics

Hardware	150,000		
Software	25,000	225,000	Traditional cost accounting
Labour	50,000		
Operational	180,000		
Capital	45,000	225,000	Capital structure
Direct	51,000		
Indirect	55,000	225,000	Benefit structure
Fixed	100,000		
Variable	125,000	225,000	Variability of costs
Subtotal Expenditure		**225,000**	

Collaboration Service Potential Value Add

Utility Optimizations			Est. value of service improvement
Warranty Enhancement	10,000		Est. value of service improvement
Subtotal Value Add		**10,000**	
Subtotal:		225,000	Current Period Funding Base
Anticipated Peak Demand Variance	20%		
Increase (Decrease)		47,000	Additional Funding Required
		282,000	
Total Service Valuation (future)		**282,000**	Future Funding Need

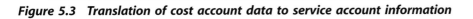

Figure 5.3   Translation of cost account data to service account information

unused capacity and the opportunity to provide additional services using the same capacity and resources is lost.

The model for **Shared Services** targets the provisioning of multiple services to one or more business units through use of shared infrastructure and resources (Figure 5.4). This concept is also widely applied throughout industry and represents significant cost savings to practitioners over the managed services model through the increased utilization of existing resources.

Utility-based Provisioning maximizes the combination of services being provisioned over the same infrastructure so that even more services are provisioned utilizing the same resources found in the Shared Services model. This is accomplished by providing services on a utility basis, dependent on how much, how often, and at what times the customer needs them. (N.B. The term 'utility' is used here with a very specific meaning, different from the meaning used in the rest of the publication.) Examples of such services would include an accounting application with primary usage at the end of each month, a reporting service that receives heavy usage only around the 1st and 15th of each month, or a production-related service used only in every other production cycle as production line outputs are changed.

This service provisioning model is the most cost-effective and the most elusive in that it requires a level of knowledge and capability missing from many IT organizations today. These cost savings are achieved primarily through leveraging a deeper understanding of technology architectures and customer needs in order to compile a service combination and architecture that enables maximum utilization of existing resources.

On-shore, Off-shore or Near-shore? The advent of off-shore service provisioning and its related success is not new. However, companies are still finding that what represents an off-shore opportunity for one firm may not necessarily be an opportunity for another. Many service elements discussed in this publication (and others discussed in the Service Design, Service Transition and Service Operations publications) are combined in an analysis of what mix of on-shore, near-shore and off-shore service provisioning is right for a specific company at a specific time.

The Financial Management impact on this decision cannot be underestimated. If a company does not understand its core service cost components and variable cost dynamics, it will typically have a difficult time making logical and fact-based decisions regarding outsourcing models, and an equally difficult time asking the right questions of providers.

Service provisioning cost analysis is the activity of statistically ranking the various forms of provisioning (and often providers) to determine the most beneficial model. A simplified example of a comparative service provisioning cost analysis that accounts for the way provisioning models could impact the cost of a service is provided. Table 5.1 is a simplified example of service cost components for the Service Desk function and how they come into play within the analysis of various provisioning models.

In this example, the scoring mechanism is normalized to a five-point scale where the lowest score is preferred. Notice that the company has ranked itself lower in some service components relative to the service quality and cost it has

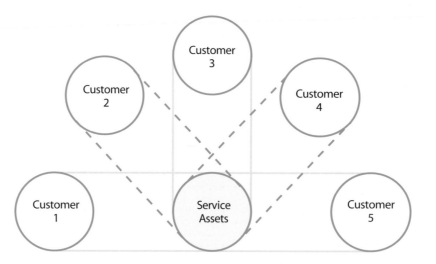

Figure 5.4 Shared services

Table 5.1 Service provisioning cost analysis

Service components	Type I provider (internal)	Managed service (on-shore provider)	Shared service (on-shore provider)	Managed service (off-shore provider)	Shared service (off-shore provider)
Cost scoring					
Tier 1 support (10 staff)	10*40000/200000=(2)	2.9	2.1	1.8	1.5
Tier 2 support (10 staff)	3	3.5	3.2	2.2	1.9
Tier 3 support (10 staff)	4	4.8	3.8	3.5	3
Service desk app hosting	1.2	1.5	1.5	1.1	0.6
Call centre infrastructure	1.5	1.5	0.8	0.5	0.4
Subtotals	11.7	14.2	11.4	9.1	7.4
Quality scoring					
Tier 1 support (10 staff)	4	3	3.5	2.9	4
Tier 2 support (10 staff)	3	2	3	3	3
Tier 3 support (10 staff)	2	3.2	3.5	3.2	3.5
Service desk app hosting	2.5	1	2	1.5	1.7
Call center infrastructure	3.5	1	2	1	1
Subtotals	15	10.2	14	11.6	13.2
TOTALS	**26.7**	**24.4**	**25.4**	**20.7**	**20.6**

determined to be available in the market from alternative providers. If only the simplified overall scores for each provider are assessed, the off-shore shared services provider appears to offer the lowest cost and highest quality for the entire portfolio of services. On closer inspection, however, the same provider offers the same

tiered support service quality as the company's existing Type I provider in all areas except Tier 3 support, estimated to be inferior to the provider.

Given that existing internal Tier 1 support has been ranked among the bottom of all alternatives, and existing Tier 3 internal support is actually superior, this provider may not offer the correct combination of cost and quality. Similar deficiencies and strengths are evident throughout the provisioning scoring example above. What conclusions can you draw from the scoring? What are some possible causes for the scoring in the presented sections? What optimized provisioning model would you conclude to be the most applicable for this company to adopt, given its current strengths and weaknesses?

5.1.3.3 Funding model alternatives

Funding addresses the financial impacts from changes to current and future demand for IT Services and the way in which IT will retain the funds to continue operations. This section offers a high-level discussion of various traditional models for the funding of IT Services. Since each model assumes a different perspective, yet rests on the same financial data, an increased ability to generate the requisite information translates to increased visibility into service costs and perceived value. The model chosen should always take into account and be appropriate for the current business culture and expectations.

Rolling Plan Funding – In a rolling plan, as one cycle completes another cycle of funding is added. This plan encourages a constant cycle of funding. However, it only addresses timing and does not necessarily increase accuracy. This type of model for funding would work well with a Service Lifecycle treatment where a commitment to fund a service is made at the beginning of the lifecycle and rolls until changes are made or the lifecycle has ended.

Trigger-Based Plans – Trigger-based funding occurs when identified critical triggers occur and set off planning for a particular event. For example, the Change Management process would be a trigger to the planning process for all approved changes that have financial impacts. Another trigger might be Capacity Planning where insight into capacity variances would affect the financial translation of IT Services. This type of planning alleviates timing issues with accounting for past events, since the process requires future planning at the time of the change. It would be a good plan to use with portfolio service management since it deals with services on a lifecycle basis.

Zero-Based Funding – This funding refers to how funding of IT occurs. Funding is only enough to bring the balance of the IT financial centre back to zero or to bring the balance of the funding of a service back to zero until another funding cycle. This equates to funding only the actual costs to deliver the IT Services.

5.1.3.4 Business Impact Analysis (BIA)

A BIA seeks to identify a company's most critical business services through analysis of outage severity translated into a financial value, coupled with operational risk. This information can help shape and enhance operational performance by enabling better decision making regarding prioritization of incident handling, problem management focus, change and release management operations, project priority, and so on. It is a beneficial tool for identifying the cost of service outage to a company, and the relative worth of a service. These two concepts are not identical.

The cost of service outage is a financial value placed on a specific service, and is meant to reflect the value of lost productivity and revenue over a specific period of time. The worth of a service relative to other services in a portfolio may not result exclusively from financial characteristics. Service Value, as discussed earlier, is derived from characteristics that may go beyond Financial Management, and represent aspects such as the ability to complete work or communicate with clients that may not be directly related to revenue generation. Both of these elements can be identified to a very adequate degree by the use of a BIA. While this section will discuss and illustrate the output of, and approach to creating a BIA, the reader should realize that the examples of BIA format and output represented here are not the only options, and alternative formats are visible throughout industry.

A number of steps need to be completed while generating a BIA. Some of the high-level activities are as follows:

1. Arrange resources from the business and IT that will work together on the analysis
2. Identify all of the top candidate services for designation as critical, secondary and tertiary (you do not need to designate them at this point)
3. Identify the core analysis points for use in assessing risk and impact, such as:
   - Lost sales revenue
   - Fines
   - Failure risk
   - Lost productivity
   - Lost opportunity
   - Number of users impacted
   - Visibility to shareholders, management etc.
   - Risk of service obsolescence
   - Harm to reputation among customers, shareholders and regulatory authorities
4. With the business, weight the identified elements of risk and impact

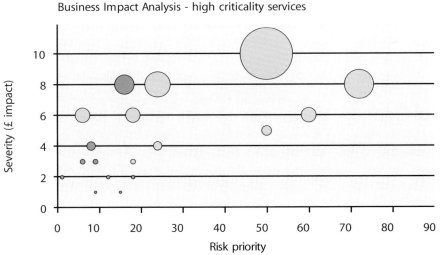

Figure 5.5 Business Impact Analysis

5 Score the candidate services against the weighted elements of risk and impact, and total their individual risk scores (you can utilize an FMEA for additional input here)

6 Generate a list of services in order of risk profile

7 Decide on a universal time period with which to standardize the translation of service outage to financial cost (1 minute, 1 hour, 1 day, etc.)

8 Calculate the financial impact of each service being analysed within the BIA using agreed methods, formulas and assumptions

9 Generate a list of services in order of financial impact

10 Utilize the risk and financial impact data generated to create charts that illustrate the company's highest risk applications that also carry the greatest financial impact. A sample output from this analysis is shown in Figure 5.5.

Figure 5.5 displays services on a comparative scale using financial impact and risk priority (in this case the probability, detectability and impact of failure) as points of analysis. For those companies that are inclined and capable, the use of Six Sigma methodologies can bring additional rigour to a BIA exercise, such as the example above, by enabling a structured approach to assessing Failure Modes and Effects (FMEA).

5.1.4 Key decisions for Financial Management

A number of concepts within the realm of Financial Management can have great impact on the development of service strategies. This section attempts to highlight some of those concepts so that the reader can determine how best to incorporate preferred alternatives into a formative strategy.

5.1.4.1 Cost recovery, value centre or accounting centre?

Whereas traditional accounting terminology refers to IT as a cost or profit centre, the real decision is not in the term used but in how funding will be replenished. Clarity around the operating model greatly contributes to understanding the requisite visibility of service provisioning costs, and funding is a good test of the business's confidence and perception of IT. Important questions should be answered when determining the premise under which the IT organization will replenish its funding for operations. The IT financial cycle starts with funding applied to resources that create output. That output is identified as value by the customer, and this in turn induces the funding cycle to begin again (Figure 5.6).

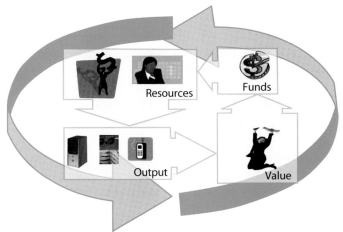

Figure 5.6 The funding lifecycle

IT is typically referred to as a cost centre, with funding based only on replenishing actual costs expended to deliver service. Compare this to the value centre or profit centre model where IT funding rests on the actual costs plus a perceived value-added amount. The capture of this additional value above actual cost is not confined to external providers, as Type I providers also have a need to continually expand their offerings and fund the analysis of provisioning alternatives and service quality enhancements.

Corporate culture plays a large role in determining the operating model. Homogeneity of business products can impact corporate culture and how each organization prefers to see IT financial models. If all product lines are similar and use IT systems similarly and equitably, then the operating model may not require the complexities of a business with very diverse product lines where each line consumes IT Services differently from one another. Similarly, the complexities of business structure (i.e. a global conglomerate versus a single operating entity), and the geographic dispersion of an organization can also greatly effect business expectations.

Replenishment of funds requires a decision about when to fund. Will funding be done on an annual basis (based on a corporate cycle) or on a constant cycle of replenishment (rolling plan model, zero-based model, trigger-based)? If the decision is made for IT to self-fund, then a higher level of perceived value will be added to the cost of services, and funding will most likely occur on a constant cycle. A constant cycle of replenishment, like in a rolling plan, is based on mutually agreed services, and removes the constraints inflicted by an annual budget since any changes to funding are agreed first by both the consumer and the provider.

5.1.4.2 Chargeback: to charge or not to charge

A 'chargeback' model for IT can provide accountability and transparency. However, if the operating model currently provides for a more simplistic annual replenishment of funds, then charging is often not necessary to provide accountability or transparency. In this instance the desired visibility would instead come from the activities and outputs of planning, demand modelling, and Service Valuation. If IT is a self-funding organization, suggesting more complexity and maturity in financial mechanisms, then some form of charging would provide added accountability and visibility.

Visibility is brought about through identification of Service Portfolios and catalogues, valuing those IT Services, and application of those values to demand or consumption models. Accountability refers to IT's ability to deliver expected services as agreed with the business, and the business's fulfilment of its obligations in funding those services. However, with no common ground as to what

service or value the business is receiving, accountability just becomes a constant struggle to explain why perceived value varies from the funding. Therefore, charging, without taking into account the operating model, typically does not deliver desired levels of accountability and visibility.

Charging should be done to encourage behavioural changes related to steering demand for IT Services. Charging must add value to the business and be in business terms, and it should have a degree of simplicity appropriate to the business culture. The most difficult and critical requirement of the model is its perceived fairness, which can be imparted if the model provides a level of predictability that the business typically desires, coupled with the mutual identification of services and service values.

Chargeback models vary based on the simplicity of the calculations and the ability for the business to understand them. Some sample chargeback models and components include:

- Notional charging – these chargeback alternatives address whether a journal entry will be made to the corporate financial systems. One option, the 'two-book' method, records costs into corporate financial systems in one fashion (for example, with IT as a cost centre), while a second book is kept but not recorded. This second book provides the same information but reflects what would have happened if the alternative method of recording had been used. This can be a good transitional model if chargeback practices are moving from one methodology to another.

- Tiered subscription – involves varying levels of warranty and/or utility offered for a service or service bundle, all of which have been priced, with the appropriate chargeback models applied. Most commonly referred to as gold, silver and bronze levels of service, the weakness of tiered subscriptions is that there is no non-repudiation and it does not encourage different behaviour with regard to usage.

- Metered usage – involves a more mature financial environment and operational capability, where demand modelling is incorporated with utility computing capabilities to provide confidence in the capture of real-time usage. This consumption information is then translated into customer charging based on various service increments that have been agreed, such as hours, days or weeks.

- Direct Plus – this is a more simplistic model where those costs that can be attributed directly to a service are charged accordingly with some percentage of indirect costs shared amongst all.

■ Fixed or user cost – The most simplistic of chargeback models, this model takes the cost and divides by an agreed denominator such as number of users. This model contributes little to affecting customer behaviour, or identifying true service demand or consumption, but does allocate the costs to the bottom line of multiple businesses in the easiest, if somewhat inequitable, fashion if so desired.

No matter which methodology is used, or none or all, it is more important to make certain that the overriding substantiation comes from providing value to the business.

5.1.4.3 Financial Management implementation checklist

The tracks indicated below serve as a sample checklist of recommended implementation steps that should be addressed. The guidance below is not intended to be a project plan, but a representation of a phased approach to implementation.

Track 1 – Plan

■ Critical questions about the business and IT culture should be addressed prior to moving forward with implementing Financial Management. Refer to previous chapters and ITIL publications for a discussion on organizational considerations that should be considered before designing processes.

■ Key to setting of practices is assessing the corporate culture. Geographical considerations, such as one location versus global distribution, will have additional regulatory and compliance considerations.

■ Identify all internal and external contacts that provide and/or receive IT financial information.

■ Be clear about IT and business expectations. What deliverables do both organizations expect from the implementation? Does the business or IT expect a chargeback system? Is there currently a Service Catalogue implemented and awaiting pricing?

■ Determine systems that are in place from which Financial Management will receive and contribute data.

■ Determine the funding or operating model to be used. This will set the tone for the way accounting and valuation will be performed.

■ Assign responsibilities for the deliverables and outline the activities to be performed.

■ Prepare the organization chart based on activities that will be performed, the size of the data that will be managed, and tools that are available.

■ Prepare a policy and operating procedures list.

Track 2 – Analyse

■ The analysis portion of the implementation should involve gathering in-depth details around the planning and funding items previously identified. The most in-depth task will be analysing the data surrounding service valuation and demand modelling.

■ If either IT or the business holds expectations about deliverables, work backwards to make certain that all processes and information required to produce the expected deliverables are accounted for as part of Financial Management responsibilities. Often, a chargeback methodology drives implementation of Financial Management with perceptions of multiple levels of service. However, as the availability of financial information is analysed, it becomes apparent that collection and reporting of the various levels of demand is not possible and there is no real value in even having multiple levels of service.

■ Become familiar with current expenses in preparation for creating new valuation and funding documents. There may be immediate issues that come into view after reviewing expenditures. Of critical importance may be the realization that not all IT expenditures are collected into one financial centre. Frequently telecommunications charges are disbursed among numerous business organizations. To properly report and account for services costs, centralization of IT expenditures is a prerequisite.

■ Once an accounting of all IT expenditures has been completed, service valuation should be performed. Reports should be produced that provide for the first element of valuation pricing of service assets. If the operating model allows for the addition of value-add pricing, then the next step is to add that value to each service to calculate the total price for an IT Service. Analysis and calculation of the value-add price will require a great amount of input from Service Level Management, Availability, Security and Capacity Management. This is a critical calculation since business perception of value and price can be miscalculated and create an unwanted effect.

■ If during the analysis phase it becomes apparent that Financial Management dependent processes are not available, the plans for implementation must be adjusted. For example, if no IT Services have already been identified, then valuation will be postponed until the catalogue of services has been agreed.

Track 3 – Design

■ The design phase creates the outputs that are expected from a Financial Management implementation. Working with key contributors and supporters is paramount during this track. Design is done around data inputs and translations, reports, methodologies and models.

- Processes – identify all processes in place within IT and design clear hooks into Financial Management.
- Valuation Models – should be prepared and tested for appropriateness to the business environment.
- Accounting processes – from the learning obtained from the initial accounting of IT expenditures, processes and procedures should be finalized. Reports should be identified that will be pertinent to the operating model and business environment, for example, cost trends by different classifications, and financial analysis of ROI, ROA and TCO.
- Chargeback methods – create the chosen chargeback methodology.
- Procedures – complete design of FM policies and procedures.
- Roles and responsibilities – prepare job descriptions and fill required roles.

Track 4 – Implement

- Implementation involves activation of planned processes. The initial input will come from corporate financial systems and Change Management processes. Key hooks to data translations come through:
  - Accounting is the first process that receives financial data for translation.
  - Change and Demand Management are the first steps in becoming aware of anticipated changes to IT.

Track 5 – Measure

- To come full cycle through implementation, measures of success need to be provided on financial trends within funding, valuing and accounting.
- It is also important to audit for any credibility gap between the value being received and price being paid as soon as possible. This can be done through providing:
  - Concise communication possibly via a balanced scorecard
  - Regular communication
  - Meaningful data
  - Making certain to always map to business strategy.

Auditing provides verification that processes are being followed. Since Financial Management is the owner of the data that translates and creates financial data, it is of obvious importance that audits be performed regularly.

5.2 RETURN ON INVESTMENT

Return on Investment (ROI) is a concept for quantifying the value of an investment. Its use and meaning are not always precise. When dealing with financial officers, ROI most likely means ROIC (Return on Invested Capital), a measure of business performance. This is not the case here. In service management, ROI is used as a measure of the ability to use assets to generate additional value. In the simplest sense, it is the net profit of an investment divided by the net worth of the assets invested. The resulting percentage is applied to either additional top-line revenue or the elimination of bottom-line cost.

It is not unexpected that companies seek to apply the ROI in deciding to adopt service management. ROI is appealing because it is self-evident. The measure either meets or does not meet a numerical criterion. The challenge is when ROI calculations focus in the short term. The application of service management has different degrees of ROI, depending on business impact. Moreover, there are often difficulties in quantifying the complexities involved in implementations.

While a service can be directly linked and justified through specific business imperatives, few companies can readily identify the financial return for the specific aspects of service management. It is often an investment that companies must make in advance of any return. Service management by itself does not provide any of the tactical benefits that business managers typically budget for. One of the greatest challenges for those seeking funding for ITIL projects is identifying a specific business imperative that depends on service management. For these reasons, this section covers three areas:

- Business case – a means to identify business imperatives that depend on service management
- Pre-Programme ROI – techniques for quantitatively analysing an investment in service management
- Post-Programme ROI – techniques for retroactively analysing an investment in service management.

5.2.1 Business case

A business case is a decision support and planning tool that projects the likely consequences of a business action. The consequences can take on qualitative and quantitative dimensions. A financial analysis, for example, is frequently central to a good business case.

Table 5.2 Sample business case structure

Business case structure
A. Introduction
Presents the business objectives addressed by the service
B. Methods and assumptions
Defines the boundaries of the business case, such as time period, whose costs and whose benefits
C. Business impacts
The financial and non-financial business case results
D. Risks and contingencies
The probability that alternative results will emerge.
E. Recommendations
Specific actions recommended.

5.2.1.1 Business objectives

The structure of a business case varies from organization to organization. A generic form is given in Table 5.2. What they all have in common is a detailed analysis of business impact or benefits. Business impact is in turn linked to business objectives. A business objective is the reason for considering a service management initiative in the first place. Objectives should start broadly. For example:

- The business objectives for commercial provider organizations are usually the objectives of the business itself, including financial and organizational performance.
- The business objectives for not-for-profit organizations are usually the objectives for the constituents, population or membership served as well as financial and organizational performance.

Table 5.3 Common business objectives

Operational	Financial	Strategic	Industry
Shorten development time	Improve return on assets	Establish or enhance strategic positioning	Increase market share
Increase productivity	Avoid costs	Introduce competitive products	Improve market position
Increase capacity	Increase discretionary spending as a percentage of budget	Improve professionalism of organization	Increase repeat business
Increase reliability	Decrease non-discretionary spending	Improve customer satisfaction	Take market leadership
Minimize risks	Increase revenues	Provide better quality	Recognized as producer of reliable or quality products or services
Improve resource utilization	Increase margins	Provide customized offerings	Recognized as low price leader
Improve efficiencies	Keep spending to within budget	Introduce new products or services	Recognized as compliant to industry standards

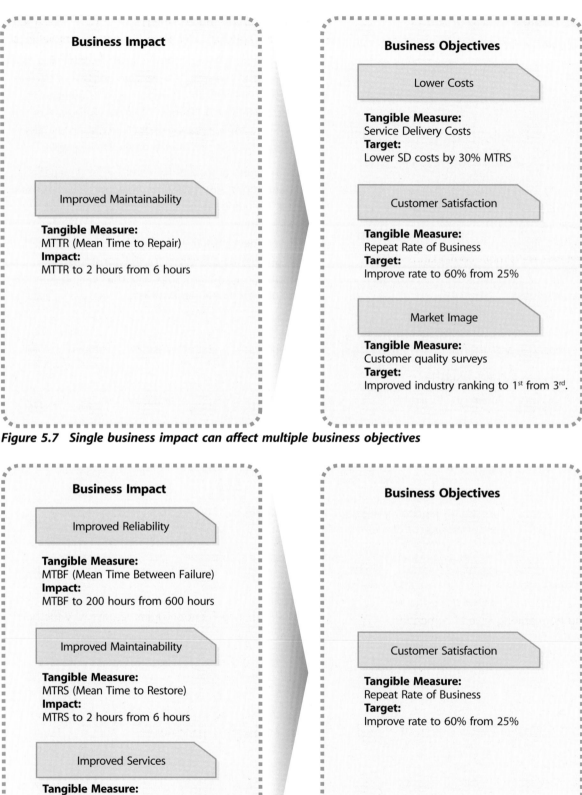

Figure 5.7   Single business impact can affect multiple business objectives

Figure 5.8   Multiple business impacts can affect a single business objective

5.2.1.2 Business impact

While most of a business case argument relies on cost analysis, there is much more to a service management initiative than financials. The scope of possible non-financial business impacts is summarized in this way: a business impact has no value unless it is linked to a business objective. There need not be a one-to-one relationship between business impact and business objective. Examples are given in Figures 5.7 and 5.8.

It is easy for a business case to focus on financial analysis and neglect non-financial impacts. The end result is a business case that is not as convincing as it should be. By incorporating business impacts linked to business objectives, a business case is more compelling.

5.2.2 Pre-programme ROI

The term capital budgeting is used to describe how managers plan significant outlays on projects that have long-term implications. A service management initiative may sometimes require capital budgeting. It is the commitment of funds now in order to receive a return in the future in the form of additional cash inflows or reduced cash outflows (earnings or savings).

Capital budgeting

Capital budgeting is the commitment of funds now in order to receive a return in the future in the form of additional cash inflows or reduced cash outflows.

Capital budgeting decisions fall into two broad categories: screening and preference decisions. Screening decisions relate to whether a proposed service management initiative passes a predetermined hurdle, minimum return for example. Preference decisions, on the other hand, relate to choosing from among several competing alternatives. Selecting between an internal Service Improvement Plan (SIP) and a service sourcing programme is an example.

5.2.2.1 Screening decisions (NPV)

An investment typically occurs early while returns do not occur until some time later. Therefore the time value of money, or discounted cash flows, should be accounted for. There are two approaches to making capital budgeting decisions using discounted cash flows: Net Present Value (NPV) and Internal Rate of Return (IRR). NPV is preferred for screening decisions for reasons discussed later. IRR is preferred for preference decisions, as explained in the next section.

Under the NPV method, the programme's cash inflows are compared to the cash outflows. The difference, called net present value, determines whether or not the investment is suitable (Table 5.4). Whenever the net present value is negative, the investment is unlikely to be suitable.

Table 5.4 NPV decisions

If the NPV is:	Then the programme is:
Positive	Acceptable. It promises a return greater than the required rate of return
Zero	Acceptable. It promises a return equal to the required rate of return.
Negative	Unacceptable. It promises a return less than the required rate of return.

Case example 11: *Net present value*

A Type I provider for a small company in South America considers investing in a service management programme. The programme is estimated to cost £50,000. The programme is expected to reduce labour costs by £16,500 per year. The company requires a minimum pre-tax return of 20% on all investment programmes. A five-year window is used for investment return.

For simplicity, ignore inflation and taxes.

Should the investment be made?

(Answer given later in this section)

What is an organization's discount rate? A company's cost of capital is typically considered the minimum required rate of return. This is the average rate of return the company must pay to its long-term shareholders or creditors for use of their funds. Therefore, the cost of capital serves as a minimum screening device.

For service management programmes, the NPV method has several advantages over the IRR method:

- NPV is generally easier to use
- IRR may require searching for a discount rate resulting in an NPV of zero.
- IRR assumes the rate of return is the rate of return on the programme, a questionable assumption for environments with minimal service management programme experience
- When NPV and IRR disagree on the attractiveness of the project, it is best to go with NPV. It makes the more realistic assumption about the rate of return.

There are other methods used for making capital budgeting decisions such as Pay-Back and Simple Rate of Return. Neither method is covered, as Pay-Back is not a true measure of the profitability of an investment while

Simple Rate of Return does not consider the time value of money.

Case example 11 (solution): *No*

The answer may appear obvious since the savings (£82,500 = 5 years x £16,500) exceeds investment (£50,000). However, it is not enough that the cost reductions cover the investment. It must also yield a return of at least 20%.

To determine the suitability of the investment, the £16,500 annual savings should be discounted to its present value. Since the company uses a 20% minimum hurdle, this rate is used in the discounting process and is called the discount rate.

See Table 5.5. Deducting the present value of the required investment from the present value of the cost savings gives the net present value of -£648. According to the analysis, the company should not proceed.

Table 5.5 provides a simple but effective expression of an NPV screening analysis for Case example 11:

- The projected cost saving is £18,000. This inflow is multiplied by 2.991 (the present value of £1 in 5 years. This factor can be found in the table in Appendix A).
- The initial investment is subtracted from the savings, providing the net present value.

In a service management NPV, the focus remains on cash flows and not on accounting net income. Managers should look for the types of cash flows shown in Table 5.6.

Although it has an effect on taxes, depreciation is not deducted. Discounted cash flow methods automatically provide for return of the original investment, thereby making a deduction for depreciation unnecessary.

Table 5.6 Types of cash flow

Typical cash outflows	Initial investment in assets, including installation costs
	Periodic outlays for maintenance
	Training and consulting
	Incremental operating costs
	Increase in working capital
Typical cash inflows	Incremental revenues
	Reduced costs
	Salvage value from old assets, either from operational retirement or project end
	Release of working capital

A simplifying assumption is made in that all cash flows other than the initial investment occur at the end of periods. This is somewhat unrealistic as cash flows typically occur throughout a period rather than just at its end.

Intangible Benefits

There are a number of techniques available when service management cash flows are uncertain. Some are very technical as they involve computer simulations and advanced skills in mathematics.

Process improvement and automation are common examples of difficult-to-estimate cash flows. The up-front and tangible costs are easy to estimate. The intangible benefits, such as lessened risk, greater reliability, quality and speed are much more difficult to estimate. They are very real in impact but nonetheless challenging in estimating cash flows. Fortunately, there is a simple procedure available.

Table 5.5 NPV of a proposed service management programme (Case example 11)

Initial investment	£50,000
Investment window	5 years
Annual cost savings	£16,500
Salvage value	£0
Required rate of return	20%

Item	Years	Amount of cash flow	20% discount	Present value of cash flow
Initial cost savings	1 to 5	£16,500	2.991*	49,352
Initial investment	Now	(£50,000)	1	-50,000
Net present value				-£648

*Present value of an annuity of £1 in 5 years arrears

Take, for example, the organization seeking to purchase service management process-automation software. The organization has an 8% discount rate. The useful life of the software is set to five years. A prior NPV analysis of the tangible costs and benefits shows an NPV of -£139,755. If the intangible benefits are large enough, the NPV could go from negative to positive. To compute the benefit required (inflow), first find the Present Value Factor in Appendix A. A look in Column 8%, Row 5-period, reveals a factor of 3.993. Now perform the following calculation:

$$\frac{\text{NPV excluding intangible benefits, £139,755}}{\text{Present value factor (8\%, 5 periods), 3.993}} = \text{£35,000}$$

The result serves as a subjective guideline for estimation. If the intangible benefits are at least £35,000, then the NPV is acceptable. The process automation should be performed. If in the judgement of senior managers, the intangible benefits are not worth £35,000, then the process automation should not be performed.

5.2.2.2 Preference decisions (IRR)

There are often many opportunities that pass the screening decision process. The bad news is not all can be acted on. Financial or resource constraints may preclude investing in every opportunity. Preference decisions, sometimes called rationing or ranking decisions, must be made. The competing alternatives are ranked.

The NPV of one project cannot be directly compared to another unless the investments are equal. As a result, the IRR is widely used for preference decisions. The higher the Internal Rate of Return, the more desirable the initiative.

The IRR, sometimes called the yield, is the rate of return over the life of an initiative. IRR is computed by finding the discount rate that equates the present value of a project's cash outflows with the present value of its inflows. That is, the IRR is the discount rate resulting in an NPV of zero.

Take, for example, Case example 11. To compute the IRR, first find the discount rate that will result in a net present value of zero. The simplest approach is to divide the investment in the project by the expected net annual cash flow. This will yield a factor from which the IRR can be found.

$$\frac{\text{Investment required (£50,000)}}{\text{Net annual cash inflow (£16,500)}} = 3.03$$

The IRR factor, 3.0303 in this case, is then located in the present value table in Appendix A to determine the rate of return it represents. Use the 5-period line since the programme has a five-year window. A scan on the 5-period line reveals that an IRR factor of 3.03 represents a rate of return between 19% and 20%.

Once the IRR is computed, compare against required rate of return. In this case, the required rate of return is 20%. Since the IRR is slightly less, it would likely be rejected during a screening decision. A summary is given in Table 5.7.

The IRR for successful candidates can be directly compared to other successful candidates. Viable projects can then be ranked by their respective IRR. The projects with the highest rank are those with the highest IRR percentages.

5.2.3 Post-programme ROI

Many companies successfully justify service management implementations through qualitative arguments, without a business case or plan, often ranking cost savings as a low business driver. But without clearly defined financial objectives, companies cannot measure the added value brought about by service management, thereby introducing future risk in the form of strong opposition from business leaders. Having experienced a history of shortfalls in past frameworks, stakeholders may question the resultant value of a service management programme. Without proof of value, executives may cease further

Table 5.7 IRR of a proposed service management programme (Case example 11)

Initial investment	£50,000
Investment window	5 years
Annual cost savings	£16,500
Salvage value	£0
Required rate of return	20%

Item	Years	Amount of cash flow	19-20% discount	Present value of cash flow
Annual cost savings	1 to 5	£16,500	3.0303	50,000
Initial investment	Now	**(£50,000)**	1	-50,000
Net present value				£0

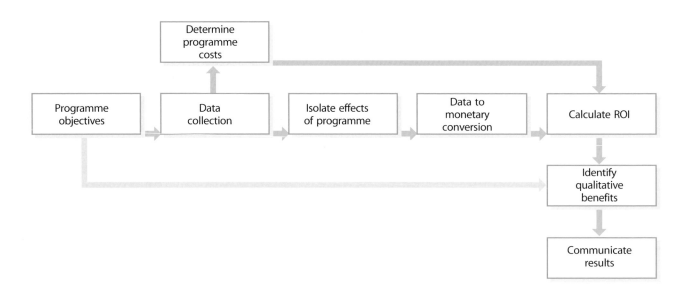

Figure 5.9 Post-programme ROI approach

investments. Therefore, if a service management initiative is initiated without prior ROI analysis, it is recommended that an analysis be conducted at an appropriate time after. The calculation of a service management ROI is illustrated in the basic model shown in Figure 5.9.

5.2.3.1 Programme objectives

Objectives should be clear, as they serve to guide the depth and scope of the ROI analysis. Objectives can range from simple terminology to the adoption of industry practices:

- Deliver consistent and repeatable service
- Lower the overall total cost of ownership
- Improve quality of service
- Implement industry-wide best practices
- Provide an overall structure and process
- Facilitate the use of common concepts and terminology.

5.2.3.2 Data collection

The collection of data is vital for a valid and quantifiable ROI result. There are two periods in which to collect data: pre- and post-implementation. Programme objectives should guide the source and nature of data points. For example:

- Metrics for quality of service
- Costs for service transactions
- Questionnaires for customer satisfaction.

Note that the data collection for process transactions will differ from data collection for a function.

5.2.3.3 Isolate the effects of the programme

By this stage, the results of the service management programme are becoming evident. By isolating the effects, there should be little doubt that the results should be attributed to the programme. There are many techniques available:

- Forecast analysis: a trend line analysis or another forecasting model is used to project data points had the programme not taken place. An example is given in Figure 5.10.
- Impact estimates: when a forecasting approach is not feasible, either due to lack of data or inconsistencies in measurements, an alternative approach in the form of estimations is performed. Simply put, customers and stakeholders estimate the level of improvements. Input is sought from organizational managers, independent experts and external assessments.
- Control group: in this technique, a pilot implementation takes place in a subset of the enterprise. That subset may be based on geography, delivery centre or organizational branch. The resultant performance is compared with a similar but unaffected subset.

5.2.3.4 Data to monetary conversion

To calculate ROI, it is essential to convert the impact data to monetary values. Only then can those values be compared to programme costs. The challenge is in assigning a value to each unit of data. The technique applied will vary and will often depend on the nature of the data:

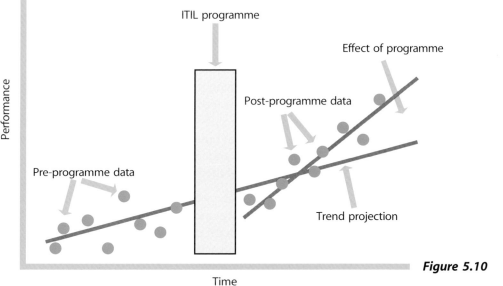

Pre-programme data

ITIL programme

Effect of programme

Post-programme data

Trend projection

Performance

Time

Figure 5.10   Trend line analysis

- A quality measure, such as a complaint or violation, is assigned or calculated, and reported as a standard value
- Staff reductions or efficiency improvements, in the form of loaded costs, are reported as a standard value
- Improvements in business performance, in the form of lessened impacts, are reported as a standard value
- Internal or external experts are used to establish the value of a measure.

5.2.3.5 Determine programme costs

This requires tracking all the related costs of the ITIL programme. It can include:

- The planning, design and implementation costs. These are pro-rated over the expected life of the programme
- The technology acquisition costs
- The education expenses.

5.2.3.6 Calculate ROI

NPV and IRR techniques are detailed in the previous sections.

5.2.3.7 Identify qualitative benefits

Qualitative benefits begin with those detailed in the business case, as described in a previous section. A second look at service management qualitative benefits is found in the Continual Service Improvement volume.

5.3   SERVICE PORTFOLIO MANAGEMENT

A Service Portfolio describes a provider's services in terms of business value. It articulates business needs and the provider's response to those needs. By definition, business value terms correspond to marketing terms, providing a means for comparing service competitiveness across alternative providers. By acting as the basis of a decision framework, a Service Portfolio either clarifies or helps to clarify the following strategic questions:

- Why should a customer buy these services?
- Why should they buy these services from us?
- What are the pricing or chargeback models?
- What are our strengths and weaknesses, priorities and risk?
- How should our resources and capabilities be allocated?

Organizations embarking on a service-orientation journey have a tendency to view it as a series of tactical programmes. Armed with a conceptual understanding of services, organizations frequently rush to industrialize service outcomes. The impulse is to launch initiatives in organizational change or process redesign. While these are important fulfilment elements, there is an order worth noting.

While this order is not absolute it does serve two purposes. First, it warns against missteps such as performing organizational design before knowing what services to offer, or performing a tool selection before optimizing processes. Second, it signals the early need for a Service Portfolio, one of the most vital yet often missing constructs for driving service strategies and managing service investments.

Financial managers tailor a portfolio of investments based on their customer's risk and reward profile. Regardless of the profile, the objective is the same: maximize return at an acceptable risk level. When conditions change, appropriate changes are made to the portfolio. There is a need for applying comparable practices when managing a portfolio of services. The value of a Service Portfolio strategy is demonstrated through the ability to anticipate change while maintaining traceability to strategy and planning.

> Service Portfolio Management is a dynamic method for governing investments in service management across the enterprise and managing them for value.

The operative word is method. Often the term portfolio is marginalized to a list of services, applications, assets or projects. A portfolio is essentially a group of investments that share similar characteristics. They are grouped by size, discipline or strategic value. There are few fundamental differences between IT portfolio management, project portfolio management and SPM. All are enabling techniques for governance. The difference is in the implementation details.

5.3.1 Business service and IT Service

A business process can be distributed across technologies and applications, span geographies, have many users, and yet still reside in one place: the data centre. To integrate business process, IT frequently employs bottom-up integration, stitching together a patchwork of technology and application components that were never designed to interact at the business process layer. What began as an elegant top-down business design frequently deteriorates into a disjointed and inflexible IT solution, disconnected from the goals of the business.

An improved strategy for engaging at the business process layer is focusing on modelled abstractions of business activities. These focal points, called business services, represent business activities with varying degrees of granularity and functionality. A business process, for example, may be represented as a single business service or a collection of business services (Figure 5.11). A business service can represent a composite application or a discrete application function. It may represent a discrete transaction or a collection of supporting fulfilment elements. In all cases, it exists in the domain of the business.

A business service is defined by the business. If IT provides a service to the business, but the business does not think of the service in any business context or semantics, then it

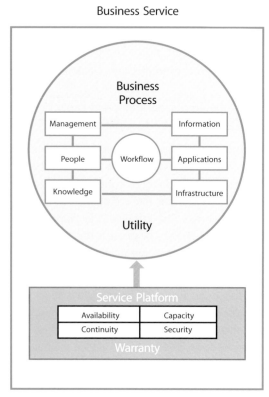
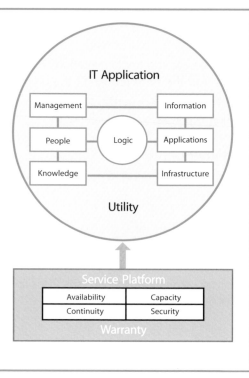

Figure 5.11 Business service and IT Service

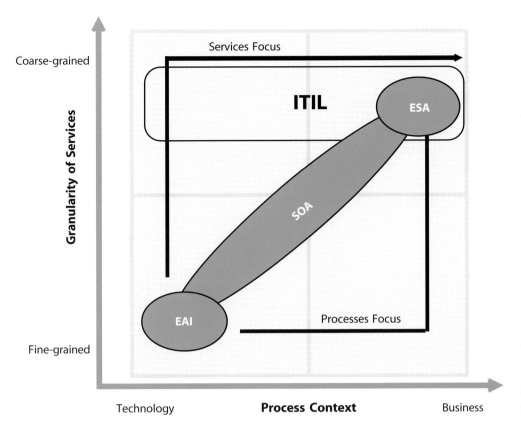

Figure 5.12 Service perspectives

is an IT Service. By considering services as a system for creating and capturing value, regardless of sourcing or underpinnings, the line between IT Services and business services begins to blur. Instead, each can be thought of as different perspectives across a spectrum. Again, the decision to adopt a business or IT perspective depends on the context of the customer. When this notion is combined with other seemingly unrelated service-oriented technologies and concepts, their relationships can be illustrated in the chart shown in Figure 5.12.

Figure 5.12 states that all services, whether they are IT Services, business services or services based on Service-oriented Architecture (SOA), Enterprise Services Architecture (ESA) or Enterprise Application Integration

(EAI), are members of the same family. They may differ by granularity (fine versus coarse) or by context (technology versus business). They each provide a basis for value and require governance, delivery and support. ITSM and BSM are each perspectives on the same concept: service management.

5.3.1.1 IT Service Management

The organization chart shown in Figure 5.13 is a collection of functional boxes representing vertical tiers of reporting relationships.

While the organization chart is a useful administrative tool, it is missing key components. It is missing the customers. It is missing the services provided to the customers. And it

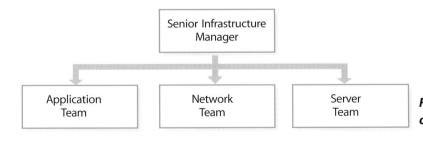

Figure 5.13 Simplified vertical view of an IT organization

is missing the workflow through which those services are provided. In other words, the organizational chart does not show what the organization does, how it does it and for whom it does it.

Goal setting and reporting are done in silos. The criteria for employees are based on expertise for a specific technology or role, rather than competencies in strategic planning, business expertise, forecasting, or managing metrics. Each technology or functional manager perceives the other as a competitor rather than a partner; positioning themselves for priority, resources, budget and advancement.

This approach prevents cross-silo issues from being resolved at low levels. Instead, the issues are escalated to functional managers who then address the issues with other functional managers. The result is then communicated downward, at which point the real work presumably begins. In other words, managers are continually forced to resolve low-level issues, taking time away from high-level customer issues. Low-level contributors, rather than resolving these issues, then see themselves as passive implementers, merely taking orders and providing technical information. Cross-functional issues frequently do not get addressed, often falling through the organizational cracks.

The opportunity for improving an organization often lies in these cracks: the white space of the organization chart.

(The 'white space' of the organization chart is examined in Rummler.[26]) It is the points at which the boxes interface and pass information. While an organizational chart does fulfil an important administrative purpose, it should not be confused with the organization itself. This confusion may lead managers to manage the organization chart, rather than the organization. Rather, they should overcome inter-silo problems by conceptualizing and managing complete processes (Figure 5.14).

Some processes can be self-contained within a functional area, while others are cross-functional. Some processes manage and produce a product or service received by a customer external to IT. Organizational performance improves as these processes allow. The discipline of these processes is commonly known as IT Service Management (ITSM). ITSM means thinking of IT as a cohesive set of business resources and capabilities. These resources and capabilities are managed through processes and ultimately represented as services.

5.3.1.2 Business Service management

IT priorities must be clearly aligned with other drivers of business value. In order for IT to organize its activities around business objectives, the organization must link to business processes and services – not just observe them. IT leadership must engage in a meaningful dialogue with line-of-business owners and communicate in terms of desired outcomes.

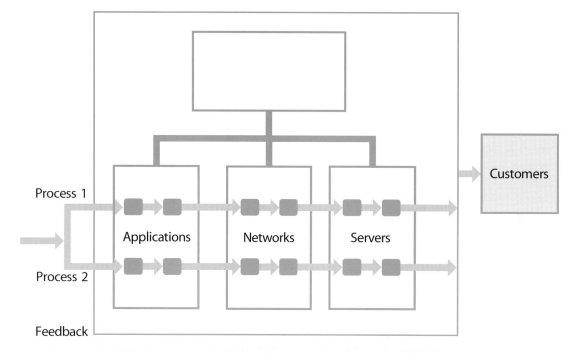

Figure 5.14 Process as a means for managing the silos of the organization chart

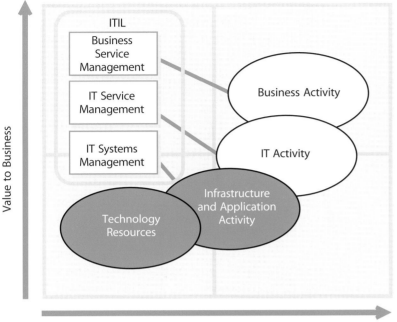

Figure 5.15 The IT management continuum

Value to IT

The transition from managing infrastructures to managing services is marked by a fundamental difference (Figure 5.15). While managing infrastructure requires a focus on component operational availability, managing services is centred on customer and business needs. Operational information about the infrastructure's health is a critical foundation but is not enough. IT organizations intuitively recognize the need to link their activities with business objectives but frequently struggle in deciding how far to go in exposing the linkages between business activities and IT execution.

Organizations are increasingly less focused on IT infrastructure and applications than on coupling applications internally and with business partners in the quest to automate end-to-end business processes and deliver business services. The challenge is to derive operational objectives from business services and to manage accordingly. Business perspectives, however, often do not easily relate to IT infrastructure.

A strategy aimed at this challenge is Business Service Management (BSM). BSM differs from previous strategic methods by offering a holistic top-down approach aimed at aligning the IT infrastructure with the business.

> Business Service Management is the ongoing practice of governing, monitoring and reporting on IT and the business service it impacts.

BSM provides the means by which the service provider manages business services. When the provider focuses its operations on business services it is better able to align investments in infrastructure and operational activities with business objectives. BSM sets forth a model for developing business-focused metrics, enabling adaptation to future needs as driven by the business requirements.

The cornerstone to BSM is the ability to link service assets to their higher-level business services. The links are based on causality instead of correlation. The view of IT infrastructure shifts from a topological map to a dependency model (Figure 5.16). This model identifies the asset-to-service linkages, allowing infrastructure events to be tied to corresponding business outcomes.

5.4 SERVICE PORTFOLIO MANAGEMENT METHODS

If we think of SPM as a dynamic and ongoing process set, it should include the following work methods (also shown in Figure 5.17):

- Define: inventory services, ensure business cases and validate portfolio data
- Analyse: maximize portfolio value, align and prioritize and balance supply and demand
- Approve: finalize proposed portfolio, authorize services and resources
- Charter: communicate decisions, allocate resources and charter services.

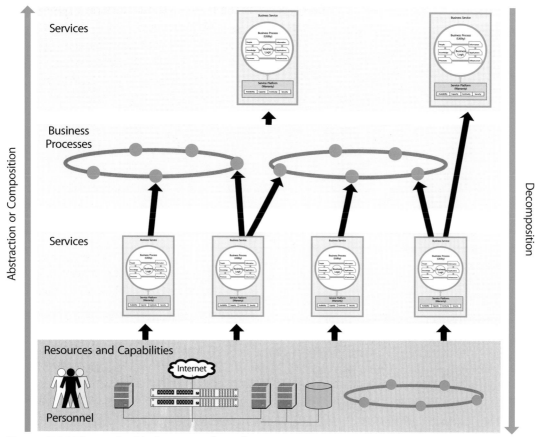

Figure 5.16 The embedded nature of services

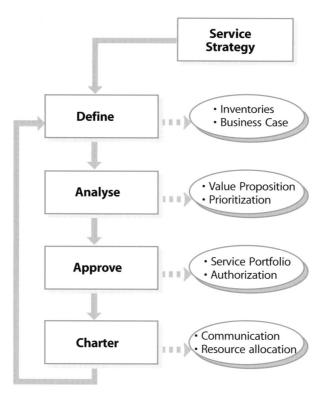

Figure 5.17 Service Portfolio process

5.4.1 Define

Begin with collecting information from all existing services as well as every proposed service. Every proposed service would include those in a conceptual phase. Namely, all services the organization would do if it had unlimited resources, capabilities and time. This documentation exercise is to understand the opportunity costs of the existing portfolio. If a service provider understands what it cannot do, then it is better able to assess if it should keep doing what it is doing or reallocate its resources and capabilities.

The next step in the process set, Analyse, should be well defined prior to beginning this phase. If the organization does not understand what analysis it will perform, it is unlikely to know the right data to collect. Data collection exercises are usually disruptive and should be as streamlined as possible.

The cyclic nature of the SPM process set means that this phase not only creates an initial inventory of services, but also validates the data on a recurring basis. Different portfolios will have different refresh cycles. Some cycles will be triggered by a particular event or business trend. For example, a Merger and Acquisition event triggers a portfolio re-examination.

Every service in the portfolio should include a business case. A business case is a model of what a service is expected to achieve. It is the justification for pursuing a course of action to meet stated organizational goals. As such, it acts as the link back to service strategy and funding. It is the assessment of a service investment in terms of potential benefits and the resources and capabilities required to provision and maintain it.

5.4.1.1 The Option Space Tool

A Service Portfolio is an expression of the provider's service strategy. Executing a service strategy involves making a sequence of major decisions. Some are made immediately while others are intentionally deferred. Some commitments once made cannot be undone. Providers can only revise their plans for future commitments. SPM sets the framework within which future strategic decisions will be made.

A useful tool for making decisions on the timing and sequencing of investments in a Service Portfolio is called an Option Space (Figure 5.18). An Option Space can guide decisions to invest and, if so, when. (This section draws on Luehrman.[27])

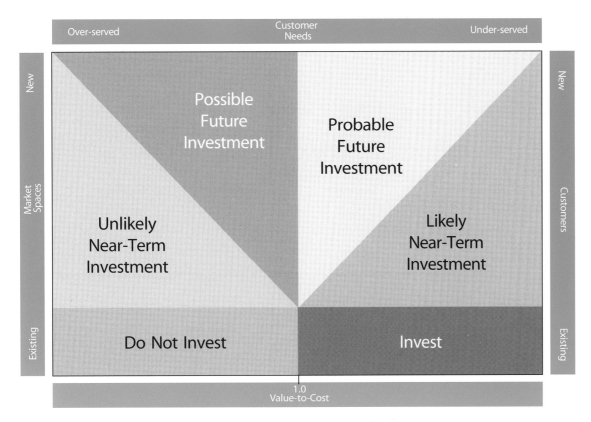

Figure 5.18 Option Space

The Value-to-Cost axis represents the ratio of a service's worth to its cost. A Value-to-Cost of less than one designates a service worth less than what it costs. When the measure is greater than one, the present value of the service is greater than its cost. Financial measures, however, need not be the only measure. Other factors can and should be incorporated such as:

- Mission imperatives
- Compliance
- Trends
- Intangible benefits
- Strategic or business fit
- Social responsibilities
- Innovation.

For example, fulfilling a legal compliance issue may on its own generate a Value-to-Cost measure of greater than one. Government agencies may generate Value-to-Cost measures on public policy while military organizations may generate measures based on mission imperatives.

The other axes are based on topics covered in other chapters: market spaces, customers and customer needs. Each is used as a guide for strategic intent. The desire of a Type I provider to serve a new business unit, for example, may take on less value because the customer needs are already over-served. If an axis is not relevant to the portfolio, disregard its guidance. If market spaces aren't

important, and a Value-to-Cost analysis isn't necessary, simply ignore the two axes.

5.4.2 Analyse

This is where strategic intent is crafted. Begin with a set of top-down questions:

- What are the long-term goals of the service organization?
- What services are required to meet those goals?
- What capabilities and resources are required for the organization to achieve those services?
- How will we get there?

In other words, what are the perspective, position, plan and patterns? The answers to these questions guide not only the analysis but also the desired outcomes of SPM. The ability to satisfactorily answer these questions requires the involvement of senior leaders and subject matter experts.

5.4.2.1 Selecting options

Senior executives have constrained and limited resources. They must understand not only the risks to the enterprise, but the impact and dependencies. Understanding these relationships allow them to make informed investment decisions in service initiatives with appropriate levels of risk and reward. These initiatives may cross business

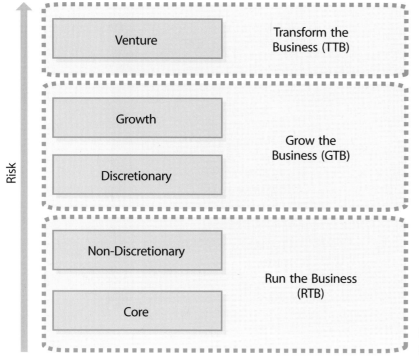

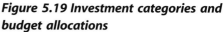

Figure 5.19 Investment categories and budget allocations

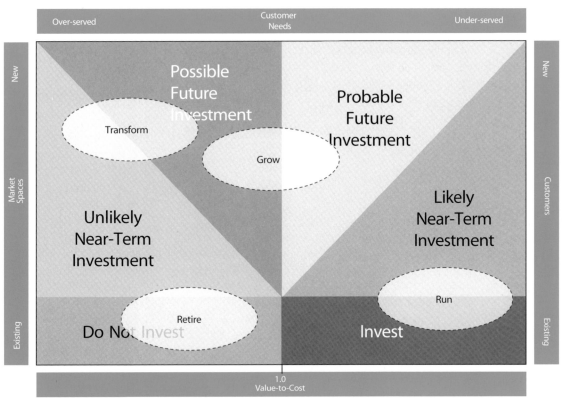

Figure 5.20 Option space: focused on maintaining services (RTB)

functions and may span short, medium and longer time frames. Moreover, the calculated value realization for each service investment should be commensurate with its level of risk.

Services investments are split between three strategic categories:

■ Run the business (RTB) – RTB investments are centred on maintaining service operations

■ Grow the business (GTB) – GTB investments are intended to grow the organization's scope of services

■ Transform the business (TTB) – TTB investments are moves into new market spaces.

The investment categories are further divided into budget allocations (as shown in Figure 5.19):

■ Venture – create services in a new market space.

■ Growth – create new services in existing market space.

■ Discretionary – provide enhancements to existing services.

■ Non-discretionary – maintain existing services

■ Core – maintain business critical services.

Retirement or divestiture

It is worth commenting on an often overlooked investment, or more accurately divestiture, category concerned with terminating services: retirement. This is potentially one of the largest hidden costs in a service provider's organization, particularly in a large enterprise with a long history. Few providers have a clear plan for retiring increasingly redundant services. Since retiring a service may temporarily exceed the cost of maintaining it, its budget allocation can shift from Non-Discretionary to Discretionary.

By determining the allocation of budget into run-the-business, grow-the-business or transform-the-business service categories, executives are not only affirming their risk tolerance on SPM, but are directly affecting the modes of operations implemented by the operational staff. The distribution of services from RTB to TTB will reflect the nature of the organization: predominantly RTB if IT is a cost centre (back-office) (Figure 5.20), predominantly TTB if IT is an investment centre (commercial provider) (Figure 5.21).

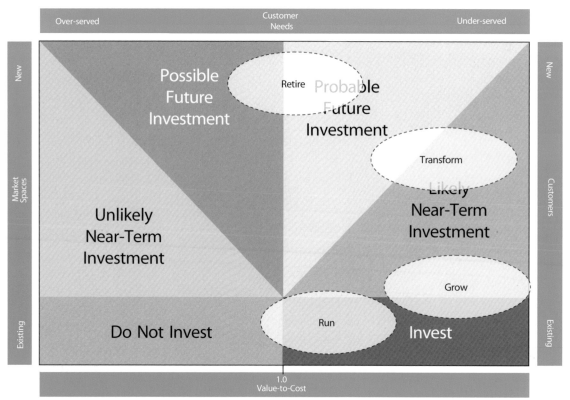

Figure 5.21 Option space: focused on expanding the scope of services (TTB)

5.4.3 Approve

The previous phases have led to a well-understood future state ('to be'). This is where deliberate approvals or disapprovals of that future state take place. With approvals, comes the corresponding authorization for new services and resources.

The outcomes for existing services fall into six categories:

- Retain – largely self-contained, with well-defined asset, process and system boundaries, these services are aligned with and are relevant to the organization's strategy.

- Replace – these services have unclear and overlapping business functionality.

- Rationalize – often organizations discover they are offering services that are composed of multiple releases of the same operating system, multiple versions of the same software and/or multiple versions of system platforms providing similar functions.

- Refactor – often services that meet the technical and functional criteria of the organization display fuzzy process or system boundaries. An example would be a service handling its own authentication or continuity

functions. In these cases, the service can often be refactored to include only the core functionality, with common services used to provide the remainder. Refactoring is also useful when a service embeds potentially reusable business services within itself.

- Renew – these services meet functional fitness criteria, but fail technical fitness. An example may be a service whose fulfilment elements include a mainframe system and frame relay network that still supports business-critical processes where the strategic direction of the organization is to retire the mainframe platform and source an MPLS (Multi-Protocol Label Switching) WAN.

- Retire – services that do not meet minimum levels of technical and functional fitness.

5.4.4 Charter

Begin with a list of decisions and action items. These are to be communicated to the organization clearly and unambiguously. These decisions should be correlated to budgetary decisions and financial plans. Budget allocations should enforce the allocation of resources.

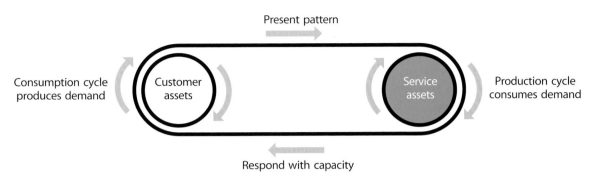

Figure 5.22 Tight coupling between demand and capacity

The expected value of each service should be built into financial forecasts and resource plans. Tracking both tracks the progress of service investments. Newly chartered services are promoted to Service Design. Existing services are refreshed in the Service Catalogue. Retired services begin their sunset to Service Transition.

5.4.4.1 Refreshing the portfolio

Conditions and markets change, invalidating prior ROI calculations. Some services may no longer be optimal due to compliance or regulatory concerns. Events occur such as mergers and acquisitions, divestitures, new public legislation or redeployed missions. The CIO must then monitor, measure, reassess and rebalance these investments, making trade-offs as business needs change. Not all services need be low risk or high reward. Instead, by seeking an efficient portfolio with optimal levels of ROI and risk, the organization is maximizing the value realization on its constrained and limited resources and capabilities.

5.5 DEMAND MANAGEMENT

5.5.1 Challenges in managing demand for services

Demand Management is a critical aspect of service management. Poorly managed demand is a source of risk for service providers because of uncertainty in demand. Excess capacity generates cost without creating value that provides a basis for cost recovery. Customers are reluctant to pay for idle capacity unless it has value for them.

There are instances in which a certain amount of unused capacity is necessary to deliver service levels. Such capacity is creating value through the higher level of

assurance made possible with higher capacity. Such capacity cannot be considered idle capacity because it is in active use for a purpose.

Insufficient capacity has impact on the quality of services delivered and limits the growth of the service. Service level agreements, forecasting, planning, and tight coordination with the customer can reduce the uncertainty in demand but cannot entirely eliminate it.

Service management faces the additional problem of synchronous production and consumption. Service production cannot occur without the concurrent presence of demand that consumes the output. It is a pull-system in which consumption cycles stimulate production cycles.

Demand Management techniques such as off-peak pricing, volume discounts and differentiated service levels can influence the arrival of demand in specific patterns. However, demand still pulls capacity. Demand cannot exist simply because capacity exists.

Consumption produces demand and production consumes demand in a highly synchronized pattern (Figure 5.22). Unlike goods, services cannot be manufactured in advance and stocked in a finished goods inventory in anticipation of demand. Demand and capacity are far more tightly coupled in service systems even when compared with just-in-time (JIT) manufacturing.

The productive capacity of resources available to a service is adjusted according to demand forecasts and patterns. Some types of capacity can be quickly increased as required and released when not in use. The arrival of demand can be influenced using pricing incentives. However, it is not possible to produce and stock service output before demand actually materializes.

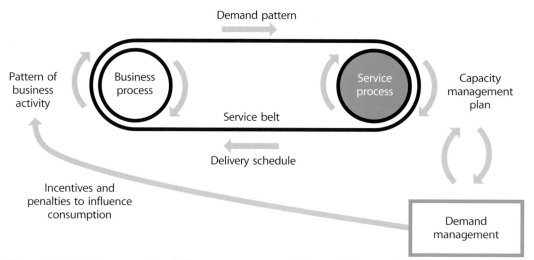

Figure 5.23 Business activity influences patterns of demand for services

5.5.2 Activity-based Demand Management

Business processes are the primary source of demand for services. Patterns of business activity (PBA) influence the demand patterns seen by the service providers (Figure 5.23). It is very important to study the customer's business to identify, analyse and codify such patterns to provide sufficient basis for Capacity Management. Visualize the customer's business activity and plans in terms of the demand for supporting services.

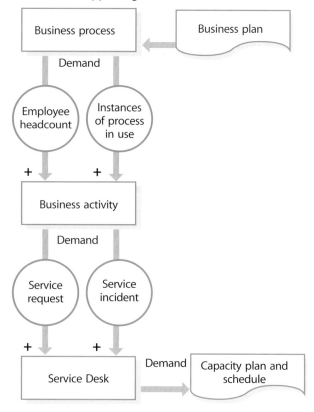

Figure 5.24 Example of activity-based Demand Management

For example, the fulfilment of a purchase order (business activity) may result in a set of requests (demand) generated by the order-to-cash process (business process of customer). Analysing and tracking the activity patterns of the business process makes it possible to predict demand for services in the catalogue that support the process. It is also possible to predict demand for underlying service assets that support those services. Every additional unit of demand generated by business activity is allocated to a unit of service capacity. Demand patterns occur at multiple levels. Activity-based Demand Management can daisy-chain demand patterns to ensure that the business plans of customers are synchronized with the service management plans of the service provider (Figure 5.24).

If a business plan calls for the allocation of human resources, the addition of an employee can be translated into additional demand for the Service Desk function in terms of service requests and service incidents. Similarly, new instances of business processes can be used as predictors of demand for the Service Demand in terms of incidents and requests. After validating the activity/demand model it is possible to make adjustments to account for variations such as new employees, changes to business processes, and technology upgrades on the customer's side.

Some of the benefits for analysing PBA are in the form of inputs to service management functions and processes such as the following:

- Service Design can then optimize designs to suit demand patterns
- Service Catalogue can map demand patterns to appropriate services

- Service Portfolio Management can approve investments in additional capacity, new services, or changes to services
- Service Operation can adjust allocation of resources and scheduling
- Service Operation can identify opportunities to consolidate demand by grouping closely matching demand patterns
- Financial Management can approve suitable incentives to influence demand

5.5.3 Business activity patterns and user profiles

Business activities drive demand for services. Customer assets such as People, Processes, and Applications generate patterns of business activity (PBA). PBA define dynamics of a business and include interactions with customers, suppliers, partners and other stakeholders. Services often directly support PBA. Since PBA generate revenue, income and costs they account for a large proportion of business outcomes.

Patterns of business activity (PBA) are identified, codified, and shared across process for clarity and completeness of detail. One or more attributes such as frequency, volume, location and duration describe business activity. They are associated with requirements such as security, privacy and latency or tolerance for delays (Table 5.8). This profile of business activity can change over time with changes and improvements in business processes, people, organization, applications and infrastructure. PBA are placed under change control.

Each PBA has to be substantially different from another PBA in order to be coded with a unique reference. Codifying patterns helps multidimensional analysis, using criteria such as likeness and nearness. This provides efficiency and robustness in developing a catalogue of patterns with simplification and standardization to reduce the number of patterns, make analysis easier, and avoid complicated solutions.

User profiles (UP) are based on roles and responsibilities within organizations for people, and functions and operations for processes and applications. As suggested earlier, business processes and applications are treated as

Table 5.8 Codifying patterns of business activity

PBA No. 45F Activities	Activity Levels					
	Hi	3	2	1	Lo	NA
Interact with customers remotely (frequency)			X			
Interact with customers on-site (frequency)				X		
Archive or handle customer information			X			
Process sensitive information (privacy)						X
Generate confidential information						X
Provide technical support (frequency)		X				
Seek technical assistance				X		
Network bandwidth requirements		X				
Data storage requirements (volume)		X				
Tolerance for delay in service response			X			
Seasonal variations in activity				X		
Print documents and images			X			
Mailing of documents using third-party systems			X			
Process transactions with wireless mobile device				X		
Email using wireless device					X	
Access work systems during domestic travel				X		
Access work systems during overseas travel					X	

users in many business contexts. Many processes are not actively executed or controlled by staff or personnel. Process automation allows for processes to consume services on their own. Processes and applications can have user profiles. Whether they should is a matter of judgment.

Each UP can be associated with one or more PBA (Table 5.9). This allows aggregations and relations between diverse PBS connected by the interactions between their respective UPs. User profiles (UP) are constructed using one ore more predefined PBA. They are also under change control. UPs represent patterns that are persistent and correlated.

Pattern matching using PBA and UP ensure a systematic approach to understanding and managing demand from customers. They also require customers to better understand their own business activities and view them as consumers of services and producers of demand. When they are used to communicate demand, service providers have the information necessary to sort and serve the demand with appropriately matched services, service levels, and service assets. This leads to improved value for both customers and service providers by eliminating waste and poor performance.

UP communicate information on the roles, responsibilities, interactions, schedules, work environments and social context of related users.

Table 5.9 User profiles matched with business activity patterns (example)

User profile	Applicable pattern of business activity (PBA)	PBA code
Senior executive (UP1)	Moderate travel-domestic and overseas; highly sensitive information; zero latency on service requests; high need for technical assistance; need to be highly available to the business	45F 45A 35D
Highly mobile executive (UP2)	Extensive travel-domestic and overseas; sensitive information; low latency on service requests; moderate need for technical assistance; high customer contact; need to be highly available to customers	45A 35D 22A
Office-based staff (UP3)	Office-based administrative staff; low travel-domestic; medium latency on service requests; low need for technical assistance; full-featured desktop needs; moderate customer contact; high volume of paperwork; need to be highly productive during work hours	22A 14B 3A
Payment processing system (UP4)	Business system; high volume; transaction-based; high security needs; low latency on service requests; low seasonal variation; mailing of documents by postal service; automatic customer notification; under regulatory compliance; need for low unit costs; need to be highly secure and transparent (audit control)	12F
Customer assistance process (UP5)	Business process; moderate volume; transaction-based; moderate security needs; very low latency on service requests; medium seasonal variation; mailing of replacement parts by express; automatic customer notification; need to be highly responsive to customers	24G 10G

5.5.4 Service packages

5.5.4.1 Core services and supporting services

Core services deliver the basic outcomes desired by the customer. They represent the value that the customer wants and for which they are willing to pay. Core services anchor the value proposition for the customer and provide the basis for their continued utilization and satisfaction. Supporting services either enable or enhance the value proposition. Enabling services are basic factors and enhancing services are excitement factors.

For example, the core service of a bank could be providing financial capital to small and medium enterprises. Value is created for the bank's customer only when the bank can provide financial capital in a timely manner (after having evaluated all the costs and risks of financing the borrower). The supporting services could include the aid offered by loan officers in assessing working capital needs and collateral, the application processing service, flexible disbursement of loan funds, and the facility of a bank account into which the borrower can electronically transfer funds. The credit-reporting service that the lending department utilizes for evaluating credit-reporting, may be a core service provided to the loan officers by internal or external service providers. It is not a supporting service to borrowers because they are not its users. Supporting services for the loan officers could include a Service Desk that provides technical support for the credit reporting service, email and voice mail. These services support the outcome of approving loans to credit-worthy customers in an efficient and timely manner, compliant with all policies, procedures and regulations.

In most markets, supporting services will either provide the basis for differentiation or represent the minimum requirements for operation. As excitement factors, enhancing services provide differentiation. As basic factors, enabling services only qualify the provider for an opportunity to serve customers. Enabling services are necessary for customers to utilize the core service effectively. Like basic factors, customers take their availability for granted and do not expect to be additionally charged for the value that such services provide. Examples of commonly offered enabling services are help desk, payment, registration, and directory services.

Examples of enhancing services are harder to provide because they tend to drift with time towards being subsumed into the core service or into becoming an enabling service, depending on the customer segment and market space. In the lending service example, the bank could provide a pre-approved banking card with which small business owners can make capital purchases and cover other business expenses. The bank can also provide a comprehensive online suite of Financial Management tools that allows the borrower to manage working capital and flow of funds connected to the loan account.

5.5.4.2 Developing differentiated offerings

The packing of core and supporting services is an essential aspect of market strategy. Service providers should conduct a thorough analysis of the prevailing conditions in their business environment, the needs of the customer segments or types they serve, and the alternatives that are available to those customers. The decisions are strategic because they hold a long-term view for maintaining value for customers even as industry practices, norms, technologies and regulations change.

Bundling of supporting services with core services has implications for the design and operation of services. Decisions have to be made whether to standardize on the core or the supporting services. One can arrive at the same level of differentiation in a service offering taking different approaches to bundling (Figure 5.25). However, the costs and risks involved may be different. Service Transition processes guide such decisions. The costs and risks for supporting services may be overlooked during

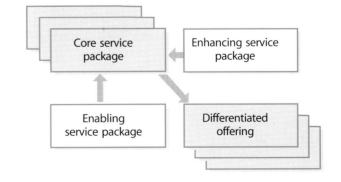

Figure 5.25 Differentiated offerings

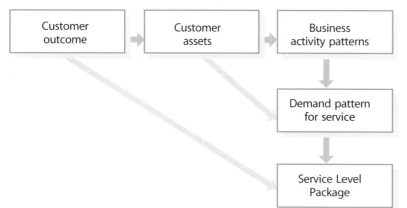

Figure 5.26 Business outcomes are the ultimate basis for service level packages

initial stages of planning and development. Not only that, since supporting services are often shared by several core services, there is often poor visibility and control over the demand for supporting services and their consumption.

While service providers must focus on the effective delivery of value from core services, they should also devote enough attention to the supporting services. Satisfaction surveys show that user dissatisfaction is often with supporting services even where the core service is being effectively delivered.

Some supporting services, such as help desk or technical support services typically bundled with most service packages can also be offered on their own. This is an important consideration in strategic planning and reviews. Service providers may adopt different strategies for core services and supporting services. For example, they can drive standardization and consolidation for supporting services to leverage economies of scale and to reduce operating costs, while developing core service packages specifically designed for particular customers. Or they may standardize the core service package and use supporting services to differentiate the offerings across customers or market segments. These strategic decisions can have enormous implications for the overall success of a service provider at the portfolio level. This is particularly important for service providers who need to balance the differing needs of, typically, not one but several enterprises or business units while trying to keep costs down across that portfolio to remain competitive.

5.5.4.3 Service level packages

Services packages come with one or more service level packages (SLP). Each SLP provides a definite level of utility or warranty from the perspective of outcomes, assets and the PBA of customers. Each SLP is capable of fulfilling one or more patterns of demand (Figure 5.26).

SLPs are associated with a set of service levels, pricing policies, and a core service package (CSP). CSPs are service packages that provide a platform of utility and warranty shared by two or more SLPs (Figure 5.27). Combinations of CSPs and SLPs are used to serve customer segments with differentiated value. Common attributes of SLPs are subsumed into the supporting CSPs. (This is like the popular game of Tetris in which the bottom-most layer of bricks gets subsumed when all its gaps are filled with the falling bricks.) This follows the principle of modularity to reduce complexity, increase asset utilization across SLPs, and to reduce the overall cost of services. CSPs and SLPs

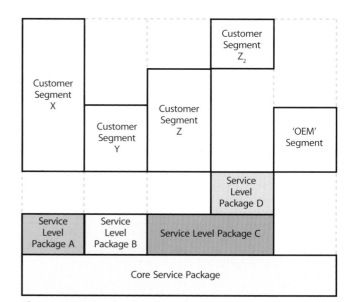

Figure 5.27 Service level packages are a means to provide differentiated services

are loosely coupled to allow for local optimization while maintaining efficiency over the entire supported Service Catalogue. Improvements made to CSPs are automatically available to all SLPs following the principle of inheritance and encapsulation. Economy of scale and economy of scope are realized at the CSP level and the savings are transmitted to the SLP and to customers as policy permits.

In certain contexts, CSPs are infrastructure services offered by a specialized service unit. This allows for greater economy, learning and growth from specialization. This is similar to the arrangements between product marketing groups and manufacturing.

5.5.4.4 Advantage of core service packages

Some enterprises have highly consolidated core infrastructure units that support the operations of business units at a very large scale with high levels of reliability and performance. An example is a global supply chain and logistics company famous for its brown delivery trucks and industrialized service. The high levels of performance and reliability translate into similar levels of service warranty offered to businesses and consumers on the delivery of parcels and documents. The strategy is tight control over core services used by all business units so that complexity is under control, economy of scale is extracted, and business outcomes are assured. Each business unit can develop SLPs based on applications and processes to serve their own market spaces, and have them hosted on top of the core infrastructure services (Figure 5.28).

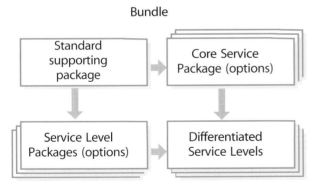

Figure 5.28 Going to market with service packages

From the business unit perspective, where the SLP is hosted has implications for exposure to quality, cost, and risks. The company is required to negotiate the best possible terms for having their SLPs supported by appropriate CSPs. The principle of separation of concerns is applied here to increase focus on customers without compromising the economy, efficiency and stability of centralized service operations and infrastructure.

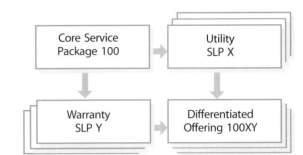

Figure 5.29 SLPs are targeted at customer segments

The infrastructure unit may offer their CSPs as third-party OEM services to other service providers who package them with their own set of SLPs. This further reduces the financial risks of service assets used to operate the CSP.

5.5.4.5 Segmentation

SLPs are effective in developing service packages for providing value to a segment of users with utility and warranty appropriate to their needs and in a cost-effective way. SLPs are combined with CSPs to build a Service Catalogue with segmentation (Figure 5.29). This avoids underserved and over-served customers and increases the economic efficiency of service agreements and contracts.

CSPs and SLPs are each made up of reusable components many of which themselves are services (Table 5.10). Other components include software applications, hardware, licences, third-party services and public infrastructure services (Figure 5.30). Some service components are assets owned by customers.

Making component services visible to customers on the Service Catalogue is a matter of policy with respect to pricing and bundling of services. Risks described in Section 9.5 have to be considered for decisions on expanding the Service Catalogue.

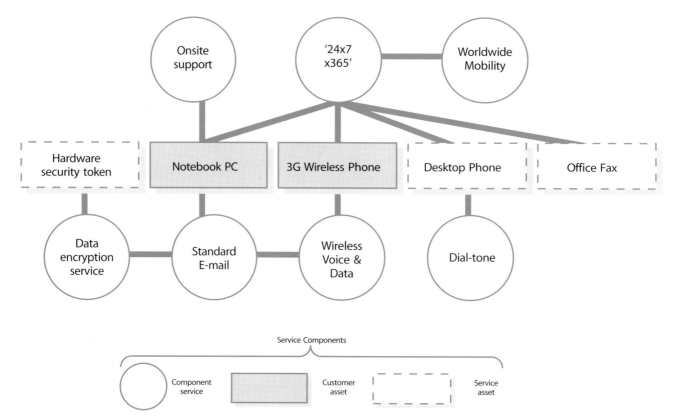

Figure 5.30 SLPs composed of service components and component services

Table 5.10 Warranty SLPs composed of service components and component services

Warranty SLP	Workspace SLP1	Workspace SLP2	Workspace SLP3
Availability SLP	24x7x365 Plan with High Availability	24x7x365 Plan with Very High Availability	9-5 Weekday Plan with Standard Availability
	Worldwide Mobility	Worldwide Mobility	Designated Office Location
	PC Notebook	PC Notebook	PC Desktop
	Wireless PDA Service	Wireless PDA Service	Desktop Phone
	Desktop Phone	Desktop Phone	Standard Wireless
	3G Wireless	3G Wireless	
Capacity SLP	Large Mailbox	Extra large Mailbox	Basic Mailbox
	Priority Broadband	Priority Broadband	Basic Broadband
			Heavy Duty Print Service
Continuity SLP	PSTN backup	PSTN backup Level-3 backup and restore	PSTN backup
	Level-2 backup and restore	Worldwide travel support	Level-1 backup and restore
	Worldwide travel support		On-site support
Security SLP	Multi-factor authentication		Multi-factor authentication
	Hardware tokens		Virtual Private Network
	Virtual Private Network		
	Secure FTP		

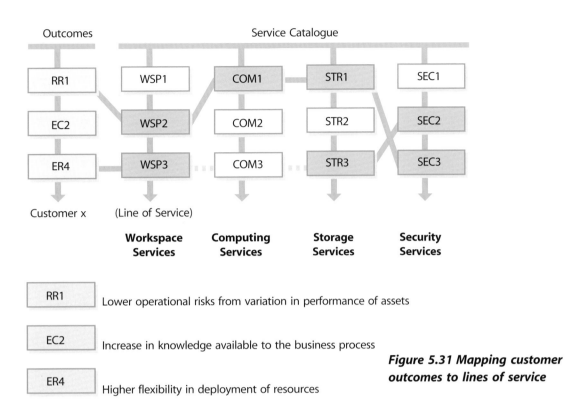

RR1 — Lower operational risks from variation in performance of assets

EC2 — Increase in knowledge available to the business process

ER4 — Higher flexibility in deployment of resources

Figure 5.31 Mapping customer outcomes to lines of service

A Service Catalogue is also a collection of Lines of Service (LOS), each under the control of a Product Manager. Section B.2 in Appendix B provides a description of the roles and responsibilities of Product Managers within the domain of service management. Each LOS provides a combination of utility and warranty most preferred by a segment of customers. Customer segments are defined in terms of business outcomes. This type of segmentation cuts across traditional market segments based on criteria such as demographics, location, size of business, purchasing behaviour, and perceived needs.[23] The links between such criteria and actual business outcomes are often weak or unstable, whereas business outcomes of customers are permanently linked with customer's perception of value. Outcome-based segmentation improves the focus and specialization for service providers in truly meeting customer needs.

Each LOS has one or more service offerings (Figure 5.31). Each service offering is made up of CSPs and SLPs. This modular approach provides multiple control perspectives within the Service Lifecycle. CSPs and SLPs can be managed by separate specialized groups within the service provider. Utility SLPs and Warranty SLPs may similarly be assigned to groups with specialized capabilities and resources, or to third parties.

It is the responsibility of the Business Relationship Manager (BRM) to identify the most suitable combination of LOS and SLP for every customer outcome they are concerned with. BRMs relate customer outcomes to the supporting UP (Figure 5.32). Each UP is then matched to the appropriate SLP to create a customized service offering for every customer outcome (Figure 5.33). The Kano Model Method[28] is applied to develop complex value-added service offerings based on service components and component services. CSPs and SLPs may be basic, performance or excitement service packages according to customer preferences and perceptions.

Figure 5.32 Services are framed by the customer outcomes they support

User Profiles   **Service Level Packages**

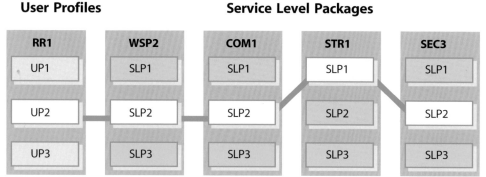

Figure 5.33 Mapping user profiles to service level packages

This component-based approach greatly reduces the cost of providing services while maintaining high levels of customer satisfaction. BRMs represent customers and work closely with Product Managers to ensure that the Service Catalogue has the right mix of LOS and SLP to fulfil the needs of the Customer Portfolio.

Strategy and organization

6

6   Strategy and organization

'I was in a warm bed, and suddenly I'm part of a plan.'
Woody Allen in *Shadows and Fog*

Organizations

Organizations are goal-directed, boundary maintaining and socially constructed systems of human activity.[29]

Organizations are designed and built for a purpose. These goals drive the behaviours of an organization's many agents who dynamically interact with each other. The many interactions produce emergent macro-level patterns of organizational behaviour. IT organizations are complex systems embedded within the larger complex system of its business, customers and industry.

The transaction costs principle is a simple and yet powerful means for explaining organizations. It argues that, in certain circumstances, organizations are more efficient mechanisms for cooperation than contracting or sourcing. IT organizations are subject to transaction costs. They must search for, negotiate, monitor, coordinate and govern resources in order to produce services. As people come together in an organization, they must learn what to do and how to work with others to perform. If this cooperation is done ineffectively, transaction costs rise. The better the organization manages its transaction costs, the better it justifies its existence. Further, certain risks are better mitigated through organizations than through contracts:

- Incomplete contracts – no contract can ever cover every possible contingency. The greater and more complex the cooperation needed with external contractors, the greater the possibility of an incomplete contract.[30]
- The hold-up problem[31] – services often require investments in specific assets such as infrastructure or facilities. The problem of incomplete contracts implies that there is always a possibility that contracts will unravel. Contractors are then stuck with these hard-to-reverse assets and may then withhold access as they seek better terms.
- Change endurance – organizations create structures that outlive the participation of their agents. These cooperative structures allow an organization to strive for complex strategies that may require years to enact.

Figure 6.1 Organizational value creation cycle

- Collective learning – much like individuals, organizations are capable of learning.[32] Despite changes in individuals, organizations act as a stabilizing and collective storehouse for knowledge while in pursuit of their goals.

Adequate scarce resources, a well-considered strategy and distinctiveness allow an organization to provide superior performance versus competing alternatives, in turn justifying the acquisition of still more scarce resources. This virtuous cycle is illustrated in Figure 6.1.

6.1 ORGANIZATIONAL DEVELOPMENT

When senior managers adopt a service management orientation, they are adopting a vision for the organization. Such a vision provides a model toward which staff can work. Organizational change, however, is not instantaneous. Senior managers often make the mistake of thinking that announcing the organizational change is the same as making it happen.

There is no one best way to organize. Elements of an organizational design, such as scale, scope and structure, are highly dependent on strategic objectives. Over time, an organization will likely outgrow its design. There is the underlying problem of structural fit. Certain organizational designs fit while others do not. The design challenge is to identify and select among often distinct choices. Thus the problem becomes much more solvable when there is an understanding of the factors that generate fit and the trade-offs involved, such as control and coordination.

When the organization performs well, the structure tends to drift towards a decentralized model where local managers possess greater autonomy (Figure 6.2). When problems persist, the tendency is to shift to a centralized model. This pendulum swing represents a lack of confidence in local decision making. Despite the extreme difficulties, there is a persistent belief that an organization is controlled from the top. But giving orders is not the same as being in control. There are no guarantees, however, that local managers will appreciate the impact of their decisions on the larger organization. Their decisions can be short-term and short-sighted. This wavering between centralized and decentralized management is attributed as the source of long-term organizational problems and has been described as, 'the illusion of being

in control'. How then, does an organization decide how to best manage its current organization and where to land along the design spectrum?

Case example 12: *Organizational development*

1   The global CIO of this Fortune 50 automotive company built an IT organization in an unusual manner. He hires divisional CIOs to correspond to business divisions: North America, Europe, Asia-Pacific, Latin America, Africa, the Middle East and finance. At the same time, he hires process information officers (PIOs) to work horizontally in different specialities across all divisions around the world: product development, supply chain management, production, customer experience and business services (HR, legal and so on).

2   The IT organization for one of the most popular sports leagues in North America flourishes under a culture of speed and entrepreneurship. Sunday game results and media events often dictate service activities with short time frames. Service processes are minimally structured, with room for improvisation and adaptation.

What are these organizational structures called?

(Answer given later in this section)

The process for major organizational change involves many events and can be a matter of years rather than months. Leading this change is difficult and should not be reduced to quick or simple fixes. The ability to lead this change is an important competence for senior executives and managers. Understanding when a service strategy is too complicated and rigid is as important as any support process.

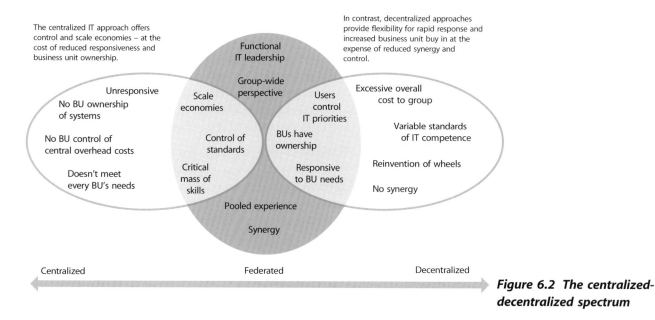

The centralized IT approach offers control and scale economies – at the cost of reduced responsiveness and business unit ownership.

In contrast, decentralized approaches provide flexibility for rapid response and increased business unit buy in at the expense of reduced synergy and control.

Unresponsive
No BU ownership of systems

No BU control of central overhead costs

Doesn't meet every BU's needs

Functional IT leadership

Scale economies

Group-wide perspective

Control of standards

Critical mass of skills

Pooled experience

Synergy

Users control IT priorities

BUs have ownership

Responsive to BU needs

Excessive overall cost to group

Variable standards of IT competence

Reinvention of wheels

No synergy

Centralized   Federated   Decentralized

Figure 6.2 The centralized-decentralized spectrum

Case example 12 (solution)

1   *Stage-5 or Matrix.* A matrix structure is a very difficult form of lateral process used for stronger collaboration with the business.

2   *Stage-1 or Network.* The focus of this organization is on the rapid, informal and ad hoc delivery of services. Informal structures are far better suited for success.

Outside forces greatly influence an organization's service strategy, which in turn determines the organizational structure. Where the lines are drawn depends on what the organization is attempting to accomplish. A service strategy then becomes an implicit blueprint for an organization's design, shaping scale and scope. Scale refers to size. Scope refers not only to the broadness of service offerings – it also describes the range of activities the organization performs. When an organization decides on a make-or-buy strategy, for example, it is determining the scope of its activities. The trade-offs are control versus coordination.

An organization's age and size affect its structure. As the organization grows and matures, changes in roles and relationships must be made or problems will arise. This is particularly important for organizations adopting a service orientation, as pressures for efficiency and discipline inevitably lead to greater formalization and complexity. The risk over time is that the organization becomes too bureaucratic and rigid.

Most IT organizations tend to grow for prolonged periods without severe setbacks. The term evolution describes the quieter periods while the term revolution describes the upheaval of management practices. Organizations are

generally characterized by a dominant management style: Network, Directive, Delegative, Coordinated or Collaborative[33] (Figure 6.3). Each style serves the needs of the organization for a period of time. As service requirements evolve, the organization encounters a dominant management challenge that must be resolved before growth can continue. The organization can no longer address its service challenge with its current management style. Nor can it be successful by retreating to a previous style – it must move ahead.

6.1.1   Stage-1: Network

The focus of a Stage-1 organization is on the rapid, informal and ad hoc delivery of services. The organization is highly technology-oriented, perhaps entrepreneurial, and is reluctant to adopt formal structures. Innovation and entrepreneurship are important organizational values. The organization learns which processes and services work and adjusts accordingly. The organization believes that informal structures are far better suited to the resources required to deliver services. Past successes reinforce this belief. As the service demands grow, this model is not sustainable. It requires great local knowledge and intense dedication on the part of the staff. Conflict is created as staff resist the creation of service structures.

As the organization grows and the need for efficient resources increases, leaders are confronted with the task of having to manage an organization. This is a very different skill from technology and entrepreneurship and often a task for which leaders find themselves ill prepared.

A common structure in this stage is called a network (Figure 6.4). A network structure is a cluster whose actions are coordinated by agreements rather than through a formal hierarchy of authority. The members work closely

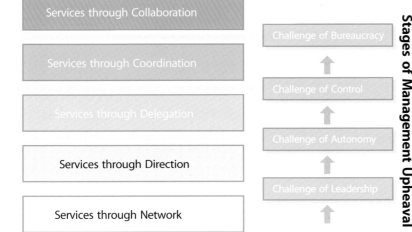

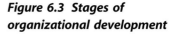

Figure 6.3 Stages of organizational development

together to complement each other's activities. The goal of the organization is to share its skills with the customer in order to allow them to become more efficient, reduce costs or improve quality.

The key advantages of a network structure:

- It avoids the high bureaucratic costs of operating a complex organizational structure
- The organization can be kept flat with fewer managers required
- The organization can quickly adapt or alter its structure.

The practical disadvantages of a network structure:

- Managers must ensure the activities of the staff are integrated
- The coordination problems are significant
- There are difficulties in externally sourcing functional activities.

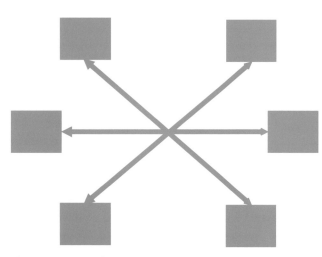

Figure 6.4 Services through network

Guidance: to grow past this challenge requires a significant change in leadership style. While this is accomplished through a variety of human performance techniques and methods, the desired outcome is a cadre of strong managers skilled and experienced in service management structures. Their influence and business focus are essential for moving to the next stage.

6.1.2 Stage-2: Directive

The Stage-1 crisis of leadership ends with a strong management team. They take responsibility for directing strategy and direct low-level managers to assume functional responsibilities (Figure 6.5).

The focus of a Stage-2 organization is on hierarchical structures that separate functional activities. Communication is more formal and basic processes are in

place. Although effort and energy are diligently applied to services, they are likely to be inefficient. Functional specialists are frequently faced with the difficult decision of whether to follow the process or take the initiative on their own.

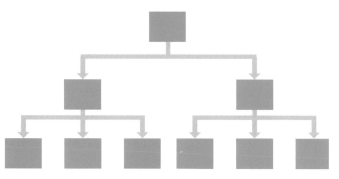

Figure 6.5 Services through direction

A crisis of autonomy arises because the centralization limits decision making and the freedom to experiment or innovate. Entrepreneurial motivation is degraded. For example, high-level approval is needed to start new projects, while successful performance at the lower levels goes unnoticed or unrewarded. Staff become frustrated with their lack of autonomy. By not solving this crisis, the organization limits its ability to grow and prosper.

Guidance: to grow past this challenge requires a shift to greater delegation. Responsibility for service processes should be driven lower in the organization, allowing process owners to be responsible for lower-level decision making and service accountability.

6.1.3 Stage-3: Delegation

The Stage-2 crisis ends with the delegation of authority to lower-level managers, linking their increased control to a corresponding reward structure (Figure 6.6). Growth through delegation allows the organization to strike a balance between technical efficiency and the need to provide room for innovation in the pursuit of new means to reduce costs or improve services.

The focus of a Stage-3 organization is on the proper application of a decentralized organizational structure. More responsibility shifts from functional owners to process owners. Process owners focus on process improvement and customer responsiveness. The challenge here is when functional and process objectives clash. Functional owners feel a loss of control and seek to regain it. At this stage, top managers intervene in decision making only when necessary.

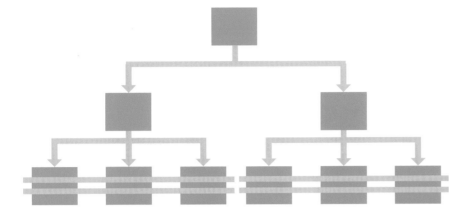

Figure 6.6 Services through delegation

Guidance: Rather than the frequent reaction of returning to a functionally centralized model, the recommended approach is to enhance the organization's coordination techniques and solutions. The most common approach is through formal systems and programmes. There are occasions when an organization attempts to resolve the coordination challenge by centralizing on a process, rather than functional model. Rather than creating a white space between functions, this leads to white space between processes. In other words, a pure process model is as problematic as a purely functional organizational model. A balance should be sought or the organization will revert back to a crisis of autonomy.

6.1.4 Stage-4: Coordination

The focus of a Stage-4 organization is on the use of formal systems in achieving greater coordination (Figure 6.7). Senior executives acknowledge the criticality of these systems and take responsibility for success of the solutions. The solutions lead to planned service management structures that are intensely reviewed and continually improved. Each service is treated as a carefully nurtured and monitored investment. Technical functions

remain centralized while service management processes are decentralized.

The challenge here is the ability to respond to business needs in an agile manner. The business often adopts a perception that IT, despite its service orientation, has become too bureaucratic and rigid. While the linkages to the business may be well understood, innovation is dampened and service procedures have taken precedence over business agility.

6.1.5 Stage-5: Collaboration

The focus of a Stage-5 organization is on stronger collaboration with the business (Figure 6.8). Relationship management is more flexible, while managers are highly skilled in teamwork and conflict resolution. The organization responds to changes in business conditions and strategy in the form of teams across functions. Experiments in new practices are encouraged. A matrix-type structure is frequently adopted in this phase.

A matrix structure is a rectangular grid that shows the vertical flow of functional responsibility and a horizontal flow of product or customer responsibility. The provider effectively has two (or more) line organizations with dual

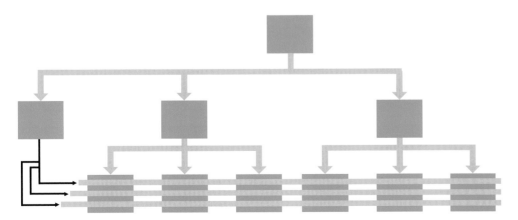

Figure 6.7 Services through coordination

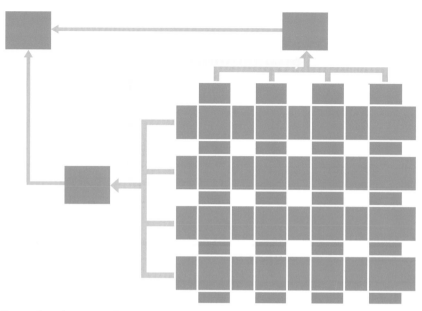

Figure 6.8 Services through collaboration

lines of authority and a balance of power; two (or more) bosses, each actively participating in strategy setting and governance.

An organization with a matrix structure adopts whatever functions the organization requires to achieve its goals. Functional personnel report to the heads of their respective functions but do not work under their direct supervision. Rather, the work of the functional staff is primarily determined by the leadership of the respective cross-functional product or customer team. The matrix relies on minimal formal vertical control and maximum horizontal control from the use of integrated teams.

The key advantages of a matrix structure:

- Reduces and overcomes functional barriers
- Increases responsiveness to changing product or customer needs
- Opens up communication between functional specialists
- Provides opportunities for team members from different functions to learn from each other
- Uses the skills of specialized employees who move from product to product, or customer to customer, as needed.

In practice, there can be many problems with a matrix structure. The disadvantages:

- Lacks a control structure that allows staff to develop stable expectations of each other
- Staff can be put off by the ambiguity and role conflict produced
- Potential conflict between functions and product or customer teams over time.

6.1.6 Deciding on a structure

Notice how each phase influences the other over time. The sequences are not always inevitable or linear. Each phase is neither right nor wrong. They are signposts to guide the organization. By understanding the current state, senior executives are better able to decide in what direction, and how far, to move along the centralized-decentralized spectrum.

The key to applying service management organizational development is understanding the following:

- Where the organization is in the sequence
- The range of appropriate options
- Each solution will bring new challenges.

6.1.7 Organizational change

No matter what type of change the organization decides on, there remains the problem of getting the organization to change. Implementing change can be thought of as a three-step process, as in Figure 6.9.

Resistance to change will force the organization to revert to previous behaviours unless steps are taken to refreeze the new changes. Role and task changes are not enough. Managers must actively manage the process.

1 The first step to change is diagnosis. Namely, acknowledge the need for change and the factors prompting it. For example, complaints about service quality have increased or operating costs have escalated. Or morale is low while turnover is high. There is little point in focusing on improving costs if the customer is concerned about quality.

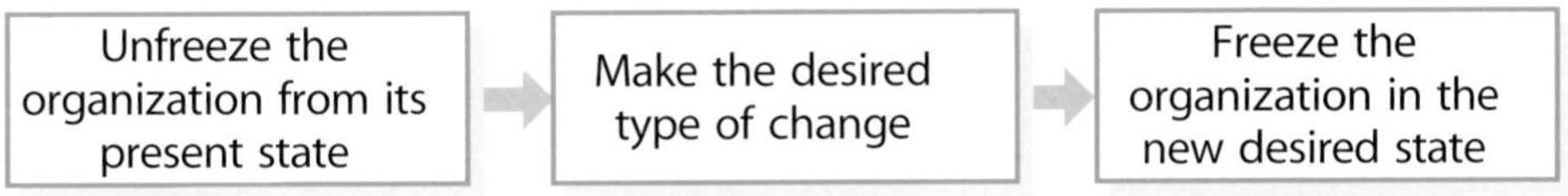

| Unfreeze the organization from its present state | → | Make the desired type of change | → | Freeze the organization in the new desired state |

Figure 6.9 Three-step change process

2 The second step is determining the desired state. While this can be a difficult planning process with alternative courses of action, it begins with the organization's strategy and desired structure. Is the strategy based on reducing costs or improving quality? Should the organization adopt a product or geographic structure?

3 The third step is implementation. This three-step process begins with identifying possible impediments to change. What obstacles are anticipated? For example, functional managers may resist reductions in power or prestige. The more severe the change then the greater the difficulties encountered. Next, decide who will be responsible for implementing changes and controlling the change process. These change agents can be external, as in consultants, or internal, as in knowledgeable managers. External change agents tend to be more objective and less likely to be perceived to be influenced by internal politics, while internal agents tend to have greater local knowledge. Last, decide on which change strategy will most effectively unfreeze, change and refreeze the organization. These techniques fall into two categories: top-down and bottom-up. Top-down is a dramatic restructuring by senior managers while bottom-up is a gradual change by low-level employees. Example techniques include:

■ Education and communication
■ Participation and empowerment
■ Facilitation
■ Bargaining and negotiation
■ Process consultation
■ Team building and inter-group training.

6.2 ORGANIZATIONAL DEPARTMENTALIZATION

It is common to think of organizational hierarchies in terms of functions. As the functional groups become larger, think of them in terms of departmentalization. A department can loosely be defined as an organizational activity involving over 20 people. When a functional group grows to departmental size, the organization can reorient the group to one of the following areas or a hybrid thereof:

■ Function – preferred for specialization, the pooling of resources and reducing duplication
■ Product – preferred for servicing businesses with strategies of diverse and new products, usually manufacturing businesses
■ Market space or customer – preferred for organizing around market structures. Provides differentiation in the form of increased knowledge of and response to customer preferences
■ Geography – the use of geography depends on the industry. By providing services in close geographical proximity, travel and distribution costs are minimized while local knowledge is leveraged
■ Process – preferred for an end-to-end coverage of a process.

Certain basic structures are preferred for certain service strategies, as shown in Table 6.1.

Table 6.1 Basic organizational structures

Basic Structure	Strategic Considerations
Functional	Specialization
	Common standards
	Small size
Product	Product focus
	Strong product knowledge
Market space or customer	Service unique to segment
	Customer service
	Buyer strength
	Rapid customer service
Geography	On-site services
	Proximity to customer for delivery and support
	Organization perceived as local
Process	Need to minimize process cycle times
	Process excellence

6.3 ORGANIZATIONAL DESIGN

The starting point for organizational design is strategy (Figure 6.10). It sets the direction and guides the criteria for each step of the design process.

It is recommended to decide on a departmentalization structure prior to designing key processes. For example, if the provider's organization will be structured by geography or aligned by customers, the process design will be guided by this criterion. Once key processes are

understood, it is appropriate to begin organizational design (Figure 6.11).

The flow depends on clearly articulated strategic criteria. Processes can be thought of as organizational software – configurable to the requirements of a service strategy. Organizational designers should see each step as an iterative cycle: create basic processes and structures, learn about current and new conditions, and adjust as learning evolves.

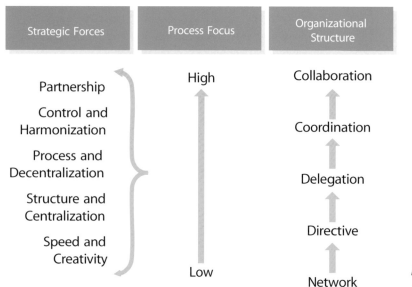

Figure 6.10 Matching strategic forces with organizational development

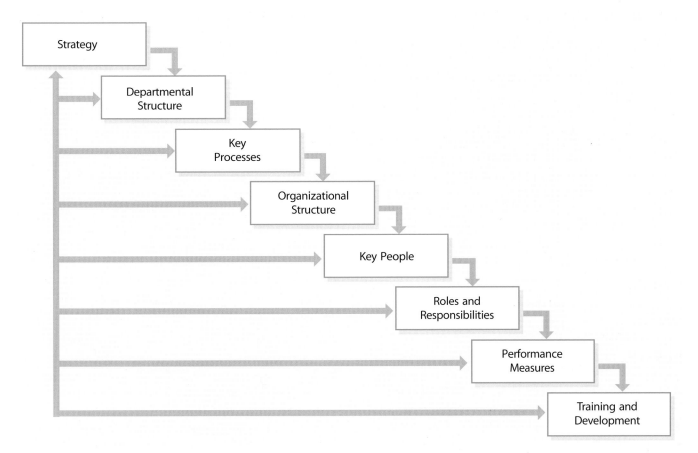

Figure 6.11 Organizational design steps

6.4 ORGANIZATIONAL CULTURE

Organizational culture is the set of shared values and norms that control the IT organization's interactions with each other and customers. Just as an organizational structure can improve performance, so, too, can an organization's culture increase organizational effectiveness.

There are two types of organizational values: terminal and instrumental.

- Terminal values are desired outcomes or end states. IT organizations can adopt any of the following as terminal values: quality, excellence, reliability, innovativeness or profitability. Terminal values are often reflected in the organization's strategic perspective.
- Instrumental values are desired modes of behaviour. IT organizations can adopt any of the following as instrumental values: high standards, respecting tradition and authority, acting cautiously and conservatively, or being frugal.

Terminal and instrumental values are key shapers of behaviour and can therefore produce very different responses in an IT organization. Many mergers and acquisitions fail because of these differences. Culture is transmitted to staff through socialization, training programmes, stories, ceremonies and language.

A service management organizational culture can be analysed through the following steps:

- Identify the terminal and instrumental values of the organization.
- Determine whether the goals, norms and rules of the organization are properly transmitting the value of the organizational culture to staff members. Are there areas for improvement?
- Assess the methods the IT organization uses to introduce new staff. Do these practices help newcomers learn the organization's culture? (Van Maanen[34] identified 12 socialization tactics that are useful in orienting newcomers to an organization's culture.)

6.5 SOURCING STRATEGY

'The next layers of value creation – whether in technology, marketing, biomedicine or manufacturing – are becoming so complex that no single firm or department is going to be able to master them alone.'

Thomas L. Friedman, *The World is Flat*

Outsourcing is the moving of a value-creating activity that was performed inside the organization to outside the organization where it is performed by another company. What prompts an organization to outsource an activity is the same logic that determines whether an organization makes or buys inputs. Namely, does the extra value generated from performing an activity inside the organization outweigh the costs of managing it? This decision can change over time.

A service strategy should enhance an organization's special strengths and core competencies. Each component should reinforce the other. Change any one and you have a different model. As organizations seek to improve their performance, they should consider which competencies are essential and know when to extend their capabilities by partnering in areas both inside and outside their enterprise. Service sourcing is another example of the Separation of Concerns (SoC) principle. This time it is a separation of the 'what' from the 'who'.

Case example 13: *Service Strategy*

During the early 2000s, companies rushed to implement a service strategy based on labour arbitrage: service providers decrease labour costs by making use of less expensive off-shore resources. The strategic intent is to make a provider's value proposition more compelling through lower cost structures.

While costs did indeed decrease for customers, providers were unable to make long-term gains to their financial bottom line.

Why?

(Answer in Section 6.5.1)

IT and business services are increasingly delivered by service providers outside the enterprise, and by the internal organization. Making an informed service sourcing decision requires finding a balance between thorough qualitative and quantitative considerations. Historically, the financial business case is the primary basis for most sourcing decisions. These analyses include pure cost savings, lower capital investments, investment redirections and long-term cost containment. Unfortunately, most

financial analyses do not include all the costs related to sourcing, leading to difficult sourcing relationships with unexpected costs and service issues. If costs are a primary driver for a sourcing decision, include financials for service transition, relationship management, legal support, incentives, training, tools licensing implications and process rationalization, among others.

6.5.1 Deciding what to source

A business's strategy formulation is the search for competitive differentiation through the redeployment of resources and capabilities. When a business decides to source services it is in essence deciding to source resources and capabilities. If candidates are only peripherally related to the business's strategic themes and are available in competitive markets then they should be considered. Once candidates for sourcing are identified, the following questions are intended to clarify matters:

- Do the candidate services improve the business's resources and capabilities?
- How closely are the candidate services connected to the business's competitive and strategic resources and capabilities?
- Do the candidate services require extensive interactions between the service providers and the business's competitive and strategic resources and capabilities?

Case example 13 (solution): *The inability to capture value*

Early adopters of a labour arbitrage strategy made great gains because, for a while, the costs of services they offered were lower than any competing alternatives. But as more and more service providers made use of off-shore resources, the cost of services was lowered for everyone. This was great for customers but bad for providers – this distinctiveness was eventually eliminated. Value was created for customers but service providers were not able to keep any of it. This ability of a service provider to keep a portion of any value created is known as 'value capture'.

The sourcing strategy was vitally important for fending off competing alternatives. However, service providers who focused solely on this strategy, at the expense of other distinctive capabilities, soon encountered strategic failure in the form 'mediocre performance versus competing alternatives'.

If the responses uncover minimal dependencies and infrequent interactions between the sourced services and the business's competitive and strategic positioning, then the candidates are strong contenders.

If candidates for sourcing are closely related to the business's competitive or strategic positioning, then care must be taken. Such sourcing structures are particularly vulnerable to:

■ Substitution – 'Why do I need the service provider when its supplier can offer the same services?' The sourced vendor develops competing capabilities and replaces the sourcing organization.

■ Disruption – The sourced vendor has a direct impact on quality or reputation of the sourcing organization.

■ Distinctiveness – The sourced vendor is the source of distinctiveness for the sourcing organization. The sourcing organization then becomes particularly dependent on the continued development and success of the second organization.

Do not confuse distinctive activities with critical activities. Critical activities do not necessarily refer to activities that may be distinctive to the service provider. Take, for example, customer service. Customers may believe it is critical, but if it does not differentiate the provider from competing alternatives then it is not distinctive, it is context.

This does not mean critical activities are not important. Contextual activities are not of secondary importance. It means they do not provide the differentiating benefit that generates value. One service provider's context may be

another's distinctiveness. What is distinctive today may over time become context. Contextual processes may be recombined into distinctive processes. Here is a basic test:

■ Does the customer or market space expect the service provider to do this activity? (context)

■ Does the customer or market space give the service provider credit for performing this activity exceptionally well? (distinctiveness)

Early adopters of airline kiosks, for example, differentiated themselves through self-service technology (Mode-E). While kiosks were a distinctive activity central to the service strategy, it was hardly critical. Years later, customers expect kiosks at all locations for every airline. Every major airline considers it a critical activity but not distinctive – it no longer differentiates. Hence airlines consolidate or source this critical activity. They collaborate with partner airlines to provide kiosks any member airline may use. They source kiosks from Type III providers who place them in corporate locations, hotels and public places.

6.5.2 Sourcing structures

The dynamics of service sourcing require businesses to formally address provisions for a sourcing strategy, the structure and role of the retained organization, and the impacted decision rights processes. When sourcing services, the enterprise retains the responsibility for the adequacy of services delivered. Therefore, the enterprise retains key overall responsibility for governance. The enterprise should adopt a formal governance approach in

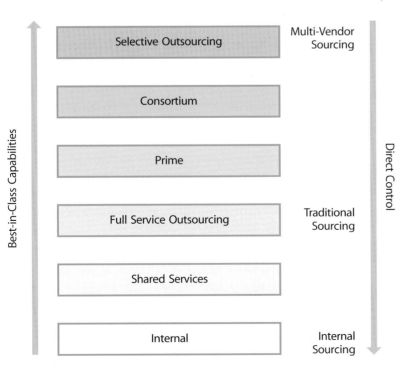

Figure 6.12 Service sourcing structures

Table 6.2 Service sourcing structures

Sourcing Structure	Description
Internal (Type I)	The provision and delivery of services by internal staff. Does not typically include standardization of service delivery across business units.
	Provides the most control but also the most limited in terms of scale.
Shared Services (Type II)	An internal business unit. Typically operates its profit and loss, and a chargeback mechanism. If cost recovery is not used, then it is Internal not Shared Services.
	Lower costs than Internal with a similar degree of control. Improved standardization but limited in terms of scale.
Full Service Outsourcing	A single contract with a single service provider. Typically involves significant asset transfer.
	Provides improved scale but limited in terms of best-in-class capabilities. Delivery risks are higher than Prime, Consortium or Selective Outsourcing as switching to an alternative is difficult.
Prime	A single contract with a single service provider who manages service delivery but engages multiple providers to do so. The contract stipulates that the prime vendor will leverage the capabilities of other best-in-class service providers.
	Capabilities and risk are improved from Single-Vendor Outsourcing but complexity is increased.
Consortium	A collection of service providers explicitly selected by the service recipient. All providers are required to come together and present a unified management interface.
	Fulfils a need that cannot be satisfied by any Single-Vendor Outsourcer. Provides best-in-class capabilities with greater control than Prime. Risk is introduced in the form of providers forced to collaborate with competitors.
Selective Outsourcing	A collection of service providers explicitly selected and managed by the service recipient.
	This is the most difficult structure to manage. The service recipient is the service integrator, responsible for gaps or cross-provider disputes.
	The term Co-Sourcing refers to a special case of Selective Outsourcing. In this variant, the service recipient maintains an Internal or Shared Services structure and combines it with external providers. The service recipient is the service integrator.

order to create a working model for managing its outsourced services as well as the assurance of value delivery. This includes planning for the organizational change precipitated by the sourcing strategy and a formal and verifiable description as to how decisions on services are made. Figure 6.12 and Table 6.2 describes the generic forms of service sourcing structures.

The selection of a sourcing structure should be balanced with acceptable risks and levels of control. The method an organization uses to manage a sourcing relationship depends greatly on the sourcing organization's characteristics such as degrees of centralization, standards and process maturity. In general, the sourcing organization should excel in establishing a set of relationship standards and processes. Other key responsibilities are to:

- Monitor the performance of the agreements and the overall relationship with providers.
- Manage the sourcing agreements.

- Provide an escalation level for issues and problems.
- Ensure prioritization for providers.

When sourcing services, enterprises should first focus on clearly defining the services. All too often the primary focus is on the reporting structures and the resources aligned to those structures. Resource alignment and organizational structures should be analysed and adjusted only after understanding the dynamics of the new or enhanced services. This affords the opportunity to remove redundancies and ambiguities, and chokepoints and dysfunctions prior to creating workflows.

Once the resource and organizational discussion begins, be sure to account for the introduction of new critical skills. While highly dynamic, these competencies generally fall into three categories: business, technical and behavioural. For example, the greater the level of outsourcing, the greater the need for business and behavioural skills. The greater the level of internal sourcing, the greater the need for technical skills.

6.5.3 Multi-vendor sourcing

The approach of sourcing services through multiple providers has emerged as a good practice. The enterprise maintains a strong relationship with each provider, spreading the risk and reducing costs. The challenges are in governance and managing the multiple providers. When sourcing multiple providers, the following issues should be carefully evaluated:

- Technical complexity: sourcing is useful for standardized service processes. Be mindful that as customization increases it is more difficult to achieve the desired efficiencies.
- Organizational interdependencies: contractual vehicles should be carefully structured to the dynamics of multiple organizations. Incentives, training, and other intangibles can have significant long-term effects.

- Integration planning: carefully consider the need for integration planning and solutions. This can take the form of standardized reporting and service reporting, or installed technology and protocols that integrate tools and data.

There are multiple approaches and varying degrees in sourcing. How far up an organization is willing to go with sourcing depends on the business objectives to be achieved and constraints to overcome (Figure 6.13). Regardless of the sourcing approach, senior executives must carefully evaluate provider attributes. The following is a useful checklist:

- Demonstrated competencies: in terms of staff, use of technologies, innovation, industry experience and certifications (ISO/IEC 20000)
- Track record: in terms of service quality attained, financial value created and demonstrated commitment to continual improvement
- Relationship dynamics: in terms of vision and strategy, the cultural fit, relative size of contract in their portfolio and quality of relationship management

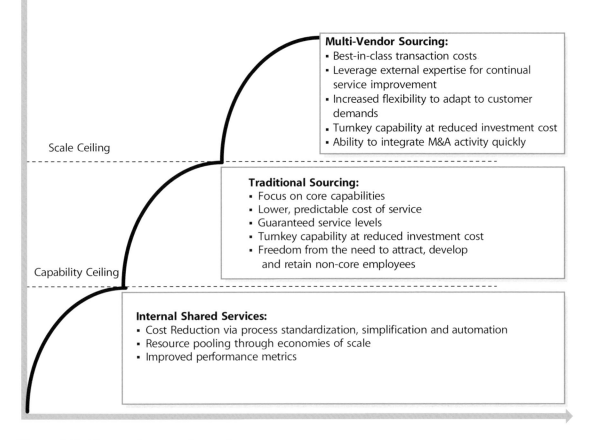

Figure 6.13 The service sourcing staircase

- Quality of solutions: relevance of services to your requirements, risk management and performance benchmarks

- Overall capabilities: in terms of financial strength, resources, management systems, and scope and range of services.

6.5.4 Service Provider Interfaces

To support development of sourcing relationships in a multi-vendor environment, guidelines and reference points (technical, procedural, organizational) are needed between the various service providers. These reference points can be provided through the use of Service Provider Interfaces (SPI) (Figure 6.14).

SPIs help coordinate end-to-end management of critical services. The Service Catalogue drives the service specifications, which are part of, or extensions to, standard process definitions. Responsibilities and service levels are negotiated at the time of service relationship contracting, and include:

- Identification of integration points between various management processes of the client and service provider

- Identification of specific roles and responsibilities for managing the ongoing systems management relationship with both parties

- Identification of relevant systems management information that needs to be communicated to the customer on an ongoing basis.

Process SPI definitions consist of:

- Technology prerequisites (e.g. management tool standards or prescribed protocols)

- Data requirements (e.g. specific events or records), formats (i.e. data layouts), interfaces (e.g. APIs, firewall ports) and protocols (e.g. SNMP, XML)

- Non-negotiable requirements (e.g. practices, activities, operating procedures)

- Required roles/responsibilities within the service provider and customer organizations

- Response times and escalations.

SPIs are defined, maintained and owned by process owners. Others involved in the definition include:

- Business representatives, who negotiate the SPI requirements and are responsible for managing the strategic relationships with and between service providers

- Service provider process coordinator(s) who take operational responsibility for ensuring the operational processes are synchronized.

6.5.5 Sourcing governance

There is a frequent misunderstanding of the definition of governance, particularly in a sourcing context. Companies have used the word interchangeably with 'vendor management,' 'retained staff,' and 'sourcing management organization'. Governance is none of these.

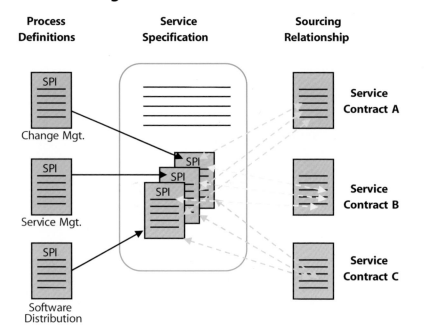

Using Service Provider Interfaces

Figure 6.14 Service provider interfaces

Management and governance are different disciplines. Management deals with making decisions and executing processes. Governance only deals with making sound decisions. It is the framework of decision rights that encourage desired behaviours in the sourcing and the sourced organization. When companies confuse management and governance, they inevitably focus on execution at the expense of strategic decision making. Both are vitally important. Further complicating matters is the requirement of sharing decision rights with the service providers. When a company places itself in a position to make operational decisions on behalf of an outsourcer, the outcomes are inevitably poor service levels and contentious relationship management.

Governance is invariably the weakest link in a service sourcing strategy. A few simple constructs have been shown to be effective at improving that weakness:

1   A governance body. By forming a manageably sized governance body with a clear understanding of the Service Sourcing strategy, decisions can be made without escalating to the highest levels of senior management. By including representation from each service provider, stronger decisions can be made.

2   Governance domains. Domains can cover decision making for a specific area of the Service Sourcing strategy. Domains can cover, for example, Service Delivery, Communication, Sourcing Strategy or Contract Management. Remember, a governance domain does not include the responsibility for its execution, only its strategic decision making.

3   Creation of a decision-rights matrix. This ties all three recommendations together. RACI or RASIC charts are common forms of a decision-rights matrix.

Partnering with providers who are ISO/IEC 20000 compliant is an important element is reducing the risk of Service Sourcing. Organizations who have achieved this certification are more likely to meet service levels on a sustained basis. This credential is particularly important in multi-sourced environments where a common framework promotes better integration. Multi-sourced environments require common language, integrated processes and a management structure between internal and external providers. ISO/IEC 20000 does not provide all of this but it provides a foundation on which it can be built.

Published in 2005, ISO/IEC 20000 is the first formal international standard specific to IT Service Management. An organization comfortable with ITIL will find no difficulty in interpreting ISO/IEC 20000.

Service providers should also consider the eSourcing Capability Model for Service Providers Version 2.0 (eSCM-SP v2) developed by a consortium of service providers led by Carnegie Mellon University. Guidance in this model is specific to sourcing of IT-enabled services. The eSCM-SP provides a framework for organizations to develop their service management capabilities from a sourcing perspective. Organizations can have their sourcing capabilities certified by Carnegie Mellon to be one of four capability levels, based on the publicly available eSCM-SP Reference Model and related Capability Determination Methods. The requirements of eSCM-SP v2 are complementary to ISO/IEC 20000.

6.5.6 Critical success factors

The factors for a Service Sourcing strategy frequently depend on:

- Desired outcomes, such as cost reduction, improved service quality or diminished business risk
- The optimal model for delivering the service
- The best location to deliver the service, such as local, off-shore or on-shore.

The recommended approach to deciding on a strategy includes:

- Analyse the organization's internal service management competencies
- Compare those findings with industry benchmarks
- Assess the organization's ability to deliver strategic value.

The approach will likely lead to these scenarios:

- If the organization's internal service management competence is high and also provides strategic value, then an internal or shared services strategy is the most likely option. The organization should continue to invest internally, leveraging high-value expert providers to refine and enhance the service management competencies.
- If the organization's internal service management competence is low but provides strategic value, then outsourcing is an option provided services can be maintained or improved through the use of high-value providers.
- If the organization's internal service management competence is high but does not provide strategic value, then there are multiple options. The business may want to invest in its service capabilities so that they do provide strategic value or it may sell off this service capability, because it may be of greater value to a third party.

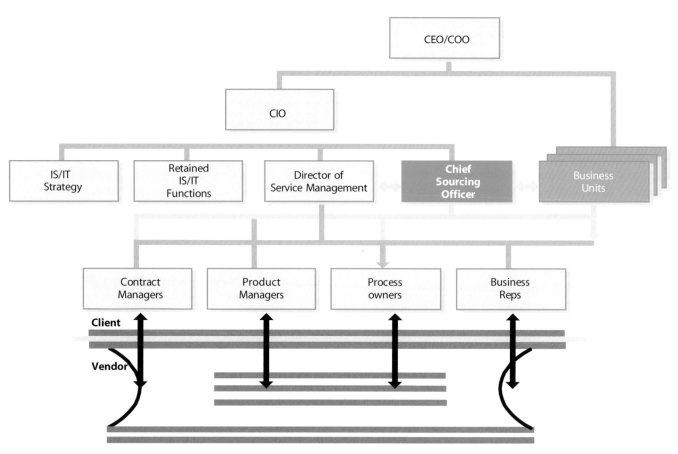

Figure 6.15 Chief Sourcing Officer

■ If the organization's internal service management competence and strategic value are low, then they should be considered candidates for outsourcing.

Prior to any implementation, an organization should establish and maintain a baseline of its performance metrics. Without such metrics, it will be difficult to assess the true impact and trends of a service sourcing implementation. Measurements can take on two forms:

■ Business metrics: financial savings, service level improvements, business process efficiency

■ Customer metrics: availability and consistency of services, increased offerings, quality of service.

6.5.7 Sourcing roles and responsibilities

A key role to champion the sourcing strategy and lead and direct the sourcing office capabilities is the Chief Sourcing Officer (Figure 6.15).

The Chief Sourcing officer

■ Champions the sourcing strategy and the sourcing office

■ Works closely with the CIO to develop a sourcing strategy that will determine which roles and

responsibilities are best assumed by internal personnel and in which areas external resources should be deployed; sets guiding principles for governance

■ Coordinates and rallies a mix of external and internal people towards goals through an empowerment-and-trust style, rather than the command-and-control hierarchical structure used with internal resources

■ Is an integrator, coordinator, communicator, leader, coach: creates a shared identity among external and internal sources so that team members identify themselves first and foremost with the initiative at hand

■ Has the ability to interact at the executive level, and to inspire and lead at the delivery level.

Other key roles should be clearly defined for coordinating activities across multiple service providers, as shown in Table 6.3.

Table 6.3 Sourcing roles and responsibilities

Role	Description	Key competencies
Director of service management	Senior executive who understands the business and defines, plans, purchases and manages all aspects of service delivery on behalf of business units	Authority and seniority to prioritise and define services for business units Large-scale service and operations management Financial and commercial management Governance, negotiation and Contract Management
Contract manager	Constructs, negotiates, monitors and manages the legal and commercial contract on behalf of the sourcing organization	Contract Management for large scale service provision Negotiation and conflict resolution Service definition and management Translation of business into contractual requirements
Product manager	Defines, plans, purchases and manages sourced elements of the service and performance on behalf of sourcing organization	Authority and seniority to prioritise and define sourcing needs for specific elements of the service
Process Owner	Interface with business users and functions to review, define and authorise current and future process models. Aim to identify and standardize best practices	Capability and process definition Process mapping Service monitoring Managing user forums e.g. Joint Application Development, Conference Room Pilot Best practice identification, capture and rollout
Business representatives	Primary service recipient on behalf of each business unit who define business requirements, monitor service, raise service requests and own budgets	Knowledge of specific business functions Requirements gathering, definition and prioritization Service monitoring Managing user forums

Strategy, tactics and operations

7

7 Strategy, tactics and operations

7.1 IMPLEMENTATION THROUGH THE LIFECYCLE

Strategic positions are converted into plans with goals and objectives for execution through the Service Lifecycle. The positions are driven by the need to serve specific customers and market spaces and influenced by strategic perspectives as a service provider (Figure 7.1). Plans are a means of achieving those positions. They include the Service Catalogue, Service Pipeline, Contract Portfolio, financial budgets, delivery schedules, and improvement programmes.

Plans ensure that each phase in the Service Lifecycle has the capabilities and resources necessary to reach strategic positions. The Service Lifecycle provides clarity and context for the development of the necessary capabilities and resources.

Plans translate the intent of strategy into action through Service Design, Service Transition, Service Operation and Service Improvement. Service Strategy provides input to each phase of the Service Lifecycle (Figure 7.2). Continual Service Improvement provides the feedback and learning mechanism by which the execution of strategy is controlled throughout the Lifecycle.

7.1.1 Top-down

For any given market space, service strategy defines the portfolio of services to be offered and the customers to be supported (Figure 7.3). This in turn determines the Contract Portfolio that needs to be supported with design, transition and operation capabilities. Lifecycle capabilities are defined in terms of the systems, processes, knowledge, skills and experience required at each phase to effectively support the Contract Portfolios. Interactions between service management capabilities are clearly defined and managed for an integrated and systematic approach to service management. Service design and operation capabilities determine the type of transition capabilities required. They determine the portfolio of service designs and the operating range of the service provider in terms of models and capacities.

Transition capabilities determine the costs and risks managed by a service provider. How quickly a service is transitioned from design to operations depends on the capabilities of the service transition phase. Transition capabilities reduce the costs and risks for customers and service providers throughout the lifecycle by maintaining visibility and control over all service management systems and processes. In this manner, transition capabilities not

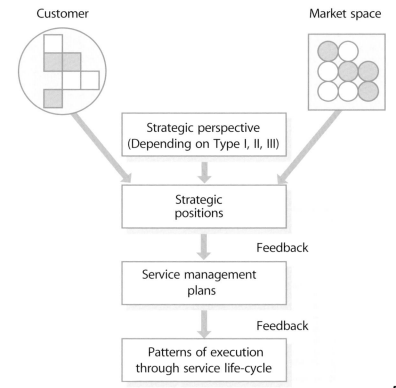

Figure 7.1 Strategic planning and control process [21]

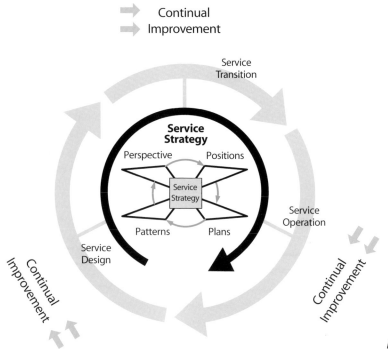

Figure 7.2 Strategy executed through the Service Lifecycle

only act as filters but also as amplifiers that increase the effectiveness of design and operation. They interact with service designs to provide new and improved service models. They interact with operation models and capacity to increase the operational effectiveness of plans and schedules. The net effect is the service levels delivered to customers in fulfilment of contracts.

Customers and service providers both face strategic risks from uncertainties. It is impossible to either control or predict all the factors in a business environment. The risks may translate into challenges or into opportunities depending on alignment between service management capabilities and the emergent needs of customers. Service Strategy requires Continual Service Improvement to drive feedback through the Lifecycle elements to ensure that challenges and opportunities are not mismanaged (Figure 7.4).

New strategic positions are adopted based on patterns that emerge from executing the Service Lifecycle. This bottom-up development of service strategy is combined

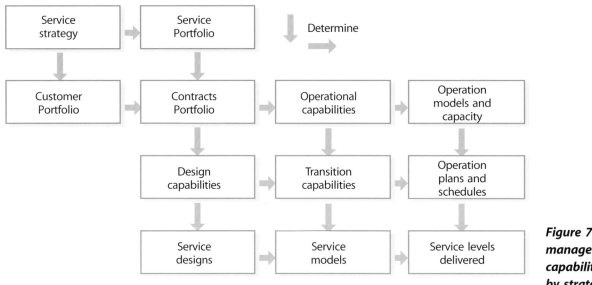

Figure 7.3 Service management capabilities driven by strategy

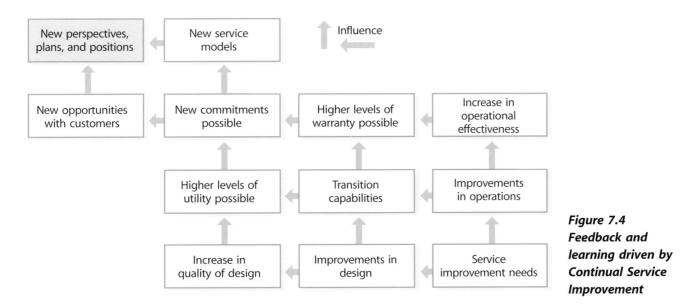

Figure 7.4 Feedback and learning driven by Continual Service Improvement

with the traditional top-down approach to form a closed-loop planning and control system for service strategies (Figure 7.5). Such feedback and learning is a critical success factor for service management to drive changes and innovation.

7.2 STRATEGY AND DESIGN

Service strategies are executed by delivering and supporting the Contract Portfolio in a given market space. Contracts specify the terms and conditions under which value is delivered to customers through services. From an operational point of view this translates into specific levels of utility and warranty for every service. Since every service is mapped to one or more market spaces, it follows that the design of a service is related to categories of customer

assets and the service models. These are the basic inputs for service design. For example, the design for managed storage services must have input into how customer assets such as business applications utilize the storage, how storage adds value to the applications, and what costs and risks the customer would like to avoid. The service model is managed services. Therefore the input to service design includes a service archetype in which the service provider takes responsibility for operating and maintaining the customer's storage systems at specified levels of availability, capacity, continuity and security. Customers provide input into the demand that needs to be supported and requirements for technical support, and indicate their willingness to pay for the services. These represent high-level inputs for service design.

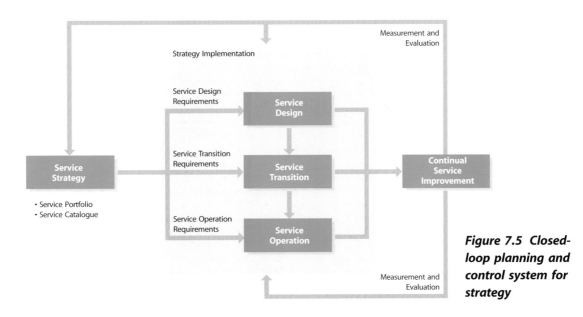

Figure 7.5 Closed-loop planning and control system for strategy

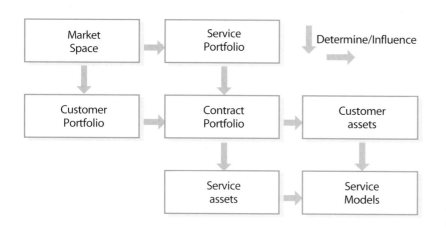

Figure 7.6 Service models are shaped by market spaces

7.2.1 Service models

Service models codify the service strategy for a market space. They are blueprints for service management processes and functions to communicate and collaborate on value creation. Service Models describe how service assets interact with customer assets and create value for a given portfolio of contracts (Figure 7.6). Interaction means demand connects with the capacity to serve. Service agreements specify the terms and conditions in which such interaction occurs with commitments and expectations on each side. The outcomes define the value to be created for the customer, which itself rests on the utility provided to customers and the warranty.

Service models codify the structure and dynamics of services. The structure and dynamics are influenced by factors of utility and warranty to be delivered to customers

(Figure 5.29). The structure and dynamics have consequences for Service Operations, which are evaluated by Service Transition (Figure 7.7).

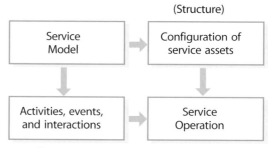
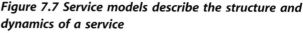

Figure 7.7 Service models describe the structure and dynamics of a service

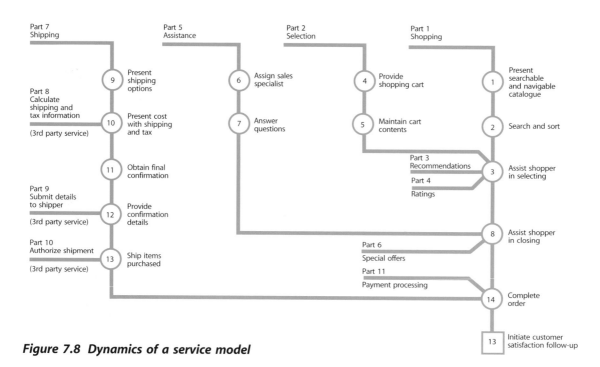

Figure 7.8 Dynamics of a service model

Table 7.1 The Kano Model[28] and service attributes

Type of attribute	Fulfilment and perceptions of utility (gain/loss)
Basic factors (B) (Must-have, non-linear)	Attributes of the service expected or taken for granted. Not fulfilling these will cause perceptions of utility loss. Fulfilling them results in utility gain but only until the neutral zone after which there is no gain.
Excitement factors (E) (Attractive utility, non-linear)	Attributes of the service that drive perceptions of utility gain but when not fulfilled do not cause perceptions of utility loss.
Performance factors (P) (Attractive utility, linear)	Attributes of the service that result in perceptions of utility gain when fulfilled and utility loss when not fulfilled in an almost linear one-dimensional pattern.
Indifferent attributes (I)	Cause neither gains nor losses in perceptions of utility regardless of whether they are fulfilled or not.
Reversed attributes (R)	Cause gains in perceptions of utility when not fulfilled and losses when fulfilled. Assumptions need to be reversed.
Questionable response (Q)	Responses are questionable possibly because questions were not clear or misinterpreted.

Structure is defined in terms of particular service assets needed and the patterns in which they are configured. Service models also describe the dynamics of value creation. Activities, flow of resources, coordination, and interactions describe the dynamics (Figure 7.8). This includes the cooperation and communication between service users and service agents. The dynamics of a service include patterns of business activity, demand patterns, exceptions and variations.

The methods and tools of systems engineering and workflow management are useful for developing the process maps, workflow diagrams, queuing models and activity patterns necessary for completeness of service models. Service Transition evaluates detailed service models to ensure they are fit for purpose and fit for use before entering Service Operation through the Service Catalogue. It is necessary for service models to be under change control because the utility and warranty of a service can have undesired variation if there are changes to the service assets or their configuration. The integrity of a service model depends on the integrity of the structure.

Service models are useful for effectiveness in Continual Service Improvement. Improvements can be made to the structure or the dynamics of a model. Service Transition evaluates the options or paths for improvements and recommends solutions that are cost-effective and low-risk. Service models continually evolve, based on external feedback received from customers and internal feedback from service management processes. CSI processes ensure the feedback to the strategy, design, transition and operation processes.

7.2.2 Design driven by outcomes

Attributes of a service are the characteristics that provide form and function to the service from a utilization perspective. The attributes are traced from business outcomes to be supported by the service. Determining which attributes to include is a design challenge. Certain attributes must be present for value creation to begin. Others add value on a sliding scale determined by how customers evaluate increments in utility and warranty. Service level agreements commonly provide for differentiated levels of service quality for different sets of users.

Some attributes are more important to customers than others. They have a direct impact on the performance of customer assets and therefore the realization of basic outcomes. Such attributes are must-have attributes.[28] Table 7.1 describes the type of attributes that influence the customer's perception of utility from a service.

Take the example of an online storage service with synchronized backup and restore capabilities. It must provide round-the-clock access, with high upload and download speeds. It must protect from corruption, unauthorized access and accidental disclosure. At the same time, it must be very accessible to the rightful owners. There is utility gain from having access to the storage service on a public network through a secure browser. The service is a substitute for a portable storage device, which needs careful handling and transport by the users to maintain access to the stored data. To an extent, security and accessibility are basic factors. Their provision does not result in utility gains for the customer. It takes utility to the level of no difference or the neutral zone

(Figure 7.9). Not providing them causes a dramatic drop in customer satisfaction.

Some users have need for a greater amount of storage than others. Within a certain range, they value an increasing amount of storage and are willing to pay a proportionally higher price. The size of storage is a performance factor with one-dimensional utility, along with which it is meaningful to offer options. Within the range, the relationship between utility and storage space is approximately linear. Outside this range, the customers have diminishing utility on additional storage or the lack of it. Another type of one-dimensional utility could be the number of 'sub-accounts' so that customers can assign different storage boxes for different purposes such as projects, media type, and personal information. More sub-accounts mean greater utility with diminishing utility after a particular number of sub-accounts.

Services can have excitement attributes, which customers do not expect but are happy to have, given a reasonable offer. The storage service may offer attributes such as scheduled backups and notification, administrator-style privileges, multiple sub-accounts, metering, access control, account administration and secure file transfer protocols. Some customers may view these as performance factors with one-dimensional utility. For others these are excitement factors. Their absence does not cause dissatisfaction. Their presence causes a dramatic increase in satisfaction at a reasonable price.

Excitement factors and performance factors are the basis for market segmentation and differentiated service levels. They are used to fulfil the needs of particular types of customers. Such attributes are necessary for any strategy involving the segmenting of customers into groups and serving them with an appropriate utility package. Basic factors are the cost of entry into the market space. Without basic factors the service provider cannot enter the market space. As time passes, excitement factors become commonly available, losing their ability to differentiate. Competition, changes in customer perceptions, and new innovations can cause excitement factors to drift towards becoming performance or basic factors.

Extensive dialogue is required with targeted customers or segments of market spaces to determine the attributes a service must have, should have, and could have in terms of must-have attractive utility. Questionnaires are used to elicit responses from customers from which further analysis is possible. The Kano Evaluation Table is a useful method (Table 7.2).

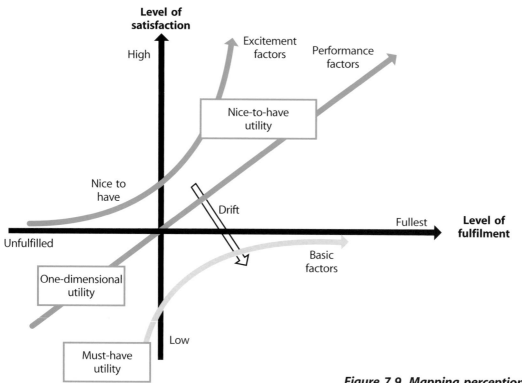

Figure 7.9 Mapping perceptions of utility [28]

Table 7.2 The Kano evaluation table[28]

Customers are asked …	Dysfunctional form (-)	How would you feel if the product *does not have* attribute X?				
Functional form (+)	Customers respond …	Like it	Expect it	Neutral	Accept it	Dislike it
How would you feel if the product *has* attribute X?	Like it	Q	E	E	E	P
	Expect it	R	I	I	I	B
	Neutral	R	I	I	I	B
	Accept it	R	I	I	I	B
	Dislike it	R	R	R	R	Q

B: Basic E: Excitement P: Performance I: Indifferent R: Reversed Q: Questionable

A well-designed service provides a combination of basic, performance and excitement attributes to deliver an appropriate level of utility for the customer. Different customers will place different weights or importance on the same combination of attributes. Furthermore, even if a particular type of customer values a particular combination, they may not find justification to pay for additional charges. The utility of a service can be under-engineered or over-engineered for a particular type of customer.

7.2.3 Design driven by constraints

Customer needs translate into attributes of a service, which in turn determine a set of design constraints. Design constraints are of various types. Their combined effect is to define a set of solutions that are feasible in terms of meeting customer needs (Figure 7.10). The shape and size of the solutions space changes with changes in any of the constraints still in effect. A constraint is no longer in effect when another constraint nullifies it. (Graphically the constraint is no longer one of the lines forming the solution space). Solutions at the corners of the space are preferred to solutions in the middle because they tend to push a constraint to its maximum limit.

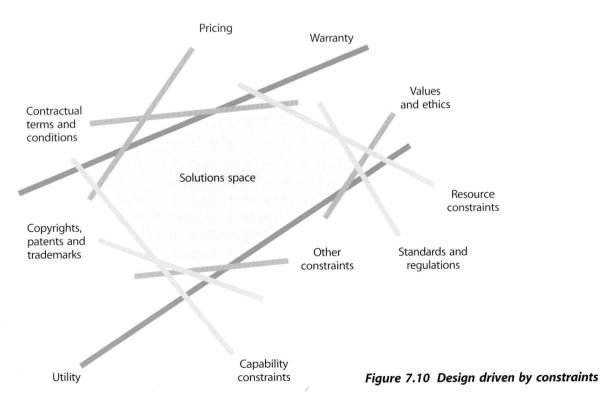

Figure 7.10 Design driven by constraints

There is no universal list of constraints for a given service. Developing the list of constraints and visualizing their combined interaction requires a team of specialists from business and technical practices to interact with customers, suppliers, partners and advisors. All five elements of the Service Lifecycle provide input for the constraints. The method is a means for Service Strategy to communicate challenges and opportunities to Service Design.

7.2.4 Pricing as a design constraint

Dissecting the customer's business model is necessary to design, develop, package and offer services that meet the business needs of customers. Service designs are better with pricing as a key design constraint. By analysing how customers create value for their own customers it is possible to correctly identify the most important attributes of the service. This leads to better design and packaging of services. What outcomes are customers aiming to achieve? What resources and constraints do they have? What is the value customers place on the achievement of those outcomes, productivity of those resources, and the removal of those constraints? Answers to those questions are the basis for weighing the individual attributes and pricing them within a service bundle.

Take, for example, an aircraft manufacturer that designs derivative aircraft as a service for subsequent lease to specific customer segments. By utilizing price as a design constraint, and applying insight gained from customers sharing their specific industry knowledge, needs, business and revenue models, the manufacturer can decompose the final product into characteristics that can then be analysed in two ways. The first analysis focuses on what combinations of characteristics can maximize customer revenue, margins and/or excitement or satisfaction. This includes the price the customer is able and willing to pay for various characteristics, given its market positioning and economic models. The second analysis focuses on what groupings of characteristics the provider can bundle to best fulfil the needs of the customer, that also represent the best opportunity for cost reductions related to provisioning those services.

A common illustration of bundling service components in a manner that generates service cost reductions for a provider, while maximizing positive service impact for the customer, can be found in a car maintenance example. For many cars, the price of replacing a timing belt is fairly high, and is composed primarily of labour. Because the time and activities required to gain access to the timing belt are the same as those required to gain access to the water pump, mechanics will offer to replace both parts

while servicing the car. By doing so, the customer can receive services for two components of great utility at a reduced rate, achieving greater piece of mind at a price substantially less than it would cost to have each component serviced separately. Conversely, while the provider sells only an incremental increase in the amount of labour, it can sell an additional piece of hardware which carries a superior margin, and increase the overall margin achieved on the service labour performed. In this example, both the provider and the customer achieve greater satisfaction from the transaction.

7.3 STRATEGY AND TRANSITION

Service Strategy is dependent on the dynamic capabilities of service providers, which allow effective responses to challenges and opportunities with customers and market spaces. Strategies often require changes to be implemented to achieve specific objectives while minimizing costs and risks. There are no cost-free and risk-free strategic plans or initiatives. There are always costs and risks with decisions such as introducing new services, entering new market spaces, and serving new customers.

In many cases, the costs are real and in other cases, they are notional. The inability to respond quickly to a business need may have opportunity costs for the service provider. They may also have real costs in terms of penalties or contract terminations. Service Transition represents one of the most important sets of service management capabilities with processes such as Change Management, Configuration Management and service deployment. The ability to drive changes rapidly in Service Portfolios and contracts is a critical success factor in certain market spaces and strategies. Therefore, Service Transition (ST) is an important capability in service management.

Service Transition systems and processes provide the decision analysis necessary to analyse, evaluate and approve strategic initiatives. They help determine the options or transition paths for changing the strategic position for a customer or market space (Figure 7.11). Service Transition evaluates the costs and risks for each path and takes into account the impact on existing contracts. Service Transition processes maintain visibility and control over service assets, configurations and current allocation of resources. To reduce risk of failures all strategic changes go through Service Transition.

Service Transition capabilities help determine good answers to the following types of questions:

■ What are the implications with each path in terms of costs, time and risks?

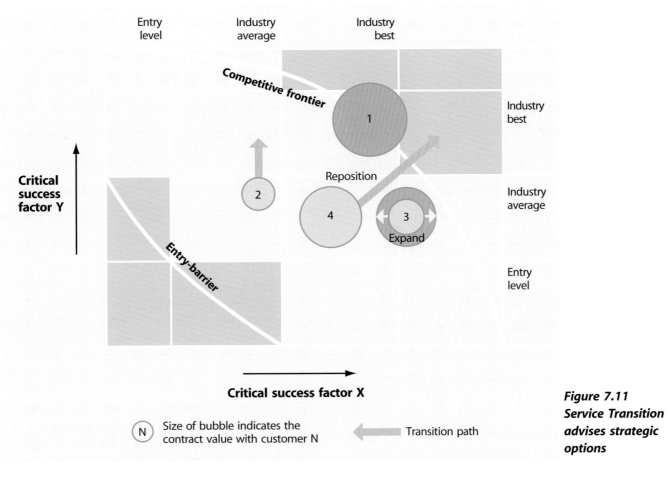

Figure 7.11
Service Transition
advises strategic
options

- In what scenarios is one path preferable to the other?
- What are the likelihoods of those scenarios?
- Can existing assets support a transition path?
- Are there contingency plans to contain the adverse impact changes?
- Can a particular change be implemented fast enough to support the strategy?

The following are examples of tactical and operations level initiatives evaluated by ST to implement strategy:

- Augment staff at call centres
- Analyse business activity patterns and redefine users
- Define Service Level Packages and revise SLA templates
- Develop knowledge assets specialized for the market space
- Add new service to the market space
- Replicate assets and configure for fault tolerance
- Offer complementary services
- Implement service-oriented architecture
- Re-engineer Incident Management process.

The planning and development of the ST functions and processes are dependent on the type of strategies pursued. The nature of the strategy, market spaces, services and customers will determine the type of transitions needed (Figure 7.12). ST requirements are filtered by the context of the Contract Portfolio.

The Contract Portfolio contains all the present and future commitments made to customers with respect to specific services. These commitments and any changes in them determine requirements for Service Design and Service Operations. Those in turn determine the Transition Requirements.

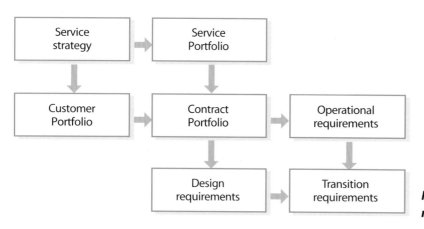

Figure 7.12 Service strategies generate requirements for Service Transition

7.4 STRATEGY AND OPERATION

Strategies are ultimately realized through Service Operation. Well-crafted strategies with great potential are pipe dreams without proper support from operations. Strategies must be mindful of operational capabilities and constraints. Operations, on the other hand, should clearly understand the outcomes necessary for a given strategy and provide adequate support with effectiveness and efficiency.

For example, some businesses have large-scale operations in several countries or regions with high levels of business activity driven by the needs of their own customers. The end-customers may be a cost-conscious but highly dependable source of revenue for the business. Many government agencies operate in similar business conditions though with different mandates. Such high-volume, low-margin, steady-stream business strategies depend on service providers being able to support them with adequate availability and capacity but at low unit costs.

7.4.1 Deployment patterns

Deploy service assets in patterns that are most effective in delivering value to customers. For example, multiple segments exist within internal and external markets. Each segment may have distinct requirements and common requirements with respect to other segments. Segments may exist within an organization such as the various user profiles and activity patterns discussed earlier in Section 5.5.3. Deployment of service assets should be in patterns that most effectively deliver the required utility and warranty in each segment across the Service Catalogue. Some segments may require dedicated capacity at one level even if they share lower levels of infrastructure with other segments (Figure 7.13). Customers are willing to pay a premium for the privilege, making it easier for such a deployment pattern to pass the requirements of Financial Management.

A template for deploying assets is defined by the need to provide high levels of warranty for services in terms of capacity and continuity. In such cases, rather than have dedicated resources, it is necessary to have shared service

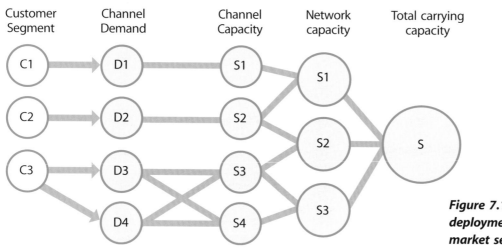

Figure 7.13 Example of a pattern for deployment of assets based on market segments

assets to provide multiple levels of redundancy (Figure 7.14). Such patterns are also useful for service providers to reduce the footprint of expensive infrastructure and to build economies of scale.

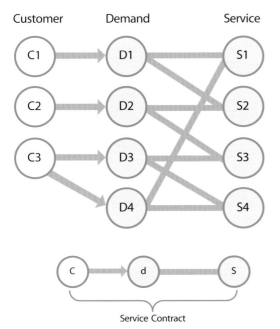

Figure 7.14 Example of a shared services pattern for capacity and continuity

Deployment patterns in Service Operation by themselves define operational strategies for customers. Apart from the deployment of service assets, such strategies may include a particular set of service designs, service level options (or limits), and charging policies that recover the costs of assets.

7.4.2 Hosting the Contract Portfolio

The need to host service contracts influences deployment patterns. Service contracts are the context within which the Service Portfolio realizes its potential for creating value for customers. Growth in the Contract Portfolio may require a system for allocating contracts to service units that can host them. Each contract has its own set of commitments made to the customer in terms of utility and warranty. Hosting decisions seek to distribute costs and risks in the Contract Portfolio across service units (Figure 7.15). For example, a follow-the-sun model involving a visualized Service Desk located in four strategically located service units may suit one contract. Other contracts may require localized Service Desks with on-site support.

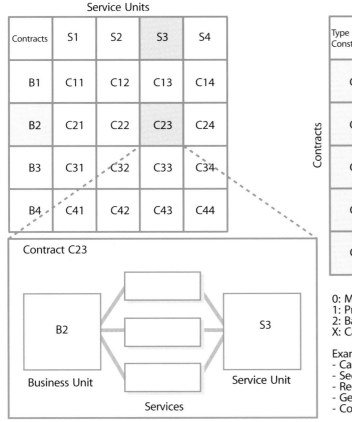

Type of Constraint	S1	S2	S3
C11	1	X	2
C12	N	1	0
C13	2	0	1
C14	1	1	2
C15	1	2	X

0: Mandatory host
1: Primary host
2: Back-up host
X: Cannot host

Examples of hosting constraints
- Carrying capacity
- Security requirements
- Regulatory compliance
- Geographic limitations
- Costing/pricing

Figure 7.15 Hosting of service contracts

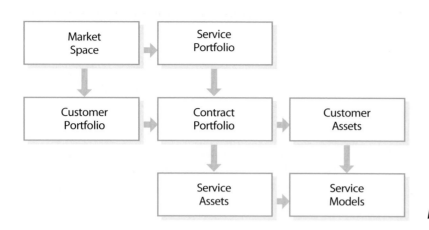

Figure 7.16 The Contract Portfolio

Hosting decisions involve close coordination between Service Strategy and Service Operation. The strategy for a market space has an influence on the contents of the Customer Portfolio and the Service Portfolio. This is because particular perspectives, positions, plans, and patterns (the Four Ps) open up or close the possibilities of what services are offered, on what contractual terms and conditions, and with what type of customers. The combination of Service Portfolios and Customer Portfolios generates the Contract Portfolio (Figure 7.16). In other words, every item in the Contract Portfolio is mapped to at least one item in the Service Portfolio and at least one item in the Customer Portfolio. The mappings are one-to-one, one-to-many and many-to-one.

Service Operation is responsible for delivering the Contract Portfolio. Service Transition enables items in the Customer Portfolio and Service Portfolio to enter the Contract Portfolio. Transition projects are of two types: services and customers. For each type of transition there are costs and risks to be evaluated by Service Transition. Items are added

to the Contract Portfolio only after the necessary service assets such as infrastructure, applications, knowledge assets and staff are made available.

7.4.3 Managing demand

Customer assets or the users of services are a source of variation in demand. Service demand is not only embedded with uncertainty – it also varies significantly based on the type of customer assets that generate demand and the patterns of business activity supported. It is therefore necessary to analyse patterns of business activity. Sources of demand with similar workload characteristics are identified and classified into distinct segments. Each segment is then expected to represent a certain type of demand distinguished by variables such as frequency, patterns, and volume of business activity. Service designs, models and assets are then specialized to serve a particular type of demand most effectively and efficiently.

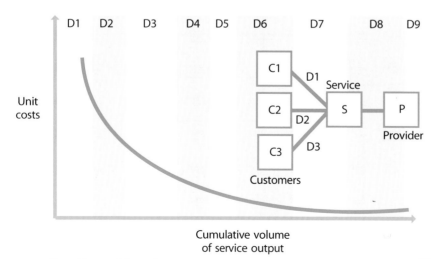

Dn = Demand from Customer n
Total Demand = D1 + D2 + D3 + ... + D9

Figure 7.17 Consolidation of demand across customers

The resulting focus leads to higher levels of customer satisfaction within each segment since service assets are now optimized to serve relatively homogeneous groups of users. Processes and systems are simplified, standardized and stabilized leading to cost-efficiencies, higher utilization levels for resources, and reduction in errors due to excessive complexity (Figure 7.17). The segmentation of demand does not mean that economies of scale are entirely lost. They are simply captured elsewhere through sharing of resources that are common across segments and service types. The same segment of users can present more than one type of demand simultaneously or under different conditions.

7.5 STRATEGY AND IMPROVEMENT

7.5.1 Quality perspectives

Industry experience shows that SLA metrics are necessary but not sufficient to measure the quality of service delivered to customers. The quality of services perceived by customers and their users rests on the utility and warranty delivered. In other words, the notions of service quality are embedded within the notions of service utility and warranty. Service quality takes into account the positive impact of the service (utility) and the certainty of impact (warranty). There are many definitions of quality that are summarized below into four broad perspectives:

- Level of excellence
- Value for money
- Conformance to specifications
- Meeting or exceeding expectations.

The dominant perspective will influence how services are measured and controlled particularly within the context of Service Level Management.

Each perspective has its own strengths and weaknesses with respect to measurement, general applicability, its usefulness to managers and relevance to customers. It is therefore a strategic decision for service providers to make, or a strategic imperative they support based on the customers they serve and distinctions they must make. One or more, if not all four, perspectives, are usually required to guide the measurement and control of service management processes (Figure 7.18).

Defining the meaning of service quality is one of the important decisions that senior leadership makes. Quality by itself is a basis of strategies in a market space and therefore the definition of quality influences strategic decisions and objectives. It influences the way services are designed and operated, and it influences internal performance measures, policies and incentives used by managers.

7.5.2 Warranty factors

7.5.2.1 Intangibility factor

There are differences and similarities in how goods and services are produced, and how their value is transferred to customers, verified and assured (Table 7.3). The activity and impact of a service can be visible or tangible in certain ways, as in the case of repaired equipment, shipped documents, printed reports, and physical records of completed transactions, installations and upgrades. Shipping of documents involves tangible changes in terms of location and possession. People are mobile with the use of wireless phones. However, the actual utility of services,

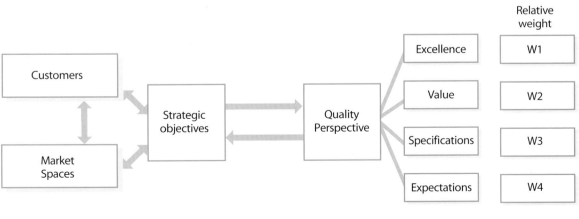

Figure 7.18 Quality perspectives and strategic imperatives influence each other

Table 7.3 Differences between goods and services

	Physical characteristics	Value transfer	Proof of transfer	Utility	Warranty
Goods	Always tangible	Embedded in objects and transferred to customers who subsequently extract it in use	Verifiable on arrival or exchange of goods in tangible form	Sometimes intangible	Assurance on utility over a fixed period under specific conditions for use; does not include normal wear and tear or misuse
Services	Sometimes tangible	Transferred on demand to customers at the time of service delivery	Not easily verified since it is embedded in the context of outcomes and conditions	Always intangible	Assurance on utility over the duration of the service contract under specific conditions for use

such as the right person having the document at the right time, the flexibility to conduct business from anywhere, and the productive state of equipment, is always intangible. A document shipped late, people moving about without a signal on their phone, and equipment repaired but not usable have no utility for the customer.

The intangibility factor makes the availability of a service almost a surrogate measure of service quality. It is more obvious than capacity, continuity and security. Users perceive the effects of capacity, continuity and security in terms of availability.

Services typically become unavailable because of failures in the underlying service assets such as applications, infrastructure, processes and people. Services are value-creating systems whose overall availability depends on a combination of factors such as reliability, maintainability, redundancy, capacity and structure. The following sections on reliability, maintainability, redundancy and accessibility refer to services simply as systems.

7.5.3 Reliability

7.5.3.1 Applications and infrastructure

Highly reliable systems function without disruptions or failures for longer periods on average. To fulfil the warranty aspect of value to customers, services must be adequately reliable. This is a critical input from Service Strategy to Service Design and Service Operation. The provision of highly reliable services can be the basis of strategic positioning. Some services need to be more reliable than others, depending on the business outcomes they support.

The reliability of a service depends on the reliability of underlying service assets and their configuration. The reliability of an asset depends on various factors such as the quality of its design, development, installation, obsolescence, maintenance, and security. Systems and components function properly within the parameters of their design. Operating conditions are an important factor in discussions on reliability. Scheduled and preventive maintenance activities that eliminate causes of potential and recurring failures are also an important factor.

The mean time between failures (MTBF) of a service asset is a measure of the reliability of that asset. To increase the reliability of service assets consider the following approaches:

- Use service assets with high MTBF
- Maintain redundant assets
- Operate the assets within design parameters
- Secure the assets.

It is possible to achieve higher reliability from using assets of superior quality that fail less often.

7.5.3.2 People and processes

All assets can fail to perform at the required level. Assets engineered and maintained for higher performance tend to have higher MTBF under the same operating conditions. This is more intuitive in the case of engineering artefacts such as hardware and software assets. It is harder to define or measure the reliability of people and process assets even where they clearly contribute to the failure of a service. The unavailability of a service staff member may cause the service to be unavailable. Procedural faults or unhandled exceptions in processes can lead to unavailability of services. The concept of MTBF applies to people and processes even if the actual metrics may be difficult or meaningless. The idea is the same. Higher MTBF means higher reliability.

This coupling between people and process assets helps improve the overall reliability of the system with improvements in one affecting the other. To reduce the stress on people assets the following motivation (M) and hygiene (H) tactics are useful:

- Ensure staff have adequate knowledge and experience (M)
- Train, educate, and supervise staff (M)
- Reward staff for performing correctly, consistently, and ethically (M)
- Develop a culture that promotes quality, efficiency, and ownership of output (M)
- Improve the work environment including workplace design, productivity tools, information design, and supporting knowledge systems (H)
- Automate tasks with monotony, complexity or low tolerance for variation (H)
- Allocate adequate resources to balance workload and to reduce stress (H)
- Design organization to improve specialization and coordination of work (H).

To reduce the stress on process assets the following tactics are useful:

- Put processes under the ownership and control of capable groups and individuals
- Ensure the processes are fed with necessary knowledge and information
- Reduce the in-process time to reduce average workload at any given moment

- Reduce the amount of rework to be fed back into processes
- Automate tasks where appropriate to reduce variation induced by people assets
- Secure the processes from unauthorized use, intrusion, and sabotage.

7.5.4 Maintainability

Services need to be recovered as quickly as possible when they become unavailable to users. Mean Time to Restore Service (MTRS) for a service, system or component is the time taken on average to restore its full functionality. This includes not only any physical repair or replacement, but also all the other factors that contribute towards full functionality. It is possible to estimate the MTRS of a service only when there is sufficient data available about the supporting configuration of service assets. MTRS is a measure that depends on several factors including the following:

- Configuration of service assets
- Mean Time to Repair (MTTR) of individual components
- Competency of support staff
- Resources available including information
- Policies, procedures, and guidelines
- Redundancy.

Adjustments to the above factors in isolation or combination increase maintainability. Analysis of the way MTRS responds to each factor is useful for improving the design of services and performance in operation. Reducing any of the following factors can reduce MTRS (Figure 7.19):

- Time to record
- Time to respond

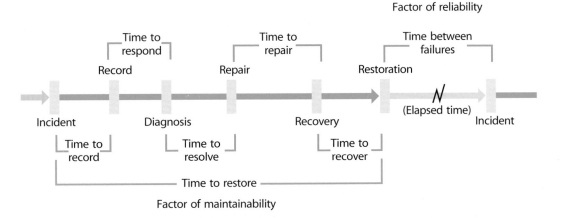

Figure 7.19 Improvement opportunities within incident lifecycle

- Time to resolve
- Time to physically repair or replace
- Time to recover.

It is normal to measure time strictly in real terms of seconds, minutes, hours and days. The periodicity of business activity varies between customers and contracts. In situations where the rate of loss to the business is linear with time, it is useful to measure the time factors indirectly in terms such as cycles, miles, transactions and trades to sense the true impact on business.

Toolbox Tip

SMethods and principles of Design of Experiments (DOE), Six Sigma and systems dynamics modelling methods are useful in developing decision models for maintainability and reliability.

7.5.5 Redundancy

Redundancy is a means of increasing reliability and maintainability of systems. High-availability systems typically have some level of redundancy built in. There are four primary types of redundancy useful selectively or in combination: active, passive, diverse and heterogeneous (Figure 7.20).

7.5.5.1 Active redundancy

Productive capacity of redundant assets is in service all the time. Their use distributes load across the system and promotes a higher MTBF at system and component level from reduced stress of each component. There is minimal disruption to the service from quick switchover to Hot Standby with replicated capabilities and resources. This type of redundancy is used to support critical services and business activity that cannot tolerate any level of disruption. This option is relatively expensive because it involves asset-specific or dedicated capacity.

7.5.5.2 Passive redundancy

Redundant assets enter service when failures occur. They are idle in the meantime or are otherwise used. There is switchover time involved. If this time is tolerable by the service or business activity, then passive redundancy could be a less expensive alternative to active redundancy. The capacity used is less asset-specific so its cost may be spread across several services or contracts.

7.5.5.3 Diverse redundancy

Diverse redundancy is from different types of service assets sharing certain capabilities but with distinctive strengths and weaknesses. This makes diverse redundancy

resistant to a single cause of failure. It is harder to implement because of the integration element between diverse types of assets. This type of redundancy is used when there is high uncertainty about the causes of failure.

7.5.5.4 Homogeneous redundancy

Homogeneous redundancy is from extra capacity of the same type of service assets. It is useful when there is high certainty about the causes of failure, and sufficient capacity is necessary to support demand. It is simpler to implement and maintain.

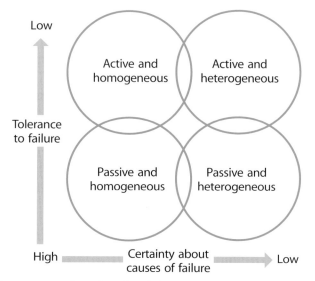

Figure 7.20 Choosing the right type of redundancy

7.5.6 Time between failures and accessibility

Reliability and maintainability are factors of service availability defined in terms of faults and failures of one or more of the underlying service assets. However, what matters to users is whether they can utilize the service or not. MTBF and MTRS mean little to them unless service levels are degraded or disrupted. The availability of services can be low even when service assets have high MTBF and low MTRS. In the time between failures, users expect the service to be easily accessible for utilization without inconvenience and undue effort on their part. Accessibility of a service is illustrated by the following examples.

An airline decides to improve customer satisfaction by increasing the number of ways for customers to purchase tickets and prepare for travel. It offers an online channel for passengers to check flight status, select seats, check in and print boarding passes before arriving at the airport. It also installs a network of self-service terminals that allow passengers with only carry-on baggage to proceed to the gates without having to wait in line at the counters. The net effect is that of virtually extending the 'surface area' of the airport check-in counter to locations convenient to the passenger, such as homes, offices and hotel rooms. The airline staff and other passengers at the airport benefit from reduced congestion. Passengers self-select between airport counters, self-service kiosks and the website channels, based on personal preference. They also respond to incentives offered by the airline to control the arrival of demand at particular locations. Similarly, a retail bank decides to make frequently requested and simple transactions available on its website and wireless devices such as telephones and personal digital assistants (PDAs).

Both businesses have effectively increased the probability that their services will be easily available for use by their customers. The improvements are not through the MTBF and MTRS factors. The primary factor has accessibility through a wider area of contact between customers and service assets through well-defined interfaces (Figure 7.21). Increasing the 'surface area' of contact of the service delivery system directly results in increased service availability from the users' perspective.

The following approaches increase the accessibility of services (Figure 7.22):

- Diversity of channels – provide multiple types of access channels so that demand goes through different channels and is safe from a single cause of failure. This is active diverse redundancy, which also provides utility to customers through preferred choices.

- Density of network – add additional service access points, nodes, or terminals of the same type to increase the capacity of the network with density of coverage. This is active homogeneous redundancy, which does not reduce vulnerability to a single cause of failure but reduces the complexity and provides economy of scale.

- Loose coupling – design interfaces based on public infrastructure, open source technologies and ubiquitous access points such as mobile phones and browsers so that the marginal cost of adding a user is low. It enables users to access the service from a wider range of locations and situations and also reduces the overall cost of maintaining a service. Advances in information security make this possible.

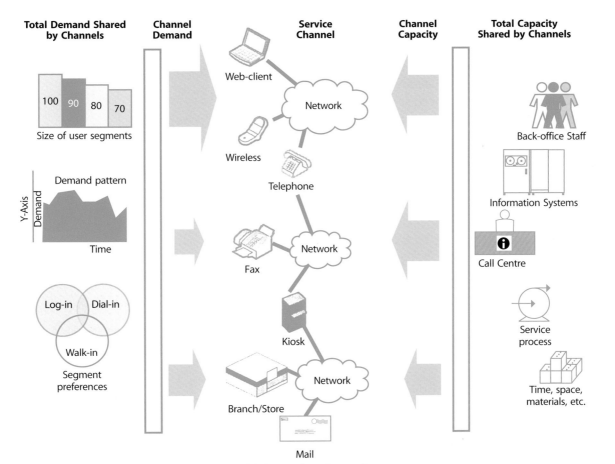

Figure 7.21 Increasing accessibility through multiple service channels

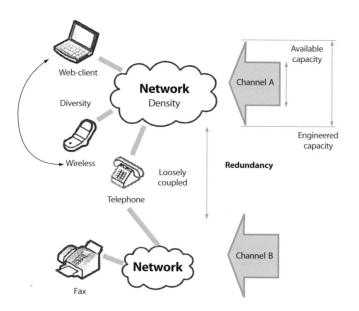

Figure 7.22 Channel capacity used for redundancy

7.5.7 Interactions between factors of availability

By balancing availability factors, the same capacity may achieve higher throughput leading to improvements in the overall operational effectiveness of the service operation. Controlling the flow of demand patterns can reduce the overall cost of service provision. Pricing and discounts can influence demand patterns. Customers can self-select as business needs justify. Self-service options are generally available at lower charges than staffed options with more expensive resources. In many countries, maintaining idle capacity of staff costs more than providing the equivalent capacity via self-service channels

such as websites, kiosks, interactive-voice response units (IVR) and new forms of service robots.

Multiple channels of service increase the level of redundancy, increase the area of contact and distribute the workload across the system. Customers value the convenience provided by a choice of multiple channels. When any one channel suffers outages or degradation in performance, it is possible to maintain the quality of service.

Underlying risks and unintended outcomes driven by feedback loops may influence the Capacity Management approach pursued. Socio-technical systems are complex with many interactions and trade-offs to be considered. The additional service channels increase not only the area of contact with customers but also the exposure to operational risks. Maintaining service levels requires additional continuity and security measures. The opening of new service channels may attract new usage patterns that need support. It is important to examine the interactions between the various factors of service availability (Figure 7.23).

Reinforcing and balancing effects are set up according to the feedback principle between factors of availability. The control levers of access, reliability and maintainability, applied in combination, provide the desired level of service availability. Considerations of capacity, cost and risks constrain each type of advantage.

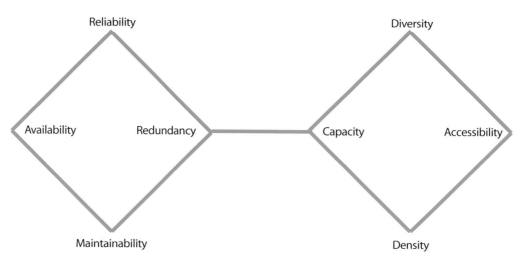

Figure 7.23 Interactions between factors of service availability

Technology and strategy

8 Technology and strategy

Herbert A. Simon of Carnegie Mellon University won the 1978 Nobel Prize in economics for his work on decision-making processes within economic organizations. According to Simon's concept of bounded rationality there are limits to the decision-making capabilities of human agents in formulating and solving complex problems and in processing information. Even the most dedicated, motivated and talented groups and individuals have limited capacity for dealing with the inherent complexity, uncertainty and conflicts or trade-offs in most socio-technical systems.

Services are socio-technical systems with service assets as the operating elements. People and processes act as concentrators of other assets in social and technical subsystems respectively (Figure 8.1). The performance of one sub-system affects the performance of the other in positive and negative ways.

The interactions between the two subsystems are in the form of dependencies (passive) and influences (active) critical to the performance of service management as a value-creating system. The following are just a few examples of how each of these interactions matter.

■ Improvements in design and engineering of activities, tasks and interfaces can compensate for limitations of people.

■ Improvements in knowledge, skills, attitudes and experience can partly compensate for poorly designed or inadequate processes, applications and infrastructure.

■ Automation of routine processes can reduce variation, allow quick adjustments to process capacity, and relieve stress on service staff during peak demand and off-hours. In some countries, automation can reduce the cost of operations attributable to expensive human resources.

■ Productivity tools can make efficient use of human resources. Communications and collaboration tools can increase the effectiveness of knowledge sharing and problem solving.

■ Analytical modelling, simulation and visualization tools are useful to analyse the impact of strategies, tactics and operations. They are useful to construct hypotheses, evaluate options and plan scenarios.

The effectiveness of Service Strategy relies on a loosely coupled but balanced and strong relationship between the social and technical subsystems. It is essential to identify and control these dependencies and influences. Reviews in Service Design, Service Transition, Service Operation and Continual Service Improvement should include analysis of possible dysfunction or lack of synchronization between the two subsystems.

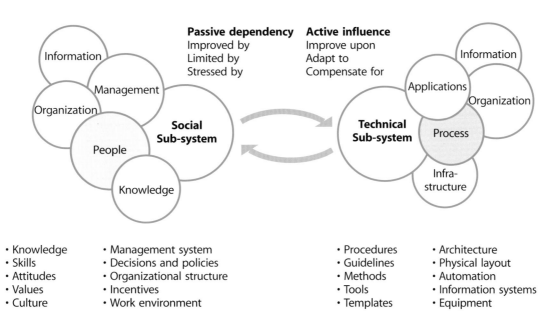

Figure 8.1 Services as socio-technical systems with people and processes as pivots

The design of socio-technical systems is an important consideration in service management. It is important to recognize that services are much more than a series of activities that produce intangible value. They are systems with complex interactions between various factors of production or service assets. The methods and principles of operations research, systems dynamics and statistical process control are very useful within the context of improving the reliability of services.

8.1 SERVICE AUTOMATION

Automation can have particularly significant impact on the performance of service assets such as management, organization, people, process, knowledge and information. Applications by themselves are a means of automation but their performance can also be improved where they need to be shared between people and process assets. Advances in artificial intelligence, machine learning and rich-media technologies have increased the capabilities of software-based service agents to handle a variety of tasks and interactions.

Automation is considered to improve the utility and warranty of services. It may offer advantages in many areas of opportunity, including the following:

- The capacity of automated resources can be more easily adjusted in response to variations in demand volumes.
- Automated resources can handle capacity with fewer restrictions on time of access; they can therefore be used to serve demand across time zones and during after hours.
- Automated systems present a good basis for measuring and improving service processes by holding constant the factor of human resources. Conversely, they can be used to measure the differential impact on service quality and costs due to varying levels of knowledge, skills and experience of human resources.
- Many optimization problems such as scheduling, routing and allocation of resources require computing power that is beyond the capacity of human agents.
- Automation is a means for capturing the knowledge required for a service process. Codified knowledge is relatively easy to distribute throughout the organization in a consistent and secure manner. It reduces the depreciation of knowledge when employees move within the organization or permanently leave.

When judiciously applied, the automation of service processes helps improve the quality of service, reduce costs and reduce risks by reducing complexity and uncertainty, and by *efficiently* resolving trade-offs. (This is the concept of Pareto efficiency, where the solution or bargain is efficient when one side of the trade-off cannot be better off without making the other side worse off.)

The following are some of the areas where service management can benefit from automation:

- Design and modelling
- Service catalogue
- Pattern recognition and analysis
- Classification, prioritization and routing
- Detection and monitoring
- Optimization.

Demand for services can be captured from simple interactions customers have with items in an automated Service Catalogue. There is a need to hide the complexity in the relationships between customer outcomes and the service assets that produce them, and present only the information the customers need to specify the utility and warranty needed with respect to any particular outcome. However, customers need choice and flexibility in presenting demand.

It is possible to handle routine service requests with some level of automation. Such requests should be identified, classified and routed to automated units or self-service options. This requires the study of business activity patterns that exist with each customer.

The variation in the performance of individuals with time, workload, motivation and nature of the task at hand can be a disadvantage in many situations. The variation in the knowledge, skills and experience of individuals can lead to variation in the performance of processes. Variations in processing times across service transactions, jobs or cycles can result in degradation of service levels, usually in the form of delays and congestion (Figure 8.2).

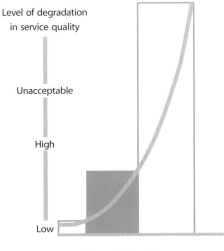

Figure 8.2 Degrading effect of variation in service processes

8.1.1 Preparing for automation

Applying automation indiscriminately can create more problems or exacerbate existing ones. The following guidelines should be applied:

Simplify the service processes before automating them. By itself, simplification of processes can reduce variations in performance because there are fewer tasks and interactions for variations to enter. Simplification should not adversely affect the outcome of the process. Removal of necessary information, tasks, or interactions makes the processes simpler but less useful. There are limits to simplification. Begin the analysis for automation at this limit.

Clarify the flow of activities, allocation of tasks, need for information, and interactions. All service agents and users should be clear about what they need to do so that the required inputs for a service transaction are available and complete. Automation itself makes the clarification easier through messaging, interactive terminals and websites. So automate, clarify, test, modify and then automate again.

In self-service situations, reduce the surface area of the contact users have with the underlying systems and processes. Needless interactions with the internals of the system can introduce avoidable variation because of mental overload and slower learning curves. Apply the principles of encapsulation and modularity to simplify the interfaces so that users see the attributes needed to present demand and extract utility.

Do not be in a hurry to automate tasks and interactions that are neither simple nor routine in terms of inputs, resources and outcomes. Recurring patterns are more suited for automation than less consistent and infrequent activities.

8.1.2 Service analytics and instrumentation

Information is necessary but not sufficient for answering questions such as why certain data is the way it is and how it is likely to change in the future. Information is static. It only becomes knowledge when placed in the context of patterns and their implications. Those patterns give a high level of predictability and reliability about how the data will change over time. By understanding patterns of information we can answer 'How?' questions such as:

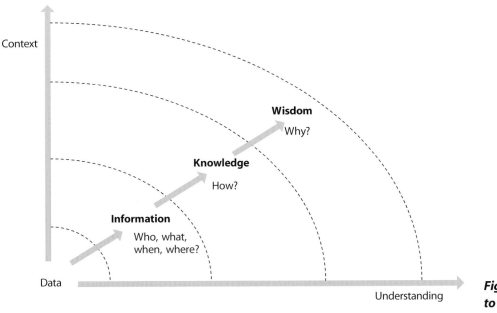

Figure 8.3 The flow from data to wisdom

Table 8.1 Instrumentation techniques

Technique	Action
Asynchronous capture	Passive listeners scan for alerts
External source	Compile data from external sources, such as Service Desk tickets, suppliers or systems (e.g. ERP, CRM)
Manual generation	Manually create or alter an event
Polling	Monitoring systems actively interrogate functional elements
Synthetic transactions	Simulate the end-user experience through known transactions

- How does this incident affect the service?
- How is the business impacted?
- How do we respond?

This is Service Analytics.

To understand things literally means to put them into a context. Service Analytics involves both analysis, to produce knowledge, and synthesis, to provide understanding. This is called the DIKW hierarchy (Figure 8.3).

While data does not answer any questions, it is a vital resource. Most organizations consider this capability in the form of instrumentation. The term instrumentation describes the technologies and techniques for measuring the behaviours of infrastructure elements. Instrumentation reports actual or potential problems and provides feedback after adjustments. Most organizations already have an installed base of instrumentation monitoring infrastructure elements similar to those in Table 8.1.

While data from element instrumentation is absolutely vital, it is insufficient for monitoring services. A service's behaviour derives from the aggregate behaviour of its supporting elements. While instrumentation can collect large amounts of raw data, greater context is needed to determine the actual relevance of any data. Information is the understanding of the relationships between pieces of data. Information answers four questions: Who, What, When and Where? This can be thought of as Event, Fault and Performance Management. The Event Management function refines instrumentation data into those that require further attention. While the line between instrumentation and Event Management can vary, the goal remains the same: create usable and actionable information. Table 8.2 describes common Event Management techniques.

A fault is an abnormal condition that requires action to repair, while an error is a single event. A fault is usually indicated by excessive errors. A fault can result from a threshold violation or a state change. Performance, on the other hand, is a measure of how well something is working. The function of the operations group begins with fault management. But as this function matures from reactive to proactive, the challenge becomes performance management. Fault management systems usually display topology maps with coloured indicators. Typically they have difficulties in dealing with complex objects that span multiple object types and geographies. Further context is needed to make this information useful for services. Begin by transitioning from information to knowledge.

Service Analytics is useful to model existing infrastructure components and support services to the higher-level business services. This model is built on dependencies

Table 8.2 Event Management techniques

Technique	Action
Compression	Consolidate multiple identical alarms into a single alarm
Correlation	See if multiple alert sources occurring during a short period of time have any relationship
Filtering	Apply rules to a single alert source over some period of time
Intelligent monitoring	Apply adaptive instrumentation
Roll-up	Compress alerts through the use of hierarchical collection structures
Verification	Actively confirm an actual incident

rather than topology – causality rather than correlation. Infrastructure events are then tied to corresponding business processes. The component-to-system-to-process linkage – also known as the Service Model – allows us to clearly identify the business impact of an event. Instead of responding to discrete events, managers can characterize the behaviour of a service. This behaviour is then compared to a baseline of the normal behaviour for that time of day or business cycle.

With Service Analytics, not only can an operations group do a better job of identifying and correcting problems from the user's standpoint, it can also predict the impact of changes to the environment. This same model can be turned around to show business demand for IT Services. This is a high leverage point when building a dynamic provisioning or on-demand environment.

This is as far along the DIKW hierarchy as modern technologies allow. It is well understood that no computer-based technology can provide wisdom. It requires people to provide evaluated understanding, to answer and appreciate the 'Why?' questions. Moreover, the application of intelligence and experience is more likely to be found in the organizational processes that define and deliver service management than in applied technologies. Section 9.4 outlines some of the challenges in measurement that can be addressed by Service Analytics.

8.2 SERVICE INTERFACES

8.2.1 Characteristics of good service interfaces

The design of service interfaces is critical to service management. Highly usable service interfaces are

necessary for service orientation. The principles of agency, specialization, coordination, encapsulation and loose coupling are possible because of effective interfaces between service assets and customer assets. Service interfaces are typically present at the point of utilization or service access points (Figure 8.4).

Service access points are associated with one or more channels of service. User interfaces include those provided for the customer's employees and other agents, as well as process-to-process interfaces. The Service interfaces should meet the basic requirements of warranty:

- They should be easily located or ubiquitous enough, or simply embedded in the immediate environment or business context, as in the case of interfaces to software applications.
- They should be available in forms or media that allow choice and flexibility for users. For example, there should be choice between staffed locations and automated self-service options, and choice between a browser and a mobile phone as access points.
- They should be available with enough capacity to avoid queuing or backlog when supporting concurrent use by many users. The presence of other users should not be noticeable (non-rival use).
- They should accommodate users with varying levels of skills, competencies, backgrounds and disabilities.
- The principle of ubiquity should be traded off with the need to keep interfaces low-profile and low-overhead to avoid undue stress on the customer's use context or the business environment.
- They should be simple and reliable having only the functions required for users to tap the utility of the service (following the principle of Ockham's Razor).

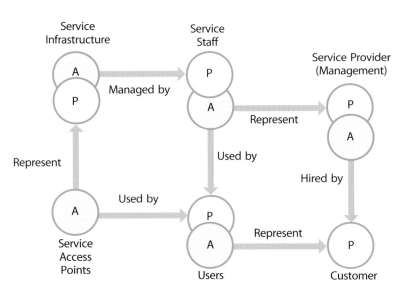

Figure 8.4 The critical role of service interfaces

■ Service interfaces should be self-reliant, requiring little or no intervention from service agents other than the dialogue necessary to carry out the service transaction.

8.2.2 Types of service technology encounters

Advances in communication technologies are having a profound effect on the manner in which service providers interact with customers. Airport kiosks, for example, have changed the interaction between airlines and their customers. There are four modes in which technology interacts with a service provider's customers (Figure 8.5).

■ Mode A: technology-free – technology is not involved in the service encounter. Consulting services, for example, may be Mode A.

■ Mode B: technology-assisted – a service encounter where only the service provider has access to the technology. For example, an airline representative who uses a terminal to check in passengers is Mode B.

■ Mode C: technology-facilitated – a service encounter where both the service provider and the customer have access to the same technology. For example, a planner in consultation with a customer can refer to 'what if' scenarios on a personal computer to illustrate capacity and availability modelling profiles.

■ Mode D: technology-mediated – a service encounter where the service provider and the customer are not in physical proximity. Communication may be through a phone. For example, a customer who receives technical support services from a Service Desk is Mode D.

■ Mode E: technology-generated – a service encounter where the service provider is represented entirely by technology, commonly known as self-service. For example, bank ATMs, online banking and distance learning are Mode E.

Encounters should be designed while considering customer assets.

■ Are customer employees technical or non-technical?

■ What are the implications of the technology encounter to the customer?

■ What are the customer expectations and perceptions?

For example, Mode E may be less effective than Mode B or C in cases where the encounter is complex or ambiguous. When the encounter is routine and explicit, as in password resets, Mode E may be preferred. Other modes may have secondary considerations. Mode D, for example, may have language or time-zone implications.

8.2.3 Self-service channels

Automation is useful to supplement the capacity of services. Self-service channels are increasingly popular among users now accustomed to human–computer interactions, devices and appliances. The ubiquitous channel of service delivery is the internet with browsers

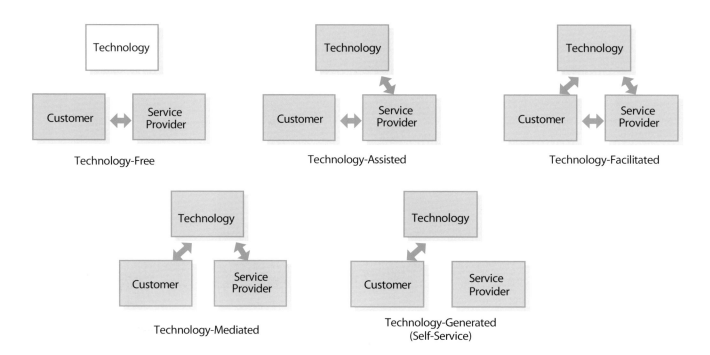

Figure 8.5 Types of service technology encounters [35]

acting as service access points that are widely distributed, standardized and highly familiar through constant use. Advances in artificial intelligence and speech recognition have improved the capabilities of software-based service agents in conducting dialogue with customers. The richness of the dialogue and the complexity of the interaction continue to increase.

The capacity of self-service channels has very low marginal cost, is highly scalable, does not suffer from fatigue, offers highly consistent performance, and is offered on a 24/7 basis at a relatively low cost. Additionally, users perceive the following disadvantages with human-to-human interactions with respect to incidents and problems:

- The emotional burden that the user is asked to carry in complaining about the service
- Variability in the experience, competence and emotional state of human agents
- Limited capacity of human resources, which causes uncertainty in wait times
- The need to schedule certain interactions with staff
- The fees associated with certain human resources.

Self-service channels are effective when appropriate knowledge and service logic is embedded into the self-service terminal. Service Design should ensure that Use Case analysis is performed to ensure usability, efficiency and ease in interactions through the automated interface.

Another example would be the use of the productive capacity of customers through self-service channels. Advances in human-computer interaction and the richness of interaction technologies, such as touch-screens, scanners and signature capture devices, allow for certain service activities to be completed without the presence or intervention of service staff.[36] This is a very intelligent way to adjust capacity that is highly sensitive to the presence of demand. Each customer brings one additional unit of productive capacity, instantly added and removed from the system without inventory-carrying costs to the service provider.

It is necessary to evaluate the level of control users are expected to assume with self-service options. The level of control should be commensurate with the proficiency and experience level of the users.[12] In almost every population of users there are differences in levels of experience, skills, aptitudes and work environments that determine preferences for methods and modes of interaction. The attributes and functions of service interfaces should take these differences into account. There will be trade-offs as different segments of users expect to be served according to their preferences. Some prefer step-by-step guidance

while others prefer efficiency and flexibility. Advances in artificial intelligences and machine learning are creating a new level of sophistication for service interfaces, which are context-aware, forgiving of new users, and capable of dialogue embedded with inquiry. The principle of forgiveness requires that the design of a service helps users avoid errors. When the errors do occur, the design should minimize negative consequences.

8.2.4 Technology-mediated service recovery

According to the peak-end rule, whereby the service providers recover well from service incidents, customers may actually retain a more positive perception of service quality than they had before the incident. This behaviour provides justification for investment in superior service support systems, processes and staff. While the strategic intent may be to reduce the occurrence of service incidents, the tactical goal would be to recover well from service incidents that are not avoided or foreseen.

Under certain conditions, the use of automation allows for quicker service recovery through fast resolution of service incidents. Users often expect nothing more than quick resolution of their problems without tedious policies and procedures. This provides a business case for simplifying, standardizing and automating certain service activities or interactions. However, when poorly designed or implemented, automated or self-service options can be especially aggravating for a user who may have suffered from a service incident. The challenge is to pick the right type of interface for a particular interaction.

Simple and routine incidents should be recovered using automation when all other factors are equal. Software-agents with diagnostic capabilities can interact with users to resolve basic technical problems. Online knowledge bases with search and navigation capabilities are useful examples of such recovery.

The approach is necessary knowledge from service management processes into automated solutions such as online technical support, self-service terminals, IVR units and software applications. Users are then presented with the self-service option as the first line of support to solve the most routine of problems. It also helps to raise the level of technical knowledge of users through well-designed documentation and self-help kits. Over time, this reduces the number of incidents that have to be handled by human resources (see example in Figure 8.4).

Example of leveraging intangible assets

The product installation and maintenance system of a major internet and telecom solutions provider generated £0.75 billion in savings (1996-98). The company made an extensive amount of technical knowledge about its solutions freely available online to its customers. Large amounts of workload were diverted away from its technical support staff and engineers, who could focus on tougher problems needing escalation. Most of the customers were themselves technical staff willing to attempt to fix problems on their own to the extent possible. This online knowledge base could be concurrently used by a large number of customers without degradation of quality or inordinate waiting times.

Baruch Lev[37]

The idea of making it convenient, quick and courteous for users to report service incidents and receive compensation is an important principle that should shape policies and guidelines. Good service culture requires it to be easy and fair for customers to file a complaint and have problems resolved, without undue burden on their time, effort, or emotion, all of which are forms of indirect costs and psychological costs of being a customer.[38] The need for that becomes particularly important where the customer or users will not receive any financial compensation. At this level of maturity, the service provider has institutionalized the true meaning of providing warranty to the customer. Preventing simple failures from turning into negative feelings will help maintain higher levels of customer satisfaction. Such service providers also demonstrate to their customers certain ethics that contribute to long-term success in the relationship.

8.3 TOOLS FOR SERVICE STRATEGY

8.3.1 Simulation

IT organizations often exhibit the counterintuitive behaviour resulting from many agents interacting over time. Long-term behaviour can be surprisingly different from short-term behaviour. System Dynamics is a methodology for understanding and managing the complex problems of IT organizations. It offers a means to capture and model the feedback processes, stocks and flows, time delays and other sources of complexity associated with IT organizations. It is a tool for evaluating the consequences of new policies and structures before putting them into action.

Just as an airline uses flight simulators to help pilots learn, System Dynamics offers simulation methods and tools available to help senior managers understand their organizations. These management flight simulators, based on mathematical models and computer simulation, can deliver useful insights for decision makers faced with enormous complexity and policy resistance.

The application of System Dynamics in the service and process domains has yielded remarkable insight for IT organizations. Some examples follow.

The Capability Trap – By pressuring staff to work harder, an organization unwittingly triggers a scenario where ever-increasing levels of effort are required to maintain the same level of performance.[39]

The Tool Trap – Although technology tools offer very useful help to an organization, they often require the development of knowledge and experience. When an organization adopts new tools, it triggers lower productivity in the short term. The increase in workload from training, learning and practice activities may unwittingly push a resource-constrained organization over its tipping point.[40]

The Firefighter Trap – When an organization rewards managers for excellence in firefighting, they may unwittingly create a dynamic harming the long-term performance of the organization. The long-term performance is instead improved by not rewarding excellence in firefighting.[40]

8.3.2 Analytical models

Analytical models are very useful where the complexity is manageable, and there is no policy resistance or interacting feedback loops. They are effective when objectives are clear, the options are well defined and the critical uncertainties are measurable. They are easy to develop when there is a fair amount of clarity on a problem or situation, the cause and effect relationships are clear and persistent, and patterns are recognizable patterns (Figures 3.6, 4.8, 4.9, 4.13, 8.2, 9.9). They also need enough historical information for assumptions on certain variables, such as costs, processing times and the load factors of resources.

Good examples of the use of analytical models are Service Desk and call centre staffing, which can be visualized as a system of queues. It is possible to gather data on the rate of arrival of requests (or incidents), how long it takes to process them on average, and how many requests are waiting to be handled. This level of knowledge is sufficient to build simple analytical models. Figure 8.6 shows an

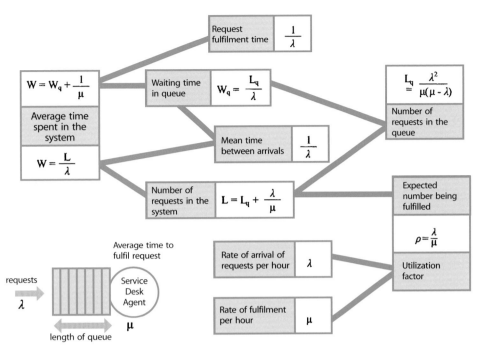

Figure 8.6 Example of simple analytical model for the Service Desk

example for a single-stage, single-agent queue at a Service Desk, with certain assumptions about the arrival pattern of requests and the processing time.

Service Desk modelling can become quite complex with the addition of numbers of service channels, multi-stage processes, dependencies and delays. However, it is useful to start with basic models and progressively elaborate them to reflect closely the reality of a problem or situation.

The following are commonly used sets of tools useful for decision making in Service Strategy:

- Decision trees, payoff matrices, analytic hierarchy process, etc.
- Linear programming (Figure 8.7) and integer programming, goal programming, etc.
- Queuing and network flow models (Figure 8.8)
- Clustering, forecasting, time-series analysis, etc.
- Analysis of variance, design of experiments, etc.

These methods can be applied to solve a variety of problems such as:

- Allocation of resources between services and contracts
- Analysis of demand patterns and segmentation of users
- Compression, correlation and filtering (Table 8.2)
- Scheduling of jobs, tasks and staff
- Location and layout of facilities and infrastructure elements

- Capital budgeting, pricing and purchase decisions
- Portfolio optimization
- Contingency planning and redundancy (coverage problems).

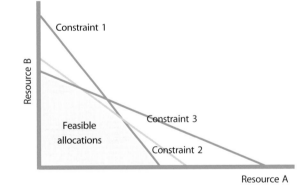

Figure 8.7 Simple LP model

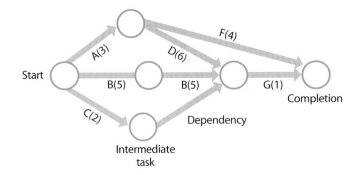

Figure 8.8 Simple network model

There is depth and diversity in analytical models, some of which have been in use for decades and have been instrumental to the maturity of disciplines such as operations management, project management and financial analysis. Service sectors such as telecommunications, transportation, logistics and financial services have achieved high levels of performance from the application of systems and industrial engineering concepts, methodologies and quality control processes to service functions and processes.[41]

There is a range of automation tools available for analytical modelling. The simplest tool available is a computer spreadsheet such as Microsoft Excel with its built-in solver function. Models with a fair amount of sophistication can be built using spreadsheets. More sophisticated models can be constructed using tools, special purpose optimization programming languages (OPL) and optimization engines. Several commercial solutions for automation in service management include functions and modules for analytical modelling and visualization.

Service Strategy and other functions and processes in the Service Lifecycle can benefit similarly from such knowledge to improve performance in the presence of technical, financial and time constraints. Six Sigma™, PMBOK® and PRINCE2® offer well-tested sets of methods based on analytical models. These should be evaluated and adopted within the context of Service Strategy and service management.

Challenges, critical
success factors and risks

9

9 Challenges, critical success factors and risks

9.1 COMPLEXITY

9.1.1 IT organizations are complex systems

A complex system is characterized by organized complexity, as opposed to disorganized complexity (random systems) or organized simplicity (simple systems). In an organizational setting, for example, the operations group is a system made up of people, process and technology. However, the components of the operations group must interact with each other to perform. Hence they are interdependent. The operations group in turn must interact with other components of the IT organization.

This complexity explains why some service organizations resist change. Complex systems behave differently from simple systems and pose unusual challenges. They are tightly coupled. They are adaptive and self-organizing. Hence they are self-stabilizing and policy resistant. Their complexity overwhelms our ability to understand them. The result: the more you try to change them, the more they resist.

The reason is due to a limited learning horizon. Organizations do not always have the ability to observe the long-term consequences of their decisions and actions. They generally fail to appreciate the time delay between action and response. They are often caught in a vicious cycle of reacting to events and attempting to predict them, rather than learning from them. Without continual learning, over a far enough horizon, today's solutions often cause tomorrow's problems. The result is policy resistance, the tendency for improvement initiatives to be defeated by the response of the organization to the initiative itself.

The natural tendency is to break services down into discrete processes managed by different groups with specialized knowledge, experience and resources. This approach is useful. However, the more divided a system, the greater the need for coordination between components. An automobile, for example, is more than a collection of parts. The parts by themselves do not have a life of their own. The most significant breakthrough in braking systems for automobiles is not from simply enhancing the performance of brake pads or rotors, but from extending the braking system to include not only the brake components, but also road and weather conditions, changing the driver's mental model of how brakes are to be applied, and the dynamic interactions between these

elements. The systems view led designers to move beyond simply continual improvements in materials science and manufacturing to the counterintuitive idea of anti-lock braking systems (ABS) which compensate for variations in weather conditions and driver skills.

Similarly, breaking services and service management down into specific processes is a suitable tactic if their interconnectedness is not lost. Service management processes are a means and not the end. They are necessary because working together they produce the characteristics of service that define value for the customer. Treated separately, some of the most significant consequences of decisions and actions may remain hidden until after major problems and incidents.

9.2 COORDINATION AND CONTROL

Decision-makers in general have limited time, attention span and personal capacity. They delegate roles and responsibilities to teams and individuals who specialize in specific systems, processes, performance and outcomes. This follows the principle of division of labour with managers acting as principals and their subordinates acting as agents. Specialization allows for development of in-depth knowledge, skills and experience. It also allows for innovation, improvements and changes to occur within a controlled space. Service management is a coherent set of specialized competencies defined around processes and lifecycle phases. An increase in the level of specialization leads to a corresponding increase in the need for coordination. This is a major challenge in service management because of the level of specialization needed for various phases of the Service Lifecycle, processes and functions. Coordination can be improved with cooperation and control between teams and individuals.

Cooperation problems involve finding a way to align groups with divergent and possibly conflicting interests and goals, to cooperate for mutual benefit. This is true not only for cooperation between internal groups but also between customers and service providers. How do you agree on the definition of service levels with respect to a given level of user satisfaction? How much should a customer agree to pay for a given service level? What is a reasonable time frame for a change request to be approved? What service levels can you impose on an internal function or service group? How can multiple service providers cooperate as an alliance in serving a common customer? Cooperation problems can be partially solved by negotiating agreements in which every party is better off. This requires the presence of mutual welfare of all groups involved. One of the reasons why relationships fail is the lop-sided nature of agreements. Type I providers are particularly vulnerable to such agreements since they have less choice and freedom in terms of their Customer Portfolio. However, as emphasized in earlier chapters, without a financially viable and self-sustaining system of value creation, service providers are bound for eventual failure. Value capture is necessary for growth and improvement in value creation.

Another means to improving coordination between groups is to maintain shared views of outcomes towards which all performance is directed. Such views are defined in terms of service strategies, objectives, policies, rewards and incentives. The views are further detailed with customer outcomes, Service Catalogues, service definitions, contracts and agreements, all described with a common vocabulary. Further coordination and control is achieved with the use of shared processes that integrate groups and functions, shared applications that integrate processes, and shared infrastructure that integrates applications. A Service Knowledge Management System allows various groups to have simultaneous but distinct control perspectives on the same reality.

Control perspectives are based on the objectives of one or more service management processes or lifecycle phases. They help managers to focus on what is important and relevant to the processes under their control and ensure that control information of good quality is available for them to be effective and efficient. Control perspectives may also be useful to determine the information requirements for implementing effective organizational learning and improvement. Financial Management provides one such control perspective. In a market-based system coordinated by prices, there is little need for customers to provide detailed specifications on service designs, to impose technical constraints, determine how service assets are to be deployed and how services are to be operated. Customers indicate the prices they are willing to pay for a given level of service quality.

The prices are indicative of the value customers place on outcomes. Service providers can then coordinate control and deploy their assets to provide services that facilitate the outcomes at a cost less than or equal to the price customers are willing to pay. They have autonomy and control over the design, development and operation of the service as well as improvements necessary over time. They can optimize, reconfigure, standardize and engineer the internals of a service as necessary while maintaining

the value delivered to the customer in specified terms. Any uncertainties in demand and delivery can be factored for either in the service level commitments, the prices, or both. This allows for management on both sides to manage by outcomes.

9.3 PRESERVING VALUE

9.3.1 Deviations in performance

Mature customers care not only about the utility and warranty they receive for the price they are being charged. They also care about the total cost of utilization (TCU). The concept of TCU is based on the principle of transaction costs discussed earlier. Customers perceive not just the direct costs of actual consumption but also all other related costs incurred indirectly in the process of receiving the committed utility and warranty.

For service providers, creating value for customers is a highly visible objective. Capturing value for their own stakeholders is also important. In the case of Type I providers, these two sets of objectives may be closely aligned. They can easily diverge or be in conflict, especially with Type III providers.

Value created for customers is easily lost to hidden costs that the customer incurs from utilizing a service. Poor management of services over the lifecycle can result in customers paying much more than the price of the service when the effect of hidden costs sets in. The enduring value for customers turns out to be much lower than the value created. Eliminating hidden costs is a challenge, a critical success factor and a risk. There is a need to reduce the total losses in the system (Figure 9.1).

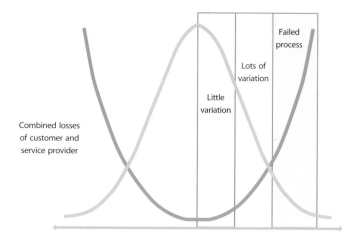

Figure 9.1 Combined losses from deviation of performance (Taguchi Loss Function)

9.3.2 Operational effectiveness and efficiency

Services ought be a beneficial undertaking from both the customer and service provider perspectives. Value creation for the customer should result in value capture for the service provider. This mutual welfare is important for the economic viability of services. It avoids losses on both sides of the relationship in real terms. Otherwise, sooner or later there will be tension in the relationship and at least one of the parties will be wishing for alternatives.

It is not unusual to start with the idea of efficiency. The notion of value itself is commonly based on efficiency. There are several notions of efficiency. The one used here is the ratio or proportionality of specific output in relation to the necessary inputs in terms of resources. Measures of efficiency depend on the type of input resource. For example, they could be based on minutes, full-time equivalents (FTE), square feet of space for facilities and equipment, gigabytes of storage, or simply financial equivalents of those units.

Efficiency goes to waste when output or outcome is not fit for purpose or fit for use. This is all too common in the case of services, because value is largely intangible. Therefore efficiency should have the guide rails of some desired effect. Effectiveness is the quality of being able to bring about a desired effect. In the context of services the two primary effects are utility and warranty (Figure 2.2).

Increasing the efficiency of a process can effectively increase remaining capacity to support additional units of demand. Increase in efficiency can result in more units of demand served from the same amount of a resource. Improvements in Service Design and Service Operation can drive such efficiency gains. There is feedback and interaction between efficiency and effectiveness (Figure 9.2).

An increase in efficiency can lead to an increase in effectiveness, which in turn can result in a further increase in efficiency until some optimization limit is reached. A shortfall in effectiveness when addressed by allocating more resources to recover the situation results in a decrease in efficiency. Efficiency losses in turn can lead to lower effectiveness because of the lower potency of each unit of output. These interactions between efficiency and effectiveness result in drifts or lifts in performance.

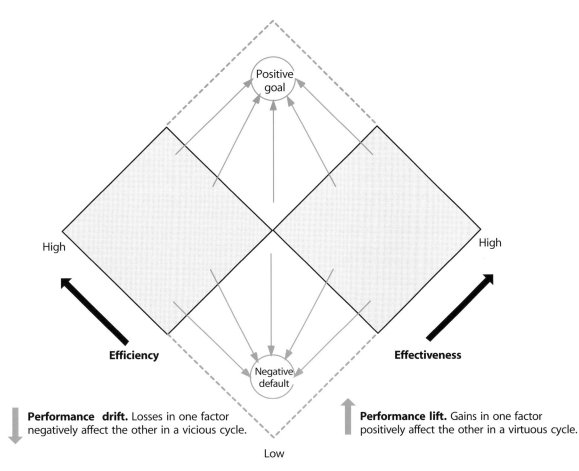

Figure 9.2 Efficiency and effectiveness

9.3.3 Reducing hidden costs

One category of hidden costs is transaction costs. These include costs for the resources that service providers spend to determine customer needs, user preferences, quality criteria that underpin value, and pricing decisions. Costs are also incurred when changes are made to services, service level agreements and demand in a trial-and-error manner. Custom-built services and low volumes of demand mean that set-up and tooling costs for the services are all borne by the customer. Standardization, shared services and reuse, coupled with segmentation and differentiated service levels should drive down transaction costs of coordination by reducing such overheads. This way, the needs of user segments are efficiently served while optimizing the use of service provider resources for maximum gain.[42] Well-defined service management processes, measurement systems, automation and communication, should drive down the transaction costs related to coordination through hierarchies. Indeed the very purpose of service governance is to drive down transaction costs. Low transaction costs are an inducement for customers to buy services instead of owning and operating non-core assets to produce the same effect on their business outcomes.

9.3.4 Substantiating hidden benefits

Customers find value in leasing assets such as applications and infrastructure rather than owning them. Part of that value comes in the form of the reduced lock-in that would otherwise exist due to high switching costs. Switching costs are high when the investment in the capital assets is high, when a major proportion of the assets come from the same vendor, and when the depreciation of the assets is slower. Faced with high switching costs, customers are often discouraged from purchasing assets. One way of reducing lock-in is to rent or lease the assets rather than buying them. Services provide an attractive alternative to asset purchases. They offer customers the utility of an asset without the related lock-in. That represents value to the customer. Another way to reduce lock-in is to contract out the maintenance and repair operations (MRO) of the assets to a third party provided a similar or better level of service is available. MRO services define a distinct category of services.

However, services by themselves can be a source of lock-in for customers. This is characterized by the disruption of learning curves of users and other people assets of the customer. It is also characterized by the changes required to processes, applications and infrastructure when switching to a new service provider. Customers value standardization in technologies, processes and industry practices to increase network externalities. Standardization helps increase the possibilities of multiple connections within a value network. When service management processes are standardized across a particular industry, then greater efficiency and flexibility can be realized from consolidation, disaggregation, and flexible configuration of business processes, infrastructure components and human resources. The risk of lock-in is reduced when it is easier to switch service providers within a value network. It also reduces operational risk to the customer's business from service provider failures. Internal service providers can be just as risky for customers as their commercial counterparts.

9.3.5 Leveraging intangible assets

Intangible assets are non-physical claims to future benefits generated by innovation, unique systems, processes, designs, organizational practices and competencies. They are combined with tangible and financial assets to create economic value for their owners.[37] Certain assets such as physical assets, human resources and financial assets are called rival or scarce assets because a specific deployment of such assets prevents their concurrent use elsewhere. Examples include bank tellers assisting customers, storage space, or financial capital invested in a certain office facility. Thus rival assets suffer opportunity costs. In contrast, intangible assets are generally non-rival because they can be replicated and concurrently deployed to serve multiple instances of demand. For the most part the concurrent deployments do not interfere with each other or reduce their utility with an increase in the number of deployments. Of course, poor system design may lead to congestion at points where underlying resources are being shared.

The use of intangible assets, such as web-based technologies and software-based automation of processes, can increase the scalability of service systems. Knowledge-intensive systems and processes can be highly leveraged with virtually zero opportunity costs. From a service management perspective, the structure of service models, designs, processes and infrastructure can be analysed to determine the ratio of intangible elements over tangible elements. Where possible, the tangible elements should be substituted with intangible ones so that the service design becomes more scalable and non-rival. Online service interfaces such as web browsers can effectively replace the many tangible assets required to interact with customers through physical channels such as branches, stores, kiosks and call centres. In other words, when services elements are well defined, it is possible to increase the throughput of the service delivery system by software-based replication, where software agents supplement human agents by taking care of some or all types of transactions.

The use of Interactive Voice Response systems with speech recognition, automated installation, automatic updates and rich-browser applications, can greatly reduce the cost of serving the same population of customers. They also reduce variations in service quality and compliance risks by reducing the workload on the human resources. The availability of services can be enhanced (or maintained in the face of an increasing workload) by the use of service interfaces or channels that rely more on intangibles than physical or human assets. It is much easier and faster to scale up an online customer support system to handle an extra million transactions through web browsers, than it is to support the same surge in demand by upgrading the voice infrastructure of a call centre or stores in a retail network. Also, the scalability does not bring the risks linked to installing additional network capacity or the training and orientation of new staff.

The non-rival or non-scarce attribute of intangibles represent the facility to deploy such assets simultaneously across a portfolio of services without diminishing their utility to any one customer. The scalability of intangibles is usually limited only by the size of the markets they can serve. The separation of intangibles from tangible assets may be difficult when they are embedded in physical assets. For example, the tacit knowledge stored in people in the form of experience, insight and certain skills is hard to codify or extract. Therefore there is considerable interaction between intangible and tangible assets in the creation of value. While this property of being embedded is a form of security for the owner, it does pose a challenge in the measurement and valuation of the intangibles.

9.4 EFFECTIVENESS IN MEASUREMENT

Case example 14: *Monitoring services*

Some time in 2004, a global automobile manufacturer sent out a call to its infrastructure outsourcing service providers. The manufacturer, with 20+ data centres and 10,000+ servers spread across the globe, was frustrated by the inability to separate the service monitoring signal from noise. It sought a better way, one where the providers received their relevant service information and the manufacturer received business impact information.

What is your response or suggestion?

(Answer at the end of the section)

Organizations have long understood the Deming principle: if you cannot measure it, you cannot manage it. Yet despite significant investments in products and processes, many IT organizations fall short in creating a holistic service analytics capability. When combined with a disjointed translation of IT components to business processes, the results are operational models lacking in proactive or predictive capabilities.

Performance measurements in service organizations are frequently out of step with the business environments they serve. This misalignment is not for the lack of measurements. Rather, traditional measurements focus more on internal goals rather than the external realities of customer satisfaction. Even the measurements of seasoned organizations emphasize control at the expense of customer response. While every organization differs, there are some common rules that are useful in designing effective measurements, as shown in Table 9.1.

Measurements focus the organization on its strategic goals, tracking progress and providing feedback. Be sure to change measurements as strategy evolves. When they conflict, older measurements will beat new goals because measurements, not strategic goals, determine rewards and promotions. Crafting new strategic goals without changing the related measurements is no change at all.

Current monitoring solutions result in the capture of only a small percentage of failures. Practice shows that monitoring discrete components is not enough. An approach that integrates with service management and promotes cross-domain coordination is more likely to afford success. Unfortunately, the common techniques are not completely satisfactory. They work well in restricted problem domains, where they focus on a particular subsystem or individual application; they don't work as well in a service management context.

The holy grail of monitoring is often referred to as 'end-to-end' visibility. Yet most of the IT organization has no visibility into the business processes. One cannot exist without the other. Indeed, the endpoints in 'end-to-end' are often misunderstood. Imagine the increased relevance that IT would gain if they could answer questions like the following:

- What is the delay, together with business impact, on the Supply Chain due to an IT problem?
- How long does it take to process procurement orders, and where are the worst delays?
- When is more than £1,000,000 worth of orders waiting to go through the distribution systems?

Table 9.1 Measurement principles

Principle	Guidance
Begin on the outside, not the inside of the service organization	A service organization should ask itself, 'What do customers really want and when?' and 'What do the best alternatives give our customers that we do not?'
	Customers, for example, frequently welcome discussion on ways to make better use of their service providers. They may also welcome personal relationships in the building of commitment from providers.
Responsiveness to customers beats all other measurement goals	Care is taken not to construct control measures that work against customer responsiveness.
	For example, organizations sometimes measure Change Management process compliance by the number of RFCs disapproved. While this measurement may be useful, it indirectly rewards slow response. An improved measurement strategy would include the number of RFCs approved in a set period of time as well as the percentage of changes that do not generate unintended consequences. Throughput, as well as compliance, is directly rewarded.
Think of process and service as equals	Focusing on services is important but be careful not to do so at the expense of process. It is easy to lose sight of process unless measurements make it equally explicit to the organization. Reward those who fix and improve process.
Numbers matter	Use a numerical and time scale that can go back far enough to cover the explanation of the current situation.
	Financial metrics are often appropriate. For non-commercial settings, adopt the same principle of measuring performance for outcomes desired. For example, 'beneficiaries served'.
Compete as an organization. Don't let overall goals get lost among the many performance measures	Be mindful of losing track of overall measures that tell you how the customer perceives your organization against alternatives. Train the organization to think of the service organization as an integrated IT system for the customer's benefit.

It is not uncommon for the business or senior managers to ask 'How?' and 'Why?' when the monitoring solution can only answer 'What?' and 'When?' Most IT organizations have deployed analytic technologies that primarily focus on the collection of monitoring data and while they are extremely effective at data collection they are ineffective in providing insight into services. This condition leads to statements such as:

'We want better Event Management so we can predict and prevent service impacts.'

The statement is a logical fallacy: one thing follows the other, therefore one thing is caused by the other. No amount of Event Management will ever provide predictive qualities; it will only give a better view of the crash. To understand why, it is helpful to borrow a construct from Knowledge Management called the DIKW hierarchy, Data-to-Information-to-Knowledge-to-Wisdom.

Case example 14 (solution): *The DIKW hierarchy and BSM*

The problem was solved through a form of the DIKW hierarchy. The multiple service providers received data and information generated through instrumentation and Event Management techniques, allowing them to perform monitoring and diagnostics.

A BSM model was crafted that linked infrastructure components to business services. The links were based on direct causality. Only those events that passed the 'causality test' were passed on to the manufacturer allowing business leaders to work off knowledge (impact) rather than information (events).

9.5 RISKS

'The number one risk factor in any organization is lack of accurate information.'

Mark Hurd, Chairman and CEO, HP

Risk is normally perceived as something to be avoided because of its association with threats. While this is generally true, risk is also to be associated with opportunity. Failure to take opportunities can be a risk in itself.[43] The opportunity costs of underserved market spaces and unfulfilled demand is a risk to be avoided. The Service Portfolio can be mapped to an underlying portfolio of risks that are to be managed. When service management is effective, services in the Catalogue and Pipeline represent opportunities to create value for customers and capture value for stakeholders. Otherwise, those services can be threats from the possibility of failure associated with the demand patterns they attract, the commitments they require and the costs they generate. Implementing strategies often requires changes to the Service Portfolio, which means managing associated risks.

Decisions about risk need to be balanced so that the potential benefits are worth more to the organization than it costs to address the risk. For example, innovation is inherently risky but could achieve major benefits in improving services. The ability of the organization to limit its exposure to risk will also be of relevance. The aim should be to make an accurate assessment of the risks in a given situation, and analyse the potential benefits. The risks and opportunities presented by each course of action should be defined in order to identify appropriate responses.[43]

For the purpose of analysis, it is sometimes useful to visualize the positive type of risks associated with opportunities, investments and innovation to the negative type from failure to take advantage of opportunities, not making enough investments, and neglecting innovation.

Case example 15: *Inbound call centre service*

A service provider operates the IT infrastructure of an inbound call centre for a business unit. A major system failure (asset impairment) leads to a reduction in the number of available call centre agents. The load for the functional on-duty agents quickly increases. As peak hours arrive, the increased traffic combined with sluggish response leads to further delays.

Increasingly frustrated by long wait times, callers become agitated. The rate of abandoned calls increases rapidly. Call centre agents observe their performance metrics plummet and respond by attempting to reduce the average length of calls. For the business unit, this drives down caller satisfaction metrics and increases opportunity costs from lost sales.

How could this have been avoided?

(Answer at the end of Section 9.5.2)

9.5.1 Definition of risk

Risk is defined as uncertainty of outcome, whether positive opportunity or negative threat. Managing risks requires the identification and control of the exposure to risk, which may have an impact on the achievement of an organization's business objectives.

Every organization manages its risk, but not always in a way that is visible, repeatable and consistently applied to support decision making. The task of management of risk is to ensure that the organization makes cost-effective use of a risk framework that has a series of well-defined steps. The aim is to support better decision making through a good understanding of risks and their likely impact. There are two distinct phases: risk analysis and risk management (Figure 9.3).

Risk analysis is concerned with gathering information about exposure to risk so that the organization can make appropriate decisions and manage risk appropriately.

Management of risk involves having processes in place to monitor risks, access to reliable and up-to-date information about risks, the right balance of control in place to deal with those risks, and decision-making processes supported by a framework of risk analysis and evaluation.

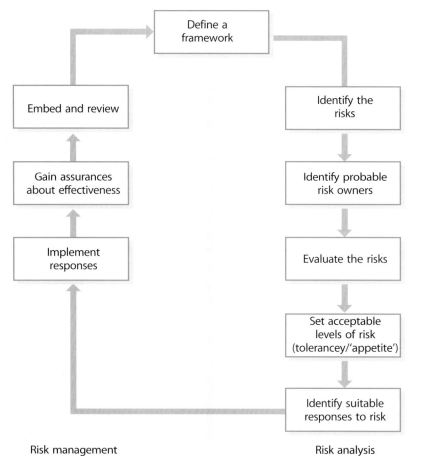

Risk management   Risk analysis

Figure 9.3 Generic framework for Risk Management [43]

Management of risk covers a wide range of topics, including Business Continuity Management (BCM), security, programme/project risk management and operational service management. These topics need to be placed in the context of an organizational framework for the management of risk. Some risk-related topics, such as security, are highly specialized and this guidance provides only an overview of such aspects.

9.5.2 Transfer of risks

Services reduce risks to the customer's business but they also transfer risk to the service provider. Risks flow both ways (Figure 9.4). For example, by maintaining and operating service assets so that customers do not have to,

the service provider is assuming risks associated with those assets. Customers compensate service providers for these transferred risks in many ways. First and foremost, the burden of risks can be accounted for in the pricing of the services.

While this may not be possible for some Type I providers it is best practice as demonstrated by their peers elsewhere. Type I providers should engage their customers in dialogue on compensation for risks within the framework of corporate policy.

When it is not possible to account for the burden of risks in pricing of services, as in the case of some Type I providers, it should nevertheless be highlighted for the

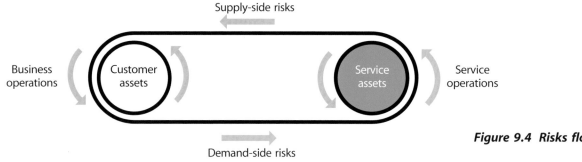

Figure 9.4 Risks flow both ways

customer. Customers compensate for risks also by assuring patterns and periods of demand that mitigate the risk of investments made by the provider in offering a catalogue of services.

This is particularly a concern for Type I providers who work with limited options in terms of market spaces, choice of customers and pricing freedom. The infrastructure must also be adaptive enough to support the differences among the business infrastructure and operative environments of several customers. Costs are a matter of fact while pricing is a matter of policy. Therefore service providers should have adequate controls to safeguard their interests in the long term, while continuing to support their customers flexibly through a wide range of scenarios.

On one hand, service providers must be sure that the compensation is complete and commensurate. On the other hand, the case they make should be reasonable. They have to take into account, for example, that certain returns on investments are not immediate but distributed over the lifetime of services and service assets. The risks they assume with new services and customers often pay off in the form of demand from other customers (from economies of scale) and demand for other services (from economies of scope).

Additions or changes to the Customer Portfolio should be preceded by an evaluation of risks that the service provider is willing to assume on behalf of the customer (Figure 9.5). Customers are similarly interested in filtering risks from service providers to an acceptable level. Risk Analysis and Risk Management should be applied to the Service Pipeline and Service Catalogue to identify, contain and mitigate risks within the Lifecycle phase.

Case example 15 (solution): *A strategy for service risks*

The service provider assures a minimum level of system availability in the event of a system failure. Though call centre services remained functional, the degradation in performance had a severe effect on the performance of business unit outcomes.

Besides protecting against system failures, there is a need to protect against service performance degradation, for instance, by isolating the business unit operations from the risks in its service provider operations. This can be done, for example, by dynamically routing callers to an alternative service unit with identical call centre service capabilities. The stand-by service unit is owned by the service provider or by a third-party service unit.

9.5.3 Service provider risks

Risks for service providers arise when uncertainty originating in the customer's business combines with uncertainty in their operations to have an adverse impact across the Service Lifecycle. Risks materialize in various forms such as technical problems, loss of control in operations, breaches in information security, delays in launching services, failure to comply with regulations, and financial short-falls. The exposure to risks and resulting damages are measured in financial terms and in terms of the loss of goodwill among customers, suppliers and partners. While financial losses are undesirable it is at least possible to account for them and write them off against gains elsewhere. It is harder to measure or recover the loss of goodwill in terms of reputation, customer confidence and credibility with prospects. However, financial measures are easier to understand and communicate across organizational boundaries and

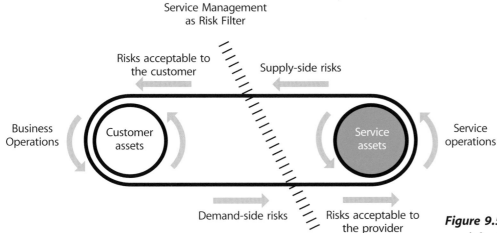

Figure 9.5 Risk management plays a crucial role in service management

cultures. To the extent possible, it is useful to communicate losses in financial terms, which are then used as indicators rather than direct measures.

Service provider risks vary by types of providers. The risk management plans and budgets of business units may cover their Type I providers. Type II providers operating with a market-based model assume a larger set of risks but stand to benefit accordingly. They assume risks similar to Type III providers in terms of marketing, new service development, financial liability and exposure to market-based competition. However, they distribute the risks across a larger customer base across the enterprise. They also have greater autonomy in managing the risks since they provide services on more commercial terms than Type I providers.

9.5.4 Contract risks

Customers depend on contracts as a means of implementing their own business strategy and achieving specific objectives, and as a means of allocating and managing most, if not all, operational risks associated with the business outcomes.[43] The concept of 'contract' includes formal, legally binding contracts as well as less formal agreements between business units and internal groups and functions. Risks that threaten the ability of the service provider to deliver on contractual commitments are strategic risks because they jeopardize not only operations in the present but also the confidence customers will place in the future. For example, failure to increase the capacity of highly leveraged assets such as infrastructure impacts a wide range of contractual commitments. Infrastructure is a strategic asset, and risks that impair such assets are strategic risks.

Risks are associated with contracts and span the Service Lifecycle. They are identified and assigned to roles and responsibilities within the functions and processes of the Lifecycle. This ensures that the risks are placed in context

and tackled with the right set of capabilities within the organization. The impact of the risks and the underlying threats and vulnerabilities may not be limited to any particular function of process (Figure 9.6). The customer does not discriminate between the origins of risks. Coordination is necessary across the Lifecycle to manage risk.

The set of risks to be managed depends on the commitments, contained in the Contract Portfolio, which define the design requirements and operational requirements to be realized through Service Models and Service Operation Plans. The combination of the two complementary sets of requirements determines the risks to be managed. Service Transition is instrumental in identifying risks in contractual commitments. The risk management is applied from the period before the commitments are made, through Service Design, until the commitments are fulfilled through Service Operation. Design risks arise from the failures or shortcomings in converting requirements into attributes of services and service models. Operational risks arise from technical and administrative failures in supporting the service model in operation. Together they determine a superset of risks to be managed actively across the Lifecycle.

9.5.5 Design risks

Customers expect services to have a particular impact on the performance of their assets, which is utility from their perspective. There is always a risk that services as designed fail to deliver the expected benefits utility. This is a performance risk (Figure 9.7). A major cause for poor performance is poor design. There is also a risk that the utility of a service diminishes with a significant change in the pattern of demand. For example, some services are designed in ways that prevent them from being scalable. In the short term, terms and conditions related to demand in service level agreements might protect the service

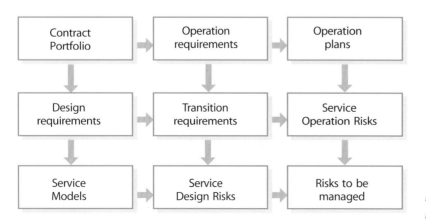

Figure 9.6 Contracts portfolios translate into a set of risks to be managed

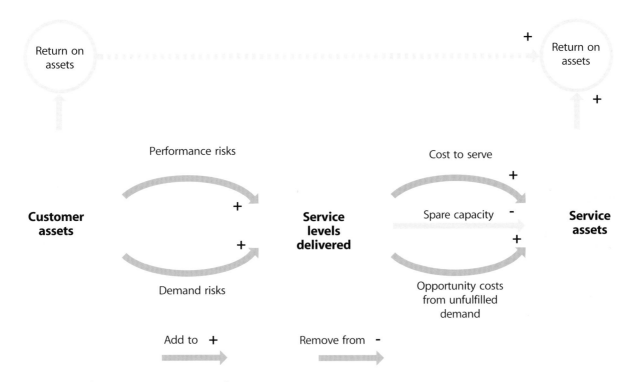

Figure 9.7 Risks from customer expectations

provider from penalties. It does not protect them from changes in customer perception about the suitability of the service.

The problem may be two-fold. There may be a lack of formal functions and processes in Service Design, which is different from the design of software applications and enterprise architecture. Service Design implements the principles of service management such as separation of concerns, modularity, loose coupling and feedback. Some Service Catalogues list as services items that are actually service components, functions and processes. These typically are applications, infrastructure and supporting systems that have been offered as services by default and not by design. Customers begin to use them only to face problems later as defects and failures emerge in actual use.

It is better to institutionalize a systematic approach to Service Design so that opportunities and resources are not wasted early in the lifecycle. Service Design processes and methods are a means to reduce the performance risks and demand risks of services. They take into account the type of customer assets to be supported, how those assets generate returns for customers, and the characteristics of demand they impose on the service to be designed. Service Design defines the best configuration of service assets that can provide the necessary performance potential and accept not only a specific pattern of demand but also tolerate variations within a specified range. Good designs also ensure that services are economical

to operate and flexible enough to modify and improve. This ensures that performance risks and demand risks do not result in high costs of utilized assets or opportunity costs from unutilized or under-utilized assets.

9.5.6 Operational risks

Operational risks are faced by every organization. Contracts are risk-sharing arrangements in which customers transfer ownership of certain types of costs and risks to service providers (Figure 9.6). Two sets of risks are considered from a service management perspective: risks faced by business units and the risks faced by the service units. A more complex view of risk is considered by taking into account the risks across an entire value net that includes partners and suppliers. This shared view of risks may be much more difficult to manage but may provide better visibility and control since the risks interact with each other. However, customers expect to be isolated from the operation risks of service providers. Poor risk management on the part of service providers may expose customer assets to risks and consequential loss. Service management prevents that from happening.

The systems and processes of Service Transition are able to filter such risks between organizations connected through services. The capabilities in Service Operation convert operational risks into opportunities to create value for customers. Their effect of removing risks from the customer's business is the core value proposition of many services.

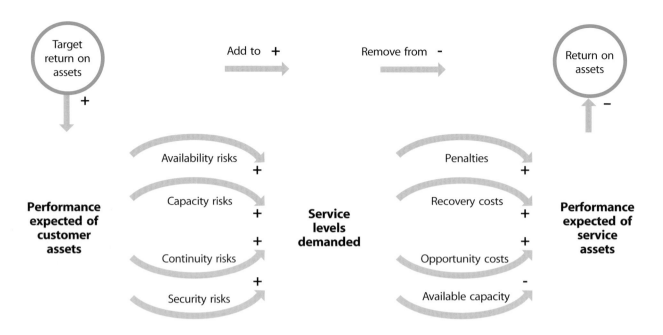

Figure 9.8 Warranty commitments are a source of risk

Procedures in Service Transition must be robust enough to ensure that this filtering capability is actualized: schedule pressures are likely to lead to demands for early delivery of new capability without the agreed level of warranty, leading to tensions when the service falls below the agreed quality.

Value to customers is realized in the Service Operation phase of the lifecycle when actual demand for services arrives. Warranty commitments require every unit of demand to be met with a unit of capacity that is available, secure and continuous within a frame of reference. There are four types of warranty risks each covering an aspect of warranty (Figure 9.8).

The Contract Portfolio is the basis for analysing short-term and long-term trends in demand from various sources. Each contract is a source of one or more streams of demand, each with its own short-term variability. Address short-term shifts in demand reallocation of resources without significant investments in new capacity. This is to avoid the risk of under-utilized assets during periods of low demand. If the trend continues, plan ahead of investments in additional capacity. Address long-term shifts with not only new capacity but also review the Service Catalogue to identify opportunities for resource sharing and consolidation. This requires engagement of not just Service Transition but also Service Design.

When shifts in average demand are long-term or permanent shifts, the solution is often to increase source capacities (an expensive option). If the increase in demand is not long-term or not sufficiently large, then increasing

capacity may result in under-utilization of assets in periods when demand is low. An option is to have 'multi-skilled' assets capable of serving more than one type of demand. Variability in capacity due to failures, outages, absenteeism, or any other forms of disruption can also be handled this way.

When demand fluctuations are short and intermittent, adjusting the capacity of certain types of resources may be difficult or not possible due to various constraints. Analyse the characteristics of various types of capacity to understand the constraints:

- **Asset specificity.** The more specialized capacity is for a service, the lower its usefulness may become for other services unless the two share a significantly high number of characteristics. A point-of-sale terminal has higher asset specificity than a PC workstation or storage device that can be repurposed. Asset specificity applies to People assets as well to a certain degree depending on the type of knowledge, experience and skills. Multi-skilled cross-trained staff with general management and administrative skills can be deployed on several tasks.

- **Scalability.** It is possible to adjust or reallocate the capacity of certain resources such as storage and network bandwidth. Other types of capacity such as facilities, hardware and headcount have tighter constraints.

- **Set-up or training costs.** It takes time, money and effort to set up and bring to productive state or redeploy an asset for a new task, purpose, or service. Set costs include adjustments, calibration and testing for the asset to perform better in the new role or context. People assets incur similar costs in terms of transition between assignments, new training and supervisory load.

■ **Dependencies.** The capacity of certain assets is unusable without free capacity of other assets. For example, a high-speed printer is not usable unless it is provisioned on a network accessible to the user domain. Similarly, it is not possible to add additional staff to a service function or process unless adequate resources such as workstations, software licences, office space and financial budgets are allocated.

■ **Overloaded assets.** Certain capacity is blocked simply because it is already overloaded beyond a factor of safety. Because of commitments made in service agreements and contracts, no further demand can be allocated to such capacity. For example, if a service contract supports a mission-critical function of a customer's business, no other service may access the capacity of resources dedicated to the contract.

A certain amount of idle capacity is required to maintain a given level of contingency. A capacity buffer or headroom is required to respond to unexpected peaks in demand. Trade-off exists between efficiency in utilization of resources and the service levels they can support (Figure 9.9). This constraint is particularly strong in shared services environments.

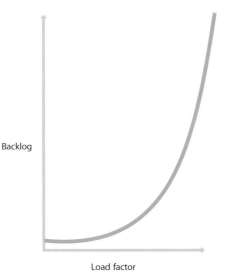

Figure 9.9 Higher load factors can create backlogs under certain conditions

Variability exists not only in demand but also capacity. The effective available capacity of a resource may vary as normal or because of failures or outages. Both types of variability affect the performance of services because of imbalance leading to backlog. Manufacturing systems overcome such problem with production planning and control techniques just as the kanban system for line balancing and redesign of process flow or assembly. Similar methods are applicable in the case of services. Six Sigma methods have been effective in service industries.

Strategic plans and initiatives that depend on the quick adjustments of productive capacity should take into consideration the inertia or resistance from capacity constraints to rapid adjustments. The processes for developing service designs, transition plans and operational plans should also include an activity or step that considers these constraints. The agility or responsiveness of a service unit depends on the mix of service assets. If service assets with high inertia dominate a service model, changes should be considered in terms of improvements or replacement of those assets.

9.5.7 Market risks

A common source of risk for all type of service providers is the choice that their customers have on sourcing decisions. In recent years, Type I providers have faced the risk of outsourcing when customers sign contracts with external providers in pursuit of strategic objectives. Customers are willing to make that switch when benefits outweigh the costs and risks of switching from one type to another. Reducing the total cost of utilization (TCU) gives customers incentives not to switch to other options. While outsourcing and shared services are the dominant trend, insourcing (or perhaps the affirmation of status quo) continues to be a valuable strategic option for customers. This is the risk faced primarily by Type III providers and to a limited extent by Type II providers. Effective service management helps reduce the levels of competitive risks faced by service providers by increasing the scale and scope of demand for a Service Catalogue. Conversely, another approach is to modify the contents of the Service Catalogue appropriately so that customers perceive the depth and width in the Catalogue with respect to their needs.

9.5.7.1 Reducing market risk through differentiation

How do you ensure good returns from investments made in service assets? How do you find new opportunities for those assets to be deployed in service of new customers? From a customer's perspective services bring to bear assets that are both scarce (i.e. customers do not have enough) and complementary (i.e. there is value in combining the customer and service assets). In a controlled and coordinated manner, service providers are allowing their assets to be used by their customers for gain. From a corresponding perspective, all service providers must maintain the assets most valued by their

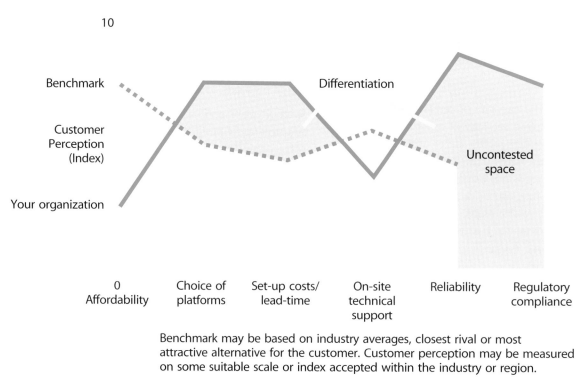

Benchmark may be based on industry averages, closest rival or most attractive alternative for the customer. Customer perception may be measured on some suitable scale or index accepted within the industry or region.

Figure 9.10 Uncontested market space based on underserved needs [25]

customers but not adequately provided by others. Unserved and underserved market spaces represent the most attractive opportunities (Figure 9.10).

For example, business process outsourcing (BPO) corresponds to the need of customers to have access to world-class business processes in functions such as finance, human resources and logistics. Customers do not want to invest their financial capital into the research and development of such processes. Customers pay a fee for using the business process, or simply for enjoying its outputs (e.g. invoices, claims or applications processes). They are free from the risk of operating or maintaining the process and keeping it efficient and compliant. They simply pay for the delivery of a given service level. Service providers have a larger basis for recovering costs in the form of service contracts, so they continue to innovate, improve and control the performance of the business processes and its enabling infrastructure. Network effects and positive feedback set in when customers receive the expected value from the BPO provider and influence the decisions of their peers.

A service provider may see this as an opportunity. It may assume the risks of investing in the design, engineering and development of a set of business processes that it would offer as services. It would also invest in the automation and staffing of the processes, and in ongoing efforts to increase their effectiveness and efficiencies. By offering these business processes as services, the provider can spread the investment across several customers and reduce the risks of not recovering its investments.

9.5.7.2 Reducing market risk through consolidation

Consolidation of demand reduces the financial risks for service providers and in turn reduces operation risks for customers. With an increase in the scale and scope of demand there is a reduction in the costs to serve the next unit of demand (Figure 9.11). The cost of unused capacity is also reduced through careful grouping of demand. Similar demand from multiple customer organizations can be hosted by the same set of service assets or service units. Fragmented pieces of demand are matched with the capacity to fulfil the demand. This leads to economy of scope for those particular service assets. On the whole there is an increase in the average return of assets realized by the service unit, and a reduction in the variation in returns.

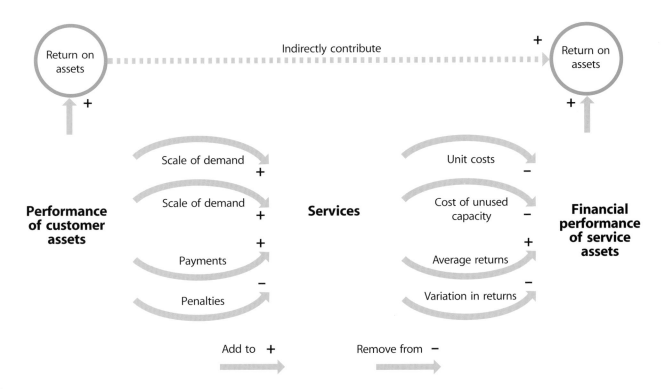

Figure 9.11 Consolidation of fragmented demand reduces financial risks

Afterword

Afterword

This publication encourages exercises in strategic thinking much needed by IT organizations and others vying to be service providers preferred by customers. It has established a strategic context for service management in the real world. But that world is about change and uncertainty. Commercial pressures, competition, legislation and environmental factors all affect business priorities and consequently also the strategies that support the business. Public sector and non-profit organizations may not have to make profits for shareholders, but they share many of the same concerns as companies and corporations. Public sector organizations, for example, have to deliver cost-effective services, and at the top level or at the internal department level run the risk of being shut down, merged or outsourced if they are not effective. This publication is about being prepared for possible scenarios, and turning threats into opportunities.

We all want to be 'not optional'. To survive and flourish, every organization, department, branch, section and individual has to understand how they create value for themselves and for their customers and the way that their suppliers enhance that value. They must appreciate the strategic choices both for their own services and those they receive from providers. Because of the environment of constant change, strategy is not something to do once, and service strategies need to be developed, applied and continually reviewed, just like all the other parts of the Service Lifecycle. If the strategy is effective, then the effort in all the other stages of the lifecycle will be applied appropriately and successfully.

Services are a predominant form in which value is created and transferred between organizations, and service management is in time maturing as a discipline. A wealth of knowledge and good practice is available for use if there is clarity on why services may be used to support the customer's business. Clarity is attained if there is a willingness to take a long-term view, to search for patterns among the noisy detail, and to be guided by business fundamentals rather than technical possibilities. Good practice is rooted in hard facts and sound principles, which are often dismissed under the pretext of being practical. Poor practice is often the blind pursuit of success in the footsteps of early champions and leaders who, unbeknownst to their followers, have been far more diligent. This publication encourages its readers to adopt a practical but principled approach to finding long-term success and durable capabilities in service management.

Appendix A: Present
value of an annuity

Appendix A: Present value of an annuity

Use Table A.1 to find the present value of an annuity of £1 in arrears.

Find the column under your discount rate (or cost of capital). Then find the horizontal row corresponding to the last year of the investment. The point at which the column and the row intersect is the present value of a series of £1 payments. Multiply this value by the number of pounds you expect to receive in each payment, in order to find the present value of the series.

Table A.1 Present value of an annuity

Present worth of £1 per period payable at end of each period

Years	3%	3.5%	4%	4.5%
1	£0.970874	£0.966184	£0.961538	£0.956938
2	£1.913470	£1.899694	£1.886095	£1.872668
3	£2.828611	£2.801637	£2.775091	£2.748964
4	£3.717098	£3.673079	£3.629895	£3.587526
5	£4.579707	£4.515052	£4.451822	£4.389977
6	£5.417191	£5.328553	£5.242137	£5.157872
7	£6.230283	£6.114544	£6.002055	£5.892701

Years	5%	5.5%	6%	6.5%
1	£0.952381	£0.947867	£0.943396	£0.938967
2	£1.859410	£1.846320	£1.833393	£1.820626
3	£2.723248	£2.697933	£2.673012	£2.648476
4	£3.545951	£3.505150	£3.465106	£3.425799
5	£4.329477	£4.270284	£4.212364	£4.155679
6	£5.075692	£4.995530	£4.917324	£4.841014
7	£5.786373	£5.682967	£5.582381	£5.484520

Years	7%	7.5%	8%	8.5%
1	£0.934579	£0.930233	£0.925926	£0.921659
2	£1.808018	£1.795565	£1.783265	£1.771114
3	£2.624316	£2.600526	£2.577097	£2.554022
4	£3.387211	£3.349326	£3.312127	£3.275597
5	£4.100197	£4.045885	£3.992710	£3.940642
6	£4.766540	£4.693846	£4.622880	£4.553587
7	£5.389289	£5.296601	£5.206370	£5.118514

Years	9%	9.5%	10%	10.5%
1	£0.917431	£0.913242	£0.909091	£0.904977
2	£1.759111	£1.747253	£1.735537	£1.723961
3	£2.531295	£2.508907	£2.486852	£2.465123
4	£3.239720	£3.204481	£3.169865	£3.135858
5	£3.889651	£3.839709	£3.790787	£3.742858
6	£4.485919	£4.419825	£4.355261	£4.292179
7	£5.032953	£4.949612	£4.868419	£4.789303

Years	11%	11.5%	12%	12.5%
1	£0.900901	£0.896861	£0.892857	£0.888889
2	£1.712523	£1.701221	£1.690051	£1.679012
3	£2.443715	£2.422619	£2.401831	£2.381344
4	£3.102446	£3.069614	£3.037349	£3.005639
5	£3.695897	£3.649878	£3.604776	£3.560568
6	£4.230538	£4.170294	£4.111407	£4.053839
7	£4.712196	£4.637035	£4.563757	£4.492301

Years	13%	13.5%	14%	14.5%
1	£0.884956	£0.881057	£0.877193	£0.873362
2	£1.668102	£1.657319	£1.646661	£1.636124
3	£2.361153	£2.341250	£2.321632	£2.302292
4	£2.974471	£2.943833	£2.913712	£2.884098
5	£3.517231	£3.474743	£3.433081	£3.392225
6	£3.997550	£3.942505	£3.888668	£3.836005
7	£4.422610	£4.354630	£4.288305	£4.223585

Years	15%	16%	17%	18%
1	£0.869565	£0.862	£0.855	£0.847
2	£1.625709	£1.605	£1.585	£1.566
3	£2.283225	£2.246	£2.210	£2.174
4	£2.854978	£2.798	£2.743	£2.690
5	£3.352155	£3.274	£3.199	£3.127
6	£3.784483	£3.685	£3.589	£3.498
7	£4.160420	£4.039	£3.922	£3.812

Years	19%	20%	21%	22%
1	£0.840	£0.833	£0.826	£0.820
2	£1.547	£1.528	£1.509	£1.492
3	£2.140	£2.106	£2.074	£2.042
4	£2.639	£2.589	£2.540	£2.494
5	£3.058	£2.991	£2.926	£2.864
6	£3.410	£3.326	£3.245	£3.167
7	£3.706	£3.605	£3.508	£3.416

Appendix B:
Supplementary guidance

B

Appendix B: Supplementary guidance

B1 DESCRIPTION OF ASSET TYPES

B1.1 Management

Management is a system that includes leadership, administration, policies, performance measures and incentives. This layer cultivates, coordinates and controls all other asset types. Management includes idiosyncratic elements such as philosophy, core beliefs, values, decision-making style and perceptions of risk. It is also the most distinctive and inimitable type of asset deeply rooted in the organization.

The term *organization* is used here to refer the enterprise or firm rather than the organization asset type. The most likely manner in which management assets can be partially extracted from an organization is by the poaching of key individuals who were instrumental in defining and developing a particular management system.

Service management itself is a type of specialized management asset like others such as Project Management, Research and Development, and Manufacturing Management.

B1.2 Organization

Organization assets are active configurations of People, Processes, Applications and Infrastructure that carry out all organizational activity through the principles of specialization and coordination. This category of assets includes the functional hierarchies, social networks of groups, teams and individuals, as well as the systems they use to work together towards shared goals and incentives. Organization assets include the patterns that People, Applications, Information and Infrastructure deploy, either by design or by self-adaptive process, to maximize the creation of value for stakeholders. Some service organizations are superior to others simply by virtue of organization. For example, networks of wireless access points, storage systems, point-of-sale terminals, databases, hardware stores and remote backup facilities. Strategic location of assets by itself is a basis for superior performance and competitive advantage.

B1.3 Process

Process assets are made of algorithms, methods, procedures and routines that direct the execution and control of activities and interactions. There is a great diversity in Process assets, which are specialized to

various degrees from generic management processes to sophisticated low-level algorithms embedded in software applications and other forms of automation. Process assets are the most dynamic of types. They signify action and transformation. Some of them are also the means by which Organization and Management assets coordinate and control each other and interact with the business environment. Process, People and Application assets execute them, Knowledge and Information assets enrich them, and Applications and Infrastructure assets enable them. Examples of Process assets are Order Fulfilment, Accounts Receivables, Incident Management, Change Management and Testing.

B1.4 Knowledge

Knowledge assets are accumulations of awareness, experience, information, insight and intellectual property that are associated with actions and context. Management, Organization, Process and Applications assets use and store knowledge assets. People assets store tacit knowledge in the form of experience, skills and talent. Such knowledge is primarily acquired through experience, observation and training. Movement of teams and individuals is an effective way to transfer tacit knowledge within and across organizations.[44] Knowledge assets in tacit form are hard for rivals to replicate but easy for owners to lose. Organizations seek to protect themselves from loss by codifying tacit knowledge into explicit forms such as knowledge embedded in Process, Applications and Infrastructure assets. Knowledge assets are difficult to manage but can be highly leveraged with increasing returns and virtually zero opportunity costs.[37] Knowledge assets include policies, plans, designs, configurations, architectures, process definitions, analytical methods, service definitions, analyses, reports and surveys. They may be owned as intellectual property and protected by copyrights, patents and trademarks. Knowledge assets can also be rented for use under licensing arrangements and service contracts.

B1.5 People

The value of People assets is the capacity for creativity, analysis, perception, learning, judgement, leadership, communication, coordination, empathy and trust. Such capacity is in teams and individuals within the organization, due to knowledge, experience and skills. Skills can be conceptual, technical and social skills. People assets are also the most convenient absorbers and carriers of all forms of Knowledge. They are the most versatile and potent of all asset types because of their ability to learn and adapt. People assets represent an organization's capabilities and resources. If capabilities are capacity for action, People assets are the actors. From the capabilities perspective, people assets are the only type that can create, combine and consume all other asset types. Their tolerance of ambiguity and uncertainty also compensates for the limitations of Processes, Applications and Infrastructure. Because of their enormous potential, People assets are often the most expensive in terms of development, maintenance and motivation. They also are assets that can be hired or rented but cannot be owned. Customers highly value services that enhance the productivity or potential of People assets.

People assets are also resources with productive capacity. Units of cost, time and effort measure their capacity as teams and individuals. They are mobile, multi-purpose and highly adaptive with the innate ability to learn. Staffing contracts, software agents and customers using self-service options augment the capacity of people assets.

B1.6 Information

Information assets are collections, patterns and meaningful abstractions of data applied in contexts such as customers, contracts, services, events, projects and operations. They are useful for various purposes including communication, coordination and control of business activities. Information assets exist in various forms such as documents, records, messages and graphs. All asset types produce them but Management, Processes, Knowledge, People and Applications primarily consume them. The value of Information assets can vary with time, location and format and depreciate very quickly. Some services create value by processing information and making it available as needed by Management, Processes, People and Applications assets. The criteria of effectiveness, efficiency, availability, integrity, confidentiality, reliability and compliance can be used to evaluate the quality of Information assets.[45]

B1.7 Applications

Applications assets are diverse in type and include artefacts, automation and tools used to support the performance of other asset types. Applications are composed of software, hardware, documents, methods, procedures, routines, scripts and instructions. They automate, codify, enable, enhance, maintain, or mimic the properties, functions and activities of Management, Organization, Processes, Knowledge, People and

Information assets. Applications derive their value in relation to these other assets. Process assets in particular commonly exist inside Applications. Applications assets consume, produce and maintain Knowledge and Information assets. They can be of various types such as general-purpose, multi-purpose and special-purpose. Some Applications are analogous to industrial tools, machinery and equipment because they enhance the performance of Processes. Others are analogous to office equipment and consumer appliances because they enhance the personal productivity of People assets. Examples of Applications are accounting software, voice mail, imaging systems, encryption devices, process control, inventory tracking, electronic design automation, mobile phones and bar code scanners. Applications are themselves supported by Infrastructure, People and Process assets. One of the most powerful attributes of Applications is that they can be creatively combined and integrated with other asset types, particularly other Applications to create valuable new assets.

B1.8 Infrastructure

Infrastructure assets have the peculiar property of existing in the form of layers defined in relation to the assets they support, especially People and Applications. They include information technology assets such as software applications, computers, storage systems, network devices, telecommunication equipment, cables, wireless links, access control devices and monitoring systems. This category of assets also includes traditional facilities such as buildings, electricity, HVAC and water supply without which it would be impossible for People, Applications and other Infrastructure assets to operate. Infrastructure assets by themselves may be composed mostly of Applications and other Infrastructure assets. Assets viewed as Applications at one level can be utilized as infrastructure at another. This is an important principle that allows service-orientation of assets.

B1.9 Financial capital

Financial assets are required to support the ownership or use of all types of assets. They also measure the economic value and performance of all types of assets. Financial assets include cash, cash equivalents and other assets such as marketable securities, and receivables that are convertible into cash with degrees of certainty and ease. Adequacy of financial assets is an important concern for all organizations including government agencies and non-profit organizations. The promise and potential of other assets is not realized in full without financial assets.

B2 PRODUCT MANAGERS

B2.1 Roles and responsibilities

Product Manager is a key role within Service Portfolio Management (Figure B.1). The role is responsible for managing services as a product over their entire lifecycle from concept to retirement through design, transition and operation. They are instrumental in the development of Service Strategy and its execution through the Service Lifecycle within a high-performing portfolio of services. Product Managers bring coordination and focus to the organization around the Service Catalogue, of which they maintain ownership. They work closely with Business Relationship Managers (BRMs) who bring coordination and focus to the Customer Portfolio.

Product Managers are recognized as the subject matter experts on Lines of Service (LOS) and the Service Catalogue (Figure B.2). They understand Service Models and their internal structure and dynamics to be able to drive changes and improvements effectively. They have a consolidated view of costs and risks across LOS, just as BRMs maintain a similar view across customers and contracts.

Product Managers evaluate new market opportunities, operating models, technologies and the emerging needs of customers. They follow variety-based positions and seek new sources of demand for items in the Service Catalogue. They negotiate internal agreements with BRMs, who represent the underserved and unserved needs of customers. When solutions are not found in the Catalogue or Pipeline, Product Managers and BRMs work together on making a business case for new service development (NSD). They involve the Sourcing Management function when there is a need to integrate third-party services and other service components for a new or existing service. They hold a position within the Sourcing Organization. This requires Product Managers to be adept in integration projects and in holding internal and external suppliers accountable via formal agreements.

Product Managers provide leadership on the development of business cases, LOS strategy, new service deployment and Service Lifecycle management schedules. They perform financial analysis in collaboration with Service Design, Service Operation and Financial Management. This requires them to be good in negotiation, managing conflict and achieving consensus in order to achieve the organization's strategic positions and financial objectives.

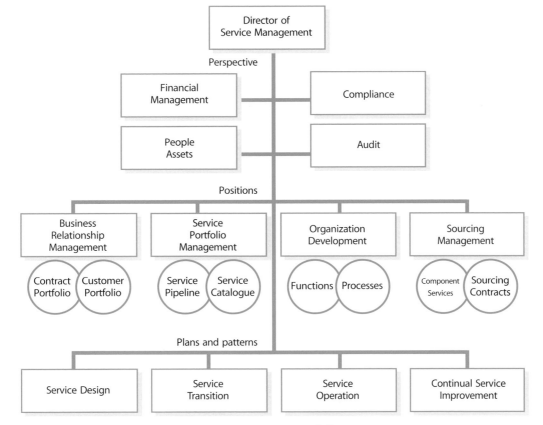

Figure B.1 Product Managers have a key role under Service Portfolio Management

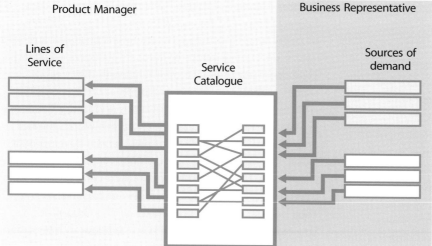

Figure B.2 Product Managers and Lines of Service (LOS)

They bring the marketing mindset necessary for an outcome-based definition of services and effectiveness in value creation. They are able to manage conflict and constraints. They balance change and innovation in the Service Pipeline with stability, dependability and financial performance of the Service Catalogue. Product Managers are able to communicate LOS strategies effectively to senior leadership, develop partnerships with other groups within the organization and outside suppliers in order to satisfy customer needs. They must be able to plan new service development programmes in response to new market opportunities, assess the impact of new technologies, and guide the creation of innovative solutions. They market the development and implementation of services that incorporate new technologies or system development. This requires extensive cross-organization communications.

B2.2 Critical knowledge, skills and experience

Product Managers should have working knowledge of the market spaces with regards to industry applications, business trends, technologies, competitive scenarios, regulations, suppliers and vendors. They also should have demonstrated sustained performance in previous assignments, sound business judgment, negotiating skills and people skills. They should have excellent communications skills and the ability to accept challenges and manage the positive and negative aspects of risks, and develop solutions on time and within cost objectives.

Product management draws from multiple disciplines, bodies of knowledge and communities of practice:

- Business strategy, competitive analysis, and portfolio management
- Design, software development and systems engineering
- Financial analysis, lifecycle Cost Management and pricing
- Project management and risk management
- Sourcing and supplier management

Education would generally include an advanced degree in Accounting, Finance, Marketing, Operations, Engineering, Information Systems or Computer Science, or equivalent experience.

Further information

Further information

REFERENCES

1   Seely Brown, John and John, Hagel III 2005. Innovation Blowback: Disruptive Management Practices from Asia. *The McKinsey Quarterly*, No. 1.

2   Coase, Ronald 1937. The Nature of the Firm. *Economica*, Vol. 4, No. 16, November 1937, 386–405.

3   Bryson, J.R., Daniels, P.W. and Warf, B. 2004. Service Worlds: People, Organisations, Technologies. Routledge.

4   McNeillis, Paul 2005. ITNOW 2005 47(6): 14–15; British Computer Society. doi:10.1093/itnow/bwi114

5   Easton, G. and Jarrell, S. 1998. The effects of total quality management on corporate performance: An empirical investigation. *Journal of Business*, 71(2), 253–307.

6   Keating, Elizabeth et al. 1999. Overcoming the Improvement Paradox. *European Management Journal*, Vol. 17, No. 2, 120–134.

7   Magretta, Joan 2002. What Management Is: How it works and why it's everyone's business. The Free Press.

8   Lovelock, Christopher and Gummesson, Evert 2004. Whither Services Marketing? In Search of A New Paradigm and Fresh Perspectives. *Journal of Service Research*, 7 (August), 20–41.

9   Malone, T.W. et al. (eds) 2003. Organizing Business Knowledge: The MIT Process Handbook.

10 Moorecroft, John et al. 2002. Systems Perspective on Resources, Capabilities, and Management Processes. Elsevier Science.

11 Goold, Michael and Campbell, Andrew 2002. Designing Effective Organizations: How to create structured networks. Jossey-Bass.

12 Lidwell, W., Holden, K. and Butler, J. 2003. Universal Principles of Design. Rockport Publishers.

13 Sterman, John D. 2000. Business Dynamics. Systems Thinking and Modeling for a Complex World. McGraw-Hill.

14 Nagle, T.N. and Holden, R.K. 2002. Strategy and tactics of pricing: A guide to profitable decision-making. 3rd Edition. Prentice-Hall.

15 Milgrom, Paul and Roberts, John 1992. Economics, Organization and Management. Prentice-Hall.

16 Tapscott, Don et al. 2000. Digital Capital: Harnessing the Power of Business Webs. Harvard Business School Press.

17 Allee, Verna 2003. The Future of Knowledge: Increasing Prosperity through value networks. Butterworth-Heinemann.

18 Porter, Michael E. 1996. What is strategy? *Harvard Business Review*. November–December 1996.

19 Breene, T., Mulani, N.P., Nunes, P.F. 2005. Marks of distinction. *Outlook Journal*, No. 2.

20 Mintzberg, Henry 1994. The Rise and Fall of Strategic Planning. Basic Books.

21 Simons, Robert 1995. Levers of Control: How Managers Use Innovative Control Systems to Drive Strategic Renewal. Harvard Business School Press, Boston, Massachusetts.

22 Gratton, Lynda and Ghoshal, Sumantra 2005. Beyond Best Practice. *MIT Sloan Management Review*. Spring 2005. Vol. 46, No. 3.

23 Ulwick, Anthony 2005. What Customers Want: Using Outcome-Driven Innovation to Create Breakthrough Products and Services. McGraw-Hill.

24 Amit, Raphael and Schoemaker, Paul 1993. Strategic assets and organizational rent. *Strategic Management Journal*, Vol. 14, 33–46.

25 Kim, W. Chan and Mauborgne, Renée 2005. Blue Ocean Strategy: How to Create Uncontested Market Space and Make Competition Irrelevant. Harvard Business School Press.

26 Rummler, Geary 1995. Improving Performance: how to manage the white space on the organization chart. Jossey-Bass.

27 Luehrman, T.A. 1998. Strategy as a portfolio of real options. *Harvard Business Review*, Vol. 76, No. 5, 89–99.

28 Kano, N., Seraku, N., Tsuji, S. and Takahashi, F. 1984. Attractive quality and must-be quality. *Hinshitsu (Quality, The Journal of Japanese Society for Quality Control)*, Vol. 14, No. 2, 39–48.

29 Aldrich, H. 1999. Organizations Evolving. Sage.

30 Williamson, O.E. and Winter, S.G. 1993. The Nature of the Firm: Origins, Evolution and Development. Oxford University Press.

31 Holmstrom, B. and Roberts, J. 1998. The Boundaries of the Firm Revisited. *Journal of Economic Perspectives.* Vol. 12, 73–94.

32 Camazine, S. et al. 2001. Self-Organization in Biological Systems. Princeton University Press.

33 Greiner, Larry E. 1998 (orig. 1972). Evolution and revolution as organizations grow. *Harvard Business Review,* May–June 1998.

34 Van Maanen, J. and Schein, E.H. 1979. Toward a theory of organizational socialization. In: B. Staw (ed) Research in Organizational Behavior 1. JAI Press, Greenwich, 209–264.

35 Froehle, C. and Roth, A.V. 2004. New measurement scales for evaluating perceptions of the technology-mediated customer service experience. *Journal of Operations Management,* **22** (1), 1–21.

36 Rayport, J.F. and Jaworski, B.J. 2004. Best Face Forward. *Harvard Business Review.* December 2004.

37 Lev, B. 2001. Intangibles: Management, Measurement, and Reporting. The Brookings Institution.

38 Tax, S.S. and Brown, S.W. 1998. Recovering and Learning from Service Failure. *Sloan Management Review,* Fall, 75–88.

39 Repenning, Nelson P. and Sterman, John D. 2001a. Nobody Ever Gets Credit for Fixing Problems that Never Happened: Creating and Sustaining Process Improvement. *California Management Review.* Vol. 43, No. 4, Summer 2001.

40 Repenning, Nelson P. et al. 2001b. Past the Tipping Point: The Persistence of Firefighting in Product Development. *California Management Review.* Vol. 43, No. 4, Summer 2001.

41 NAE (National Academy of Engineering) 2003. The Impact of Academic Research on Industrial Performance. The National Academies Press.

42 Edmondson and Frei 2002. Transformation at the IRS. Harvard Business School.

43 OGC (Office of Government Commerce) 2007. Management of Risk: Guidance for Practitioners. The Stationery Office.

44 Argote 2000. Knowledge Transfer: A Basis for Competitive Advantage in Firms. *Organizational Behaviour and Human Decision Processes.* Vol. 82, No. 1, May, 150–169.

45 ITGI 2005. COBIT 4.0: Control Objectives, Management Guidelines, and Maturity Models. IT Governance Institute.

FURTHER READING

The following publications have influenced the thinking of authors and shaped the contents of this book. They are indicative of the breadth and depth and diversity of knowledge available to interested readers. Some of these are seminal works in their respective fields, notable for their enduring influence several decades after publication. Others are contemporary works addressing new challenges and opportunities facing organizations.

Burner, Mike 2004. Service Orientation and Its Role in Your Connected Systems Strategy. Microsoft Corporation. July 2004. MSDN. URL: http://msdn2.microsoft.com/en-us/library/ms954826.aspx

Carr, Nicholas 2005. The End of Corporate Computing. *MIT Sloan Management Review.* Spring 2005, Vol. 46, No. 3, 67–73.

Cherbakov et al. 2005. Impact of service orientation at the business level. *IBM Systems Journal,* Vol. 44, No. 4.

Forrester, Jay W. 1961. Industrial Dynamics. MIT Press.

Forrester, Jay W. 1971. Principles of Systems. Wright-Allen Press.

Grant, Robert M. 1991. The Resource-Based Theory of Competitive Advantage: Implications for Strategy Formulation. *California Management Review,* Vol. 33, No. 3.

Grönroos, Christian 2001. Service management and Marketing: A Customer Relationship Management Approach. John Wiley and Sons.

Hill, Peter 1977. On Goods and Services. *The Review of Income and Wealth,* 23: 315–338.

Iravani, S.M. et al. 2005. Structural Flexibility: A New Perspective on the Design of Manufacturing and Service Operations. *Management Science,* Vol. 51, No. 2, February 2005, 151–166.

ITSqc, 2004. ITSqc Global Strategic Service Management Symposium. [ITSqc Working Paper CMU-ITSQC-WP-04-001a]. Carnegie Mellon University, Pittsburgh, PA, USA.

Jones, Gareth R. 2007. Organizational Theory, Design and Change. Pearson Prentiss Hall.

Judd, R.C. 1964. The Case for Redefining Services. *Journal of Marketing,* Vol. 28, 58–59.

Luftman, Jerry and Brier, Tom 1999. Achieving and Sustaining Business–IT Alignment. *California Management Review*. Vol. 42, No. 1. Fall 1999.

Rathmell, J.M. 1966. What Is Meant by Services? *Journal of Marketing*, Vol. 30, 1966, 32–36.

Senge, Peter 1990. The Fifth Discipline. Currency Doubleday.

Glossary

Acronyms List

ACD	Automatic Call Distribution		FMEA	Failure Modes and Effects Analysis
AM	Availability Management		FTA	Fault Tree Analysis
AMIS	Availability Management Information System		IRR	Internal Rate of Return
ASP	Application Service Provider		ISG	IT Steering Group
BCM	Business Capacity Management		ISM	Information Security Management
BCM	Business Continuity Management		ISMS	Information Security Management System
BCP	Business Continuity Plan		ISO	International Organization for Standardization
BIA	Business Impact Analysis		ISP	Internet Service Provider
BRM	Business Relationship Manager		IT	Information Technology
BSI	British Standards Institution		ITSCM	IT Service Continuity Management
BSM	Business Service Management		ITSM	IT Service Management
CAB	Change Advisory Board		itSMF	IT Service Management Forum
CAB/EC	Change Advisory Board/Emergency Committee		IVR	Interactive Voice Response
CAPEX	Capital Expenditure		KEDB	Known Error Database
CCM	Component Capacity Management		KPI	Key Performance Indicator
CFIA	Component Failure Impact Analysis		LOS	Line of Service
CI	Configuration Item		M_o_R	Management of Risk
CMDB	Configuration Management Database		MTBF	Mean Time Between Failures
CMIS	Capacity Management Information System		MTBSI	Mean Time Between Service Incidents
CMM	Capability Maturity Model		MTRS	Mean Time to Restore Service
CMMI	Capability Maturity Model Integration		MTTR	Mean Time to Repair
CMS	Configuration Management System		NPV	Net Present Value
COTS	Commercial off the Shelf		OGC	Office of Government Commerce
CSF	Critical Success Factor		OLA	Operational Level Agreement
CSI	Continual Service Improvement		OPEX	Operational Expenditure
CSIP	Continual Service Improvement Plan		OPSI	Office of Public Sector Information
CSP	Core Service Package		PBA	Pattern of Business Activity
CTI	Computer Telephony Integration		PFS	Prerequisite for Success
DIKW	Data–to–Information–to–Knowledge –to–Wisdom		PIR	Post-Implementation Review
			PSO	Projected Service Outage
ELS	Early Life Support		QA	Quality Assurance
eSCM–CL	eSourcing Capability Model for Client Organizations		QMS	Quality Management System
			RCA	Root Cause Analysis
eSCM–SP	eSourcing Capability Model for Service Providers		RFC	Request for Change

ROI	Return on Investment
RPO	Recovery Point Objective
RTO	Recovery Time Objective
SAC	Service Acceptance Criteria
SACM	Service Asset and Configuration Management
SCD	Supplier and Contract Database
SCM	Service Capacity Management
SDP	Service Design Package
SFA	Service Failure Analysis
SIP	Service Improvement Plan
SKMS	Service Knowledge Management System
SLA	Service Level Agreement
SLM	Service Level Management
SLP	Service Level Package
SLR	Service Level Requirement
SMO	Service Maintenance Objective
SoC	Separation of Concerns
SOP	Standard Operating Procedures
SOR	Statement of requirements
SPI	Service Provider Interface
SPM	Service Portfolio Management
SPO	Service Provisioning Optimization
SPOF	Single Point of Failure
TCO	Total Cost of Ownership
TCU	Total Cost of Utilization
TO	Technical Observation
TOR	Terms of Reference
TQM	Total Quality Management
UC	Underpinning Contract
UP	User Profile
VBF	Vital Business Function
VOI	Value on Investment
WIP	Work in Progress

Definitions list

The publication names included in parentheses after the name of a term identify where a reader can find more information about that term. This is either because the term is primarily used by that publication or because additional useful information about that term can be found there. Terms without a publication name associated with them may be used generally by several publications, or may not be defined in any greater detail than can be found in the glossary, i.e. we only point readers to somewhere they can expect to expand on their knowledge or to see a greater context. Terms with multiple publication names are expanded on in multiple publications.

Where the definition of a term includes another term, those related terms are highlighted in a second colour. This is designed to help the reader with their understanding by pointing them to additional definitions that are all part of the original term they were interested in. The form 'See also Term X, Term Y' is used at the end of a definition where an important related term is not used with the text of the definition itself.

Account Manager

(Service Strategy) A Role that is very similar to Business Relationship Manager, but includes more commercial aspects. Most commonly used when dealing with External Customers.

Accounting

(Service Strategy) The Process responsible for identifying actual costs of delivering IT Services, comparing these with budgeted costs, and managing variance from the Budget.

Activity

A set of actions designed to achieve a particular result. Activities are usually defined as part of Processes or Plans, and are documented in Procedures.

Agreement

A Document that describes a formal understanding between two or more parties. An Agreement is not legally binding, unless it forms part of a Contract. See also Service Level Agreement.

Alert

(Service Operation) A warning that a threshold has been reached, something has changed, or a Failure has occurred. Alerts are often created and managed by System Management tools and are managed by the Event Management Process.

Analytical modelling

(Service Strategy) (Service Design) (Continual Service Improvement) A technique that uses mathematical Models to predict the behaviour of a Configuration Item or IT Service. Analytical Models are commonly used in Capacity Management and Availability Management. See also Modelling.

Application

Software that provides Functions that are required by an IT Service. Each Application may be part of more than one IT Service. An Application runs on one or more Servers or Clients.

Architecture

(Service Design) The structure of a System or IT Service, including the Relationships of Components to each other and to the environment they are in. Architecture also includes the Standards and Guidelines that guide the design and evolution of the System.

Assessment

Inspection and analysis to check whether a Standard or set of Guidelines is being followed, that Records are accurate, or that Efficiency and Effectiveness targets are being met. See also Audit.

Asset

(Service Strategy) Any Resource or Capability. Assets of a Service Provider including anything that could contribute to the delivery of a Service. Assets can be one of the following types: Management, Organization, Process, Knowledge, People, Information, Applications, Infrastructure, and Financial Capital.

Asset Management

(Service Transition) Asset Management is the Process responsible for tracking and reporting the value and ownership of financial assets throughout their Lifecycle. Asset Management is part of an overall Service Asset and Configuration Management Process.

Attribute

(Service Transition) A piece of information about a Configuration Item. Examples are: name, location, Version number, and cost. Attributes of CIs are recorded in the Configuration Management Database (CMDB). *See also* Relationship.

Audit

Formal inspection and verification to check whether a Standard or set of Guidelines is being followed, that Records are accurate, or that Efficiency and Effectiveness targets are being met. An Audit may be carried out by internal or external groups. *See also* Certification, Assessment.

Availability

(Service Design) Ability of a Configuration Item or IT Service to perform its agreed Function when required. Availability is determined by Reliability, Maintainability, Serviceability, Performance, and Security. Availability is usually calculated as a percentage. This calculation is often based on Agreed Service Time and Downtime. It is best practice to calculate Availability using measurements of the business output of the IT Service.

Availability Management

(Service Design) The Process responsible for defining, analysing, Planning, measuring and improving all aspects of the Availability of IT Services. Availability Management is responsible for ensuring that all IT Infrastructure, Processes, Tools, Roles, etc. are appropriate for the agreed Service Level Targets for Availability.

Backup

(Service Design) (Service Operation) Copying data to protect against loss of Integrity or Availability of the original.

Balanced scorecard

(Continual Service Improvement) A management tool developed by Drs. Robert Kaplan (Harvard Business School) and David Norton. A balanced scorecard enables a Strategy to be broken down into Key Performance Indicators. Performance against the KPIs is used to demonstrate how well the Strategy is being achieved. A balanced scorecard has four major areas, each of which has a small number of KPIs. The same four areas are considered at different levels of detail throughout the Organization.

Baseline

(Continual Service Improvement) A Benchmark used as a reference point. For example:

- An ITSM Baseline can be used as a starting point to measure the effect of a Service Improvement Plan

- A Performance Baseline can be used to measure changes in Performance over the lifetime of an IT Service

- A Configuration Management Baseline can be used to enable the IT infrastructure to be restored to a known Configuration if a Change or Release fails.

Benchmark

(Continual Service Improvement) The recorded state of something at a specific point in time. A Benchmark can be created for a Configuration, a Process, or any other set of data. For example, a benchmark can be used in:

- Continual Service Improvement, to establish the current state for managing improvements

- Capacity Management, to document performance characteristics during normal operations.

See also Benchmarking, Baseline.

Benchmarking

(Continual Service Improvement) Comparing a Benchmark with a Baseline or with best practice. The term Benchmarking is also used to mean creating a series of Benchmarks over time, and comparing the results to measure progress or improvement.

Best practice

Proven Activities or Processes that have been successfully used by multiple Organizations. ITIL is an example of best practice.

British Standards Institution

The UK National Standards body, responsible for creating and maintaining British Standards. See www.bsi-global.com for more information. *See also* ISO.

Budget

A list of all the money an Organization or business unit plans to receive, and plans to pay out, over a specified period of time. *See also* Budgeting, Planning.

Budgeting

The Activity of predicting and controlling the spending of money. Consists of a periodic negotiation cycle to set future Budgets (usually annual) and the day-to-day monitoring and adjusting of current Budgets.

Business

(Service Strategy) An overall corporate entity or Organization formed of a number of business units. In the context of ITSM, the term business includes public sector and not-for-profit organizations, as well as companies. An IT Service Provider provides IT Services to a Customer within a business. The IT Service Provider may be part of the same business as its Customer (internal service provider), or part of another business (external service provider).

Business Case

(Service Strategy) Justification for a significant item of expenditure. Includes information about costs, benefits, options, issues, Risks, and possible problems.

Business Continuity Management

(Service Design) The business process responsible for managing Risks that could seriously affect the business. BCM safeguards the interests of key stakeholders, reputation, brand and value-creating activities. The BCM Process involves reducing Risks to an acceptable level and planning for the recovery of business processes should a disruption to the business occur. BCM sets the Objectives, Scope and Requirements for IT Service Continuity Management.

Business customer

(Service Strategy) A recipient of a product or a Service from the business. For example, if the business is a car manufacturer then the business customer is someone who buys a car.

Business Impact Analysis

(Service Strategy) BIA is the Activity in Business Continuity Management that identifies Vital Business Functions and their dependencies. These dependencies may include Suppliers, people, other business processes, IT Services, etc. BIA defines the recovery requirements for IT Services.

These requirements include Recovery Time Objectives, Recovery Point Objectives and minimum Service Level Targets for each IT Service.

Business objective

(Service Strategy) The Objective of a Business Process, or of the business as a whole. Business objectives support the Business Vision, provide guidance for the IT Strategy, and are often supported by IT Services.

Business operations

(Service Strategy) The day-to-day execution, monitoring and management of business processes.

Business perspective

(Continual Service Improvement) An understanding of the Service Provider and IT Services from the point of view of the business, and an understanding of the business from the point of view of the Service Provider.

Business process

A Process that is owned and carried out by the business. A business process contributes to the delivery of a product or Service to a business customer. For example, a retailer may have a purchasing Process that helps to deliver Services to its business customers. Many business processes rely on IT Services.

Business Relationship Manager

(Service Strategy) A Role responsible for maintaining the Relationship with one or more Customers. This Role is often combined with the Service Level Manager Role. *See also* Account Manager.

Business service

An IT Service that directly supports a Business Process, as opposed to an infrastructure service, which is used internally by the IT Service Provider and is not usually visible to the business.

The term business service is also used to mean a Service that is delivered to business customers by business units. For example, delivery of financial services to Customers of a bank, or goods to the Customers of a retail store. Successful delivery of business services often depends on one or more IT Services.

Business Service Management

(Service Strategy) (Service Design) An approach to the management of IT Services that considers the business processes supported and the business value provided.

This term also means the management of business services delivered to business customers.

Business unit

(Service Strategy) A segment of the business that has its own Plans, Metrics, income and costs. Each business unit owns Assets and uses these to create value for Customers in the form of goods and Services.

Call

(Service Operation) A telephone call to the Service Desk from a User. A Call could result in an Incident or a Service Request being logged.

Call centre

(Service Operation) An Organization or business unit that handles large numbers of incoming and outgoing telephone calls. *See also* Service Desk.

Capability

(Service Strategy) The ability of an Organization, person, Process, Application, Configuration Item or IT Service to carry out an Activity. Capabilities are intangible Assets of an Organization. *See also* Resource.

Capacity

(Service Design) The maximum Throughput that a Configuration Item or IT Service can deliver whilst meeting agreed Service Level Targets. For some types of CI, Capacity may be the size or volume, for example a disk drive.

Capacity Management

(Service Design) The Process responsible for ensuring that the Capacity of IT Services and the IT infrastructure is able to deliver agreed Service Level Targets in a cost-effective and timely manner. Capacity Management considers all Resources required to deliver the IT Service, and plans for short-, medium- and long-term business requirements.

Capacity Planning

(Service Design) The Activity within Capacity Management responsible for creating a Capacity Plan.

Capital Expenditure

(Service Strategy) The cost of purchasing something that will become a financial asset, for example computer equipment and buildings. The value of the Asset is Depreciated over multiple accounting periods.

Capital item

(Service Strategy) An Asset that is of interest to Financial Management because it is above an agreed financial value.

Capitalization

(Service Strategy) Identifying major cost as Capital, even though no Asset is purchased. This is done to spread the impact of the cost over multiple accounting periods. The most common example of this is software development, or purchase of a software licence.

Category

A named group of things that have something in common. Categories are used to group similar things together. For example, Cost Types are used to group similar types of cost. Incident Categories are used to group similar types of Incident, CI Types are used to group similar types of Configuration Item.

Certification

Issuing a certificate to confirm Compliance to a Standard. Certification includes a formal Audit by an independent and Accredited body. The term Certification is also used to mean awarding a certificate to verify that a person has achieved a qualification.

Change

(Service Transition) The addition, modification or removal of anything that could have an effect on IT Services. The Scope should include all IT Services, Configuration Items, Processes, Documentation, etc.

Change Management

(Service Transition) The Process responsible for controlling the Lifecycle of all Changes. The primary objective of Change Management is to enable beneficial Changes to be made, with minimum disruption to IT Services.

Change request

See Request for Change.

Charging

(Service Strategy) Requiring payment for IT Services. Charging for IT Services is optional, and many Organizations choose to treat their IT Service Provider as a Cost Centre.

Classification

The act of assigning a Category to something. Classification is used to ensure consistent management and reporting. CIs, Incidents, Problems, Changes, etc. are usually classified.

Client

A generic term that means a Customer, the business or a business customer. For example, Client Manager may be used as a synonym for Account Manager.

The term client is also used to mean:

■ A computer that is used directly by a User, for example a PC, Handheld Computer, or Workstation

■ The part of a Client-Server Application that the User directly interfaces with. For example an e-mail Client.

COBIT

(Continual Service Improvement) Control Objectives for Information and related Technology (COBIT) provides guidance and best practice for the management of IT Processes. COBIT is published by the IT Governance Institute. See www.isaca.org for more information.

Compliance

Ensuring that a Standard or set of Guidelines is followed, or that proper, consistent accounting or other practices are being employed.

Component

A general term that is used to mean one part of something more complex. For example, a computer System may be a component of an IT Service, an Application may be a Component of a Release Unit. Components that need to be managed should be Configuration Items.

Confidentiality

(Service Design) A security principle that requires that data should only be accessed by authorized people.

Configuration

(Service Transition) A generic term, used to describe a group of Configuration Items that work together to deliver an IT Service, or a recognizable part of an IT Service. Configuration is also used to describe the parameter settings for one or more CIs.

Configuration Management

(Service Transition) The Process responsible for maintaining information about Configuration Items required to deliver an IT Service, including their Relationships. This information is managed throughout the Lifecycle of the CI. Configuration Management is part of an overall Service Asset and Configuration Management Process.

Configuration Management Database

(Service Transition) A database used to store Configuration Records throughout their Lifecycle. The Configuration Management System maintains one or more CMDBs, and each CMDB stores attributes of CIs, and Relationships with other CIs.

Configuration Management System

(Service Transition) A set of tools and databases that are used to manage an IT Service Provider's Configuration data. The CMS also includes information about Incidents, Problems, Known Errors, Changes and Releases; and may contain data about employees, Suppliers, locations, business units, Customers and Users. The CMS includes tools for collecting, storing, managing, updating, and presenting data about all Configuration Items and their Relationships. The CMS is maintained by Configuration Management and is used by all IT Service Management Processes. *See also* Configuration Management Database.

Continual Service Improvement

(Continual Service Improvement) A stage in the Lifecycle of an IT Service and the title of one of the Core ITIL publications. Continual Service Improvement is responsible for managing improvements to IT Service Management Processes and IT Services. The Performance of the IT Service Provider is continually measured and improvements are made to Processes, IT Services and IT infrastructure in order to increase Efficiency, Effectiveness, and cost effectiveness. *See also* Plan–Do–Check–Act.

Contract

A legally binding Agreement between two or more parties.

Contract Portfolio

(Service Strategy) A database or structured Document used to manage Service Contracts or Agreements between an IT Service Provider and their Customers. Each IT Service delivered to a Customer should have a Contract or other Agreement that is listed in the Contract Portfolio. *See also* Service Portfolio, Service Catalogue.

Control

A means of managing a Risk, ensuring that a business objective is achieved, or ensuring that a Process is followed. Example Controls include Policies, Procedures, Roles, RAID, door locks, etc. A control is sometimes called a Countermeasure or safeguard. Control also means to manage the utilization or behaviour of a Configuration Item, System or IT Service.

Control Objectives for Information and related Technology (COBIT)

See COBIT.

Control perspective

(Service Strategy) An approach to the management of IT Services, Processes, Functions, Assets, etc. There can be several different Control Perspectives on the same IT Service, Process, etc., allowing different individuals or teams to focus on what is important and relevant to their specific Role. Example Control Perspectives include Reactive and Proactive management within IT Operations, or a Lifecycle view for an Application Project team.

Core service

(Service Strategy) An IT Service that delivers basic Outcomes desired by one or more Customers. *See also* Supporting Service, Core service package.

Core service package

(Service Strategy) A detailed description of a core service that may be shared by two or more Service Level Packages. *See also* Service Package.

Cost

The amount of money spent on a specific Activity, IT Service, or business unit. Costs consist of real cost (money), notional cost such as people's time, and Depreciation.

Cost Centre

(Service Strategy) A business unit or Project to which costs are assigned. A Cost Centre does not charge for Services provided. An IT Service Provider can be run as a Cost Centre or a Profit Centre.

Cost effectiveness

A measure of the balance between the effectiveness and cost of a service, process or activity, a cost-effective Process is one that achieves its Objectives at minimum cost. *See also* Return on Investment, Value for Money.

Cost element

(Service Strategy) The middle level of category to which costs are assigned in Budgeting and Accounting. The highest-level category is Cost Type. For example a Cost Type of 'people' could have cost elements of payroll, staff benefits, expenses, training, overtime, etc. Cost elements can be further broken down to give Cost Units. For example the cost element 'expenses' could include Cost Units of Hotels, Transport, Meals, etc.

Cost Management

(Service Strategy) A general term that is used to refer to Budgeting and Accounting, sometimes used as a synonym for Financial Management.

Cost Type

(Service Strategy) The highest level of category to which costs are assigned in Budgeting and Accounting. For example hardware, software, people, accommodation, external and Transfer. *See also* Cost element, Cost Unit.

Cost Unit

(Service Strategy) The lowest level of category to which costs are assigned, Cost Units are usually things that can be easily counted (e.g. staff numbers, software licences) or things easily measured (e.g. CPU usage, Electricity consumed). Cost Units are included within cost elements. For example a cost element of 'expenses' could include Cost Units of Hotels, Transport, Meals, etc. *See also* Cost Type.

Course corrections

Changes made to a Plan or Activity that has already started to ensure that it will meet its Objectives. Course corrections are made as a result of Monitoring progress.

Critical success factor

Something that must happen if a Process, Project, Plan, or IT Service is to succeed. KPIs are used to measure the achievement of each CSF. For example a CSF of 'protect IT Services when making Changes' could be measured by KPIs such as 'percentage reduction of unsuccessful Changes', 'percentage reduction in Changes causing Incidents', etc.

Culture

A set of values that is shared by a group of people, including expectations about how people should behave, their ideas, beliefs, and practices. *See also* Vision.

Customer

Someone who buys goods or Services. The Customer of an IT Service Provider is the person or group that defines and agrees the Service Level Targets. The term Customers is also sometimes informally used to mean Users, for example 'this is a Customer-focused Organization'.

Customer Portfolio

(Service Strategy) A database or structured Document used to record all Customers of the IT Service Provider. The Customer Portfolio is the Business Relationship Manager's view of the Customers who receive Services from the IT Service Provider. *See also* Contract Portfolio, Service Portfolio.

Data-to-Information-to-Knowledge-to-Wisdom

A way of understanding the relationships between data, information, knowledge, and wisdom. DIKW shows how each of these builds on the others.

Deliverable

Something that must be provided to meet a commitment in a Service Level Agreement or a Contract. Deliverable is also used in a more informal way to mean a planned output of any Process.

Demand Management

Activities that understand and influence Customer demand for Services and the provision of Capacity to meet these demands. At a Strategic level Demand Management can involve analysis of patterns of business activity and User Profiles. At a tactical level it can involve use of Differential Charging to encourage Customers to use IT Services at less busy times. *See also* Capacity Management.

Dependency

The direct or indirect reliance of one Process or Activity on another.

Deployment

(Service Transition) The Activity responsible for movement of new or changed hardware, software, documentation, Process, etc. to the Live Environment. Deployment is part of the Release and Deployment Management Process.

Depreciation

(Service Strategy) A measure of the reduction in value of an Asset over its life. This is based on wearing out, consumption or other reduction in the useful economic value.

Design

(Service Design) An Activity or Process that identifies Requirements and then defines a solution that is able to meet these Requirements. *See also* Service Design.

Detection

(Service Operation) A stage in the Incident Lifecycle. Detection results in the Incident becoming known to the Service Provider. Detection can be automatic, or can be the result of a user logging an Incident.

Development

(Service Design) The Process responsible for creating or modifying an IT Service or Application. Also used to mean the Role or group that carries out Development work.

Diagnosis

(Service Operation) A stage in the Incident and Problem Lifecycles. The purpose of Diagnosis is to identify a Workaround for an Incident or the Root Cause of a Problem.

Direct cost

(Service Strategy) A cost of providing an IT Service which can be allocated in full to a specific Customer, Cost Centre, Project, etc. For example, the cost of providing non-shared servers or software licences. *See also* Indirect Cost.

Directory service

(Service Operation) An Application that manages information about IT infrastructure available on a network, and corresponding User access Rights.

Document

Information in readable form. A Document may be paper or electronic. For example, a Policy statement, Service Level Agreement, Incident Record, diagram of computer room layout. *See also* Record.

Driver

Something that influences Strategy, Objectives or Requirements. For example, new legislation or the actions of competitors.

Economies of scale

(Service Strategy) The reduction in average cost that is possible from increasing the usage of an IT Service or Asset. *See also* Economies of scope.

Economies of scope

(Service Strategy) The reduction in cost that is allocated to an IT Service by using an existing Asset for an additional purpose. For example, delivering a new IT Service from existing IT infrastructure. *See also* Economies of scale.

Effectiveness

(Continual Service Improvement) A measure of whether the Objectives of a Process, Service or Activity have been achieved. An Effective Process or activity is one that achieves its agreed Objectives.

Efficiency

(Continual Service Improvement) A measure of whether the right amount of resources have been used to deliver a Process, Service or Activity. An Efficient Process achieves its Objectives with the minimum amount of time, money, people or other resources.

Environment

(Service Transition) A subset of the IT infrastructure that is used for a particular purpose. For example: Live Environment, Test Environment, Build Environment. It is possible for multiple Environments to share a Configuration Item, for example Test and Live Environments may use different partitions on a single mainframe computer. Also used in the term Physical Environment to mean the accommodation, air conditioning, power system, etc.

Environment is also used as a generic term to mean the external conditions that influence or affect something.

Error

(Service Operation) A design flaw or malfunction that causes a Failure of one or more Configuration Items or IT Services. A mistake made by a person or a faulty Process that affects a CI or IT Service is also an Error.

Escalation

(Service Operation) An Activity that obtains additional Resources when these are needed to meet Service Level Targets or Customer expectations. Escalation may be needed within any IT Service Management Process, but is most commonly associated with Incident Management, Problem Management and the management of Customer complaints. There are two types of Escalation: Functional Escalation and Hierarchic Escalation.

eSourcing Capability Model for Service Providers

(Service Strategy) A framework to help IT Service Providers develop their IT Service Management Capabilities from a Service Sourcing perspective. eSCM–SP was developed by Carnegie Mellon University, US.

Estimation

The use of experience to provide an approximate value for a Metric or cost. Estimation is also used in Capacity and Availability Management as the cheapest and least accurate Modelling method.

Evaluation

(Service Transition) The Process responsible for assessing a new or Changed IT Service to ensure that Risks have been managed and to help determine whether to proceed with the Change.

Evaluation is also used to mean comparing an actual Outcome with the intended Outcome, or comparing one alternative with another.

Event

(Service Operation) A change of state that has significance for the management of a Configuration Item or IT Service.

The term Event is also used to mean an Alert or notification created by any IT Service, Configuration Item or Monitoring tool. Events typically require IT Operations personnel to take actions, and often lead to Incidents being logged.

Event Management

(Service Operation) The Process responsible for managing Events throughout their Lifecycle. Event Management is one of the main Activities of IT Operations.

External service provider

(Service Strategy) An IT Service Provider that is part of a different Organization to its Customer. An IT Service Provider may have both Internal Customers and External Customers. *See also* Type III Service Provider.

Failure

(Service Operation) Loss of ability to Operate to Specification, or to deliver the required output. The term Failure may be used when referring to IT Services, Processes, Activities, Configuration Items, etc. A Failure often causes an Incident.

Failure Modes and Effects Analysis

An approach to assessing the potential Impact of Failures. FMEA involves analysing what would happen after Failure of each Configuration Item, all the way up to the effect on the business. FMEA is often used in Information Security Management and in IT Service Continuity Planning.

Fast Recovery

(Service Design) A Recovery Option that is also known as Hot Standby. Provision is made to Recover the IT Service in a short period of time: typically less than 24 hours. Fast Recovery typically uses a dedicated Fixed Facility with computer Systems, and software configured ready to run the IT Services. Immediate Recovery may take up to 24 hours if there is a need to Restore data from Backups.

Fault

See Error.

Fault tolerance

(Service Design) The ability of an IT Service or Configuration Item to continue to Operate correctly after Failure of a Component part.

Financial Management

(Service Strategy) The Function and Processes responsible for managing an IT Service Provider's Budgeting, Accounting and Charging Requirements.

Fit for purpose

An informal term used to describe a Process, Configuration Item, IT Service, etc. that is capable of meeting its objectives or Service Levels. Being fit for purpose requires suitable design, implementation, control and maintenance.

Fixed cost

(Service Strategy) A cost that does not vary with IT Service usage. For example the cost of Server hardware. *See also* Variable Cost.

Follow the Sun

(Service Operation) A methodology for using Service Desks and Support Groups around the world to provide seamless 24 * 7 Service. Calls, Incidents, Problems and Service Requests are passed between groups in different time zones.

Fulfilment

Performing Activities to meet a need or Requirement. For example, by providing a new IT Service, or meeting a Service Request.

Function

A team or group of people and the tools they use to carry out one or more Processes or Activities. For example the Service Desk.

The term Function also has two other meanings:

- An intended purpose of a Configuration Item, Person, Team, Process, or IT Service. For example one Function of an e-mail Service may be to store and forward outgoing mails, one Function of a business process may be to dispatch goods to Customers.

- To perform the intended purpose correctly, 'The computer is Functioning'.

Governance

Ensuring that Policies and Strategy are actually implemented, and that required Processes are correctly followed. Governance includes defining Roles and responsibilities, measuring and reporting, and taking actions to resolve any issues identified.

Guideline

A Document describing best practice, which recommends what should be done. Compliance with a guideline is not normally enforced. *See also* Standard.

Help desk

(Service Operation) A point of contact for Users to log Incidents. A help desk is usually more technically focused than a Service Desk and does not provide a Single Point of Contact for all interaction. The term help desk is often used as a synonym for Service Desk.

High Availability

(Service Design) An approach or design that minimizes or hides the effects of Configuration Item Failure on the users of an IT Service. High Availability solutions are designed to achieve an agreed level of Availability and make use of techniques such as fault tolerance, Resilience and Fast Recovery to reduce the number of Incidents, and the Impact of Incidents.

Hot Standby

See Fast Recovery or Immediate Recovery.

Immediate Recovery

(Service Design) A Recovery Option that is also known as Hot Standby. Provision is made to Recover the IT Service with no loss of Service. Immediate Recovery typically uses Mirroring, Load Balancing and Split Site technologies.

Impact

(Service Operation) (Service Transition) A measure of the effect of an Incident, Problem or Change on business processes. Impact is often based on how Service Levels will be affected. Impact and Urgency are used to assign Priority.

Incident

(Service Operation) An unplanned interruption to an IT Service or reduction in the Quality of an IT Service. Failure of a Configuration Item that has not yet affected Service is also an Incident. For example Failure of one disk from a mirror set.

Incident Management

(Service Operation) The Process responsible for managing the Lifecycle of all Incidents. The primary Objective of Incident Management is to return the IT Service to Customers as quickly as possible.

Indirect cost

(Service Strategy) A cost of providing an IT Service, which cannot be allocated in full to a specific customer. For example, the Cost of providing shared Servers or software licences. Also known as Overhead. *See also* Direct cost.

Information Security Management

(Service Design) The Process that ensures the Confidentiality, Integrity and Availability of an Organization's Assets, information, data and IT Services. Information Security Management usually forms part of an Organizational approach to Security Management that has a wider scope than the IT Service Provider, and includes handling of paper, building access, phone calls, etc., for the entire Organization.

Information Technology

The use of technology for the storage, communication or processing of information. The technology typically includes computers, telecommunications, Applications and other software. The information may include business data, voice, images, video, etc. Information Technology is often used to support business processes through IT Services.

Infrastructure service

An IT Service that is not directly used by the business, but is required by the IT Service Provider so they can provide other IT Services. For example directory services, naming services, or communication services.

Integrity

(Service Design) A security principle that ensures data and Configuration Items are modified only by authorized personnel and Activities. Integrity considers all possible causes of modification, including software and hardware Failure, environmental Events, and human intervention.

Interactive Voice Response

(Service Operation) A form of Automatic Call Distribution that accepts User input, such as key presses and spoken commands, to identify the correct destination for incoming Calls.

Internal Rate of Return

(Service Strategy) A technique used to help make decisions about capital expenditure. IRR calculates a figure that allows two or more alternative investments to be compared. A larger IRR indicates a better investment. *See also* Net Present Value, Return on Investment.

Internal service provider

(Service Strategy) An IT Service Provider that is part of the same Organization as its Customer. An IT Service Provider may have both Internal Customers and External Customers. *See also* Type I Service Provider, Type II Service Provider.

Internal sourcing

(Service Strategy) Using an Internal Service Provider to manage IT Services. *See also* Service Sourcing, Type I Service Provider, Type II Service Provider.

International Organization for Standardization

The International Organization for Standardization (ISO) is the world's largest developer of Standards. ISO is a non-governmental organization that is a network of the national standards institutes of 156 countries. See www.iso.org for further information about ISO.

ISO 9000

A generic term that refers to a number of international Standards and Guidelines for Quality Management Systems. See www.iso.org for more information. *See also* ISO.

ISO/IEC 20000

ISO Specification and Code of Practice for IT Service Management. ISO/IEC 20000 is aligned with ITIL best practice.

ISO/IEC 27001

(Service Design) (Continual Service Improvement) ISO Specification for Information Security Management. The corresponding Code of Practice is ISO/IEC 17799. *See also* Standard.

IT infrastructure

All of the hardware, software, networks, facilities, etc. that are required to develop, Test, deliver, Monitor, Control or support IT Services. The term IT infrastructure includes all of the Information Technology but not the associated people, Processes and documentation.

IT Operations

(Service Operation) Activities carried out by IT Operations Control, including Console Management, Job Scheduling, Backup and Restore, and Print and Output Management. IT Operations is also used as a synonym for Service Operation.

IT Operations Management

(Service Operation) The Function within an IT Service Provider that performs the daily Activities needed to manage IT Services and the supporting IT infrastructure. IT Operations Management includes IT Operations Control and Facilities Management.

IT Service

A Service provided to one or more Customers by an IT Service Provider. An IT Service is based on the use of Information Technology and supports the Customer's business processes. An IT Service is made up from a combination of people, Processes and technology and should be defined in a Service Level Agreement.

IT Service Management

The implementation and management of Quality IT Services that meet the needs of the business. IT Service Management is performed by IT Service Providers through an appropriate mix of people, Process and Information Technology. *See also* Service Management.

IT Service Provider

(Service Strategy) A Service Provider that provides IT Services to Internal Customers or External Customers.

ITIL

A set of best practice guidance for IT Service Management. ITIL is owned by the OGC and consists of a series of publications giving guidance on the provision of Quality IT Services, and on the Processes and facilities needed to support them. See www.itil.co.uk for more information.

Job description

A Document that defines the Roles, responsibilities, skills and knowledge required by a particular person. One job description can include multiple Roles, for example the Roles of Configuration Manager and Change Manager may be carried out by one person.

Kano Model

Service Strategy) A Model developed by Noriaki Kano that is used to help understand Customer preferences. The Kano Model considers attributes of an IT Service grouped into areas such as basic factors, excitement factors, performance factors, etc.

Knowledge base

(Service Transition) A logical database containing the data used by the Service Knowledge Management System.

Knowledge Management

(Service Transition) The Process responsible for gathering, analysing, storing and sharing knowledge and information within an Organization. The primary purpose of Knowledge Management is to improve Efficiency by reducing the need to rediscover knowledge. *See also* Data-to-Information-to-Knowledge-to-Wisdom.

Lifecycle

The various stages in the life of an IT Service, Configuration Item, Incident, Problem, Change, etc. The Lifecycle defines the Categories for Status and the Status transitions that are permitted. For example:

- The Lifecycle of an Application includes Requirements, Design, Build, Deploy, Operate, Optimize
- The Expanded Incident Lifecycle includes Detect, Respond, Diagnose, Repair, Recover, Restore
- The Lifecycle of a Server may include: Ordered, Received, In Test, Live, Disposed, etc.

Line of Service

(Service Strategy) A core service or Supporting Service that has multiple Service Level Packages. A Line of Service is managed by a Product Manager and each Service Level Package is designed to support a particular market segment.

Maintainability

(Service Design) A measure of how quickly and Effectively a Configuration Item or IT Service can be restored to normal working after a Failure. Maintainability is often measured and reported as MTRS.

Maintainability is also used in the context of Software or IT Service Development to mean ability to be Changed or Repaired easily.

Managed Services

(Service Strategy) A perspective on IT Services which emphasizes the fact that they are managed. The term Managed Services is also used as a synonym for Outsourced IT Services.

Management System

The framework of Policy, Processes and Functions that ensures an Organization can achieve its Objectives.

Marginal Cost

(Service Strategy) The cost of continuing to provide the IT Service. Marginal Cost does not include investment already made, for example the cost of developing new software and delivering training.

Market Space

(Service Strategy) All opportunities that an IT Service Provider could exploit to meet business needs of Customers. The Market Space identifies the possible IT Services that an IT Service Provider may wish to consider delivering.

Maturity

(Continual Service Improvement) A measure of the Reliability, Efficiency and Effectiveness of a Process, Function, Organization, etc. The most mature Processes and Functions are formally aligned to business objectives and Strategy, and are supported by a framework for continual improvement.

Mean Time Between Failures

(Service Design) A Metric for measuring and reporting Reliability. MTBF is the average time that a Configuration Item or IT Service can perform its agreed Function without interruption. This is measured from when the CI or IT Service starts working, until it next fails.

Mean Time To Repair

The average time taken to repair a Configuration Item or IT Service after a Failure. MTTR is measured from when the CI or IT Service fails until it is repaired. MTTR does not include the time required to Recover or Restore. MTTR is sometimes incorrectly used to mean Mean Time to Restore Service.

Mean Time to Restore Service

The average time taken to restore a Configuration Item or IT Service after a Failure. MTRS is measured from when the CI or IT Service fails until it is fully restored and delivering its normal functionality. *See also* Maintainability, Mean Time to Repair.

Metric

(Continual Service Improvement) Something that is measured and reported to help manage a Process, IT Service or Activity.

Mission Statement

The Mission Statement of an Organization is a short but complete description of the overall purpose and intentions of that Organization. It states what is to be achieved, but not how this should be done.

Model

A representation of a System, Process, IT Service, Configuration Item, etc. that is used to help understand or predict future behaviour.

Modelling

A technique that is used to predict the future behaviour of a System, Process, IT Service, Configuration Item, etc. Modelling is commonly used in Financial Management, Capacity Management and Availability Management.

Monitoring

(Service Operation) Repeated observation of a Configuration Item, IT Service or Process to detect Events and to ensure that the current status is known.

Near-shore

(Service Strategy) Provision of Services from a country near the country where the Customer is based. This can be the provision of an IT Service, or of supporting Functions such as Service Desk. *See also* On-shore, Off-shore.

Net Present Value

(Service Strategy) A technique used to help make decisions about capital expenditure. NPV compares cash inflows with cash outflows. Positive NPV indicates that an investment is worthwhile. *See also* Internal Rate of Return, Return on Investment.

Notional Charging

(Service Strategy) An approach to Charging for IT Services. Charges to Customers are calculated and Customers are informed of these charges, but no money is actually transferred. Notional Charging is sometimes introduced to ensure that Customers are aware of the costs they incur, or as a stage during the introduction of real Charging.

Objective

The defined purpose or aim of a Process, an Activity or an Organization as a whole. Objectives are usually expressed as measurable targets. The term Objective is also informally used to mean a Requirement. *See also* Outcome.

Office of Government Commerce

OGC owns the ITIL brand (copyright and trademark). OGC is a UK Government department that supports the delivery of the government's procurement agenda through its work in collaborative procurement and in raising levels of procurement skills and capability with departments. It also provides support for complex public sector projects.

Off-shore

(Service Strategy) Provision of Services from a location outside the country where the Customer is based, often in a different continent. This can be the provision of an IT Service, or of supporting Functions such as Service Desk. *See also* On-shore, Near-shore.

On-shore

(Service Strategy) Provision of Services from a location within the country where the Customer is based. *See also* Off-shore, Near-shore.

Operate

To perform as expected. A Process or Configuration Item is said to Operate if it is delivering the Required outputs. Operate also means to perform one or more Operations. For example, to Operate a computer is to do the day-to-day Operations needed for it to perform as expected.

Operation

(Service Operation) Day-to-day management of an IT Service, System, or other Configuration Item. Operation is also used to mean any pre-defined Activity or Transaction. For example loading a magnetic tape, accepting money at a point of sale, or reading data from a disk drive.

Operational

The lowest of three levels of Planning and delivery (Strategic, Tactical, Operational). Operational Activities include the day-to-day or short-term Planning or delivery of a business process or IT Service Management Process. The term Operational is also a synonym for Live.

Operations Management

See IT Operations Management.

Opportunity Cost

(Service Strategy) A cost that is used in deciding between investment choices. Opportunity Cost represents the revenue that would have been generated by using the Resources in a different way. For example the Opportunity Cost of purchasing a new Server may include not carrying out a Service Improvement activity that the money could have been spent on. Opportunity cost analysis is used as part of decision making processes, but is not treated as an actual cost in any financial statement.

Optimize

Review, Plan and request Changes, in order to obtain the maximum Efficiency and Effectiveness from a Process, Configuration Item, Application, etc.

Organization

A company, legal entity or other institution. Examples of Organizations that are not companies include International Standards Organization or itSMF. The term Organization is sometimes used to refer to any entity that has People, Resources and Budgets. For example a Project or business unit.

Outcome

The result of carrying out an Activity; following a Process; delivering an IT Service, etc. The term Outcome is used to refer to intended results, as well as to actual results. *See also* Objective.

Outsourcing

(Service Strategy) Using an external service provider to manage IT Services. *See also* Service Sourcing.

Overhead

See Indirect cost.

Partnership

A relationship between two Organizations that involves working closely together for common goals or mutual benefit. The IT Service Provider should have a Partnership with the business, and with Third Parties who are critical to the delivery of IT Services. *See also* Value Network.

Pattern of business activity

(Service Strategy) A Workload profile of one or more business activities. Patterns of business activity are used to help the IT Service Provider understand and plan for different levels of business activity. *See also* User Profile.

Performance

A measure of what is achieved or delivered by a System, person, team, Process, or IT Service.

Performance Anatomy

(Service Strategy) An approach to Organizational Culture that integrates, and actively manages, leadership and strategy, people development, technology enablement, performance management and innovation.

Performance Management

(Continual Service Improvement) The Process responsible for day-to-day Capacity Management Activities. These include monitoring, threshold detection, Performance analysis and Tuning, and implementing changes related to Performance and Capacity.

Pilot

(Service Transition) A limited Deployment of an IT Service, a Release or a Process to the Live Environment. A pilot is used to reduce Risk and to gain User feedback and Acceptance. *See also* Test, Evaluation.

Plan

A detailed proposal that describes the Activities and Resources needed to achieve an Objective. For example a Plan to implement a new IT Service or Process. ISO/IEC 20000 requires a Plan for the management of each IT Service Management Process.

Plan–Do–Check–Act

(Continual Service Improvement) A four-stage cycle for Process management, attributed to Edward Deming. Plan–Do–Check–Act is also called the Deming Cycle.

PLAN: Design or revise Processes that support the IT Services.

DO: Implement the Plan and manage the Processes.

CHECK: Measure the Processes and IT Services, compare with Objectives and produce reports.

ACT: Plan and implement Changes to improve the Processes.

Planning

An Activity responsible for creating one or more Plans. For example, Capacity Planning.

PMBOK

A Project management Standard maintained and published by the Project Management Institute. PMBOK stands for Project Management Body of Knowledge. See www.pmi.org for more information. *See also* PRINCE2.

Policy

Formally documented management expectations and intentions. Policies are used to direct decisions, and to ensure consistent and appropriate development and implementation of Processes, Standards, Roles, Activities, IT infrastructure, etc.

Practice

A way of working, or a way in which work must be done. Practices can include Activities, Processes, Functions, Standards and Guidelines. *See also* Best practice.

Pricing

(Service Strategy) The Activity for establishing how much Customers will be Charged.

PRINCE2

The standard UK government methodology for Project management. See www.ogc.gov.uk/prince2 for more information. *See also* PMBOK.

Priority

(Service Transition) (Service Operation) A Category used to identify the relative importance of an Incident, Problem or Change. Priority is based on Impact and Urgency, and is used to identify required times for actions to be taken. For example the SLA may state that Priority 2 Incidents must be resolved within 12 hours.

Problem

(Service Operation) A cause of one or more Incidents. The cause is not usually known at the time a Problem Record is created, and the Problem Management Process is responsible for further investigation.

Problem Management

(Service Operation) The Process responsible for managing the Lifecycle of all Problems. The primary objectives of Problem Management are to prevent Incidents from happening, and to minimize the Impact of Incidents that cannot be prevented.

Procedure

A Document containing steps that specify how to achieve an Activity. Procedures are defined as part of Processes.

Process

A structured set of Activities designed to accomplish a specific Objective. A Process takes one or more defined inputs and turns them into defined outputs. A Process may include any of the Roles, responsibilities, tools and management Controls required to reliably deliver the outputs. A Process may define Policies, Standards, Guidelines, Activities, and Work Instructions if they are needed.

Process Control

The Activity of planning and regulating a Process, with the Objective of performing the Process in an Effective, Efficient, and consistent manner.

Process Owner

A Role responsible for ensuring that a Process is fit for purpose. The Process Owner's responsibilities include sponsorship, Design, Change Management and continual improvement of the Process and its Metrics. This Role is often assigned to the same person who carries out the Process Manager Role, but the two Roles may be separate in larger Organizations.

Profit Centre

(Service Strategy) A business unit that charges for Services provided. A Profit Centre can be created with the objective of making a profit, recovering costs, or running at a loss. An IT Service Provider can be run as a Cost Centre or a Profit Centre.

Programme

A number of Projects and Activities that are planned and managed together to achieve an overall set of related Objectives and other Outcomes.

Project

A temporary Organization, with people and other Assets required to achieve an Objective or other Outcome. Each Project has a Lifecycle that typically includes initiation, Planning, execution, Closure, etc. Projects are usually managed using a formal methodology such as PRINCE2.

PRojects IN Controlled Environments (PRINCE2)

See PRINCE2.

Qualification

(Service Transition) An Activity that ensures that IT infrastructure is appropriate, and correctly configured, to support an Application or IT Service.

Quality

The ability of a product, Service, or Process to provide the intended value. For example, a hardware Component can be considered to be of high Quality if it performs as expected and delivers the required Reliability. Process Quality also requires an ability to monitor Effectiveness and Efficiency, and to improve them if necessary.

RACI

(Service Design) (Continual Service Improvement) A Model used to help define Roles and Responsibilities. RACI stands for Responsible, Accountable, Consulted and Informed. *See also* Stakeholder.

Record

A Document containing the results or other output from a Process or Activity. Records are evidence of the fact that an activity took place and may be paper or electronic. For example, an Audit report, an Incident Record, or the minutes of a meeting.

Recovery

(Service Design) (Service Operation) Returning a Configuration Item or an IT Service to a working state. Recovery of an IT Service often includes recovering data to a known consistent state. After Recovery, further steps may be needed before the IT Service can be made available to the Users (Restoration).

Redundancy

See Fault tolerance.

The term Redundant also has a generic meaning of obsolete, or no longer needed.

Relationship

A connection or interaction between two people or things. In Business Relationship Management it is the interaction between the IT Service Provider and the business. In Configuration Management it is a link between two Configuration Items that identifies a dependency or connection between them. For example Applications may be linked to the Servers they run on, IT Services have many links to all the CIs that contribute to them.

Release

(Service Transition) A collection of hardware, software, documentation, Processes or other Components required to implement one or more approved Changes to IT Services. The contents of each Release are managed, tested, and deployed as a single entity.

Release Management

(Service Transition) The Process responsible for Planning, scheduling and controlling the movement of Releases to Test and Live Environments. The primary Objective of Release Management is to ensure that the integrity of the Live Environment is protected and that the correct Components are released. Release Management is part of the Release and Deployment Management Process.

Reliability

(Service Design) (Continual Service Improvement) A measure of how long a Configuration Item or IT Service can perform its agreed Function without interruption. Usually measured as MTBF or MTBSI. The term Reliability can also be used to state how likely it is that a Process, Function, etc. will deliver its required outputs. *See also* Availability.

Repair

(Service Operation) The replacement or correction of a failed Configuration Item.

Request for Change

(Service Transition) A formal proposal for a Change to be made. An RFC includes details of the proposed Change, and may be recorded on paper or electronically. The term RFC is often misused to mean a Change Record, or the Change itself.

Requirement

(Service Design) A formal statement of what is needed. For example, a Service Level Requirement, a Project Requirement or the required Deliverables for a Process.

Resolution

(Service Operation) Action taken to repair the Root Cause of an Incident or Problem, or to implement a Workaround. In ISO/IEC 20000, Resolution Processes is the Process group that includes Incident and Problem Management.

Resource

(Service Strategy) A generic term that includes IT Infrastructure, people, money or anything else that might help to deliver an IT Service. Resources are considered to be Assets of an Organization. *See also* Capability, Service Asset.

Response Time

A measure of the time taken to complete an Operation or Transaction. Used in Capacity Management as a measure of IT infrastructure Performance, and in Incident Management as a measure of the time taken to answer the phone, or to start Diagnosis.

Responsiveness

A measurement of the time taken to respond to something. This could be Response Time of a Transaction, or the speed with which an IT Service Provider responds to an Incident or Request for Change, etc.

Restore

(Service Operation) Taking action to return an IT Service to the Users after Repair and Recovery from an Incident. This is the primary Objective of Incident Management.

Retire

(Service Transition) Permanent removal of an IT Service, or other Configuration Item, from the Live Environment. Retired is a stage in the Lifecycle of many Configuration Items.

Return on Investment

(Service Strategy) (Continual Service Improvement) A measurement of the expected benefit of an investment. In the simplest sense it is the net profit of an investment divided by the net worth of the assets invested. *See also* Net Present Value.

Review

An evaluation of a Change, Problem, Process, Project, etc. Reviews are typically carried out at predefined points in the Lifecycle, and especially after Closure. The purpose of a Review is to ensure that all Deliverables have been provided, and to identify opportunities for improvement.

Rights

(Service Operation) Entitlements, or permissions, granted to a User or Role. For example the Right to modify particular data, or to authorize a Change.

Risk

A possible event that could cause harm or loss, or affect the ability to achieve Objectives. A Risk is measured by the probability of a Threat, the Vulnerability of the Asset to that Threat, and the Impact it would have if it occurred.

Risk Management

The Process responsible for identifying, assessing and controlling Risks.

Role

A set of responsibilities, Activities and authorities granted to a person or team. A Role is defined in a Process. One person or team may have multiple Roles, for example the Roles of Configuration Manager and Change Manager may be carried out by a single person.

Scalability

The ability of an IT Service, Process, Configuration Item, etc. to perform its agreed Function when the Workload or Scope changes.

Scope

The boundary, or extent, to which a Process, Procedure, Certification, Contract, etc. applies. For example the Scope of Change Management may include all Live IT Services and related Configuration Items, the Scope of an ISO/IEC 20000 Certificate may include all IT Services delivered out of a named data centre.

Security

See Information Security Management.

Separation of Concerns

(Service Strategy) An approach to Designing a solution or IT Service that divides the problem into pieces that can be solved independently. This approach separates 'what' is to be done from 'how' it is to be done.

Server

(Service Operation) A computer that is connected to a network and provides software Functions that are used by other Computers.

Service

A means of delivering value to customers by facilitating outcomes customers want to achieve without the ownership of specific costs and risks.

Service Analytics

(Service Strategy) A technique used in the assessment of the business impact of Incidents. Service Analytics models the dependencies between Configuration Items, and the dependencies of IT Services on Configuration Items.

Service Asset

Any Capability or Resource of a Service Provider. *See also* Asset.

Service Catalogue

(Service Design) A database or structured Document with information about all Live IT Services, including those available for Deployment. The Service Catalogue is the only part of the Service Portfolio published to Customers, and is used to support the sale and delivery of IT Services. The Service Catalogue includes information about deliverables, prices, contact points, ordering and request Processes. *See also* Contract Portfolio.

Service Contract

(Service Strategy) A Contract to deliver one or more IT Services. The term Service Contract is also used to mean any Agreement to deliver IT Services, whether this is a legal Contract or an SLA. *See also* Contract Portfolio.

Service Culture

A Customer-oriented Culture. The major Objectives of a Service Culture are Customer satisfaction and helping Customers to achieve their business objectives.

Service Design

(Service Design) A stage in the Lifecycle of an IT Service. Service Design includes a number of Processes and Functions and is the title of one of the Core ITIL publications. *See also* Design.

Service Desk

(Service Operation) The Single Point of Contact between the Service Provider and the Users. A typical Service Desk manages Incidents and Service Requests, and also handles communication with the Users.

Service Level

Measured and reported achievement against one or more Service Level Targets. The term Service Level is sometimes used informally to mean Service Level Target.

Service Level Agreement

(Service Design) (Continual Service Improvement) An Agreement between an IT Service Provider and a Customer. The SLA describes the IT Service, documents Service Level Targets, and specifies the responsibilities of the IT Service Provider and the Customer. A single SLA may cover multiple IT Services or multiple customers.

Service Level Management

(Service Design) (Continual Service Improvement) The Process responsible for negotiating Service Level Agreements, and ensuring that these are met. SLM is responsible for ensuring that all IT Service Management Processes, Operational Level Agreements, and Underpinning Contracts, are appropriate for the agreed Service Level Targets. SLM monitors and reports on Service Levels, and holds regular Customer reviews.

Service Level Package

(Service Strategy) A defined level of Utility and Warranty for a particular Service Package. Each SLP is designed to meet the needs of a particular pattern of business activity. *See also* Line of Service.

Service Level Requirement

(Service Design) (Continual Service Improvement) A Customer Requirement for an aspect of an IT Service. SLRs are based on business objectives and are used to negotiate agreed Service Level Targets.

Service Management

Service Management is a set of specialized organizational capabilities for providing value to customers in the form of services.

Service Management Lifecycle

An approach to IT Service Management that emphasizes the importance of coordination and Control across the various Functions, Processes, and Systems necessary to manage the full Lifecycle of IT Services. The Service Management Lifecycle approach considers the Strategy, Design, Transition, Operation and Continuous Improvement of IT Services.

Service Operation

(Service Operation) A stage in the Lifecycle of an IT Service. Service Operation includes a number of Processes and Functions and is the title of one of the Core ITIL publications. *See also* Operation.

Service Package

(Service Strategy) A detailed description of an IT Service that is available to be delivered to Customers. A Service Package includes a Service Level Package and one or more core services and Supporting Services.

Service Pipeline

(Service Strategy) A database or structured Document listing all IT Services that are under consideration or Development, but are not yet available to Customers. The Service Pipeline provides a business view of possible future IT Services and is part of the Service Portfolio that is not normally published to Customers.

Service Portfolio

(Service Strategy) The complete set of Services that are managed by a Service Provider. The Service Portfolio is used to manage the entire Lifecycle of all Services, and includes three Categories: Service Pipeline (proposed or in Development); Service Catalogue (Live or available for Deployment); and Retired Services. *See also* Service Portfolio Management, Contract Portfolio.

Service Portfolio Management

(Service Strategy) The Process responsible for managing the Service Portfolio. Service Portfolio Management considers Services in terms of the business value that they provide.

Service Potential

(Service Strategy) The total possible value of the overall Capabilities and Resources of the IT Service Provider.

Service Provider

(Service Strategy) An Organization supplying Services to one or more Internal Customers or External Customers. Service Provider is often used as an abbreviation for IT Service Provider. *See also* Type I Service Provider, Type II Service Provider, Type III Service Provider.

Service Provider Interface

(Service Strategy) An interface between the IT Service Provider and a User, Customer, business process, or a Supplier. Analysis of Service Provider Interfaces helps to coordinate end-to-end management of IT Services.

Service Provisioning Optimization

(Service Strategy) Analysing the finances and constraints of an IT Service to decide if alternative approaches to service delivery might reduce costs or improve Quality.

Service Reporting

(Continual Service Improvement) The Process responsible for producing and delivering reports of achievement and trends against Service Levels. Service Reporting should agree the format, content and frequency of reports with Customers.

Service Request

(Service Operation) A request from a User for information, or advice, or for a Standard Change or for Access to an IT Service. For example to reset a password, or to provide standard IT Services for a new User. Service Requests are usually handled by a Service Desk, and do not require an RFC to be submitted.

Service Sourcing

(Service Strategy) The Strategy and approach for deciding whether to provide a Service internally or to outsource it to an External Service Provider. Service Sourcing also means the execution of this Strategy.

Service Sourcing includes:

- Internal sourcing – Internal or Shared Services using Type I or Type II Service Providers
- Traditional Sourcing – Full Service Outsourcing using a Type III Service Provider
- Multi-vendor Sourcing – Prime, Consortium or Selective Outsourcing using Type III Service Providers.

Service Strategy

(Service Strategy) The title of one of the Core ITIL publications. Service Strategy establishes an overall Strategy for IT Services and for IT Service Management.

Service Transition

(Service Transition) A stage in the Lifecycle of an IT Service. Service Transition includes a number of Processes and Functions and is the title of one of the Core ITIL publications. *See also* Transition.

Service Utility

(Service Strategy) The Functionality of an IT Service from the Customer's perspective. The business value of an IT Service is created by the combination of Service Utility (what the Service does) and Service Warranty (how well it does it). *See also* Utility.

Service Valuation

(Service Strategy) A measurement of the total cost of delivering an IT Service, and the total value to the business of that IT Service. Service Valuation is used to help the business and the IT Service Provider agree on the value of the IT Service.

Service Warranty

(Service Strategy) Assurance that an IT Service will meet agreed Requirements. This may be a formal Agreement such as a Service Level Agreement or Contract, or may be a marketing message or brand image. The business value of an IT Service is created by the combination of Service Utility (what the Service does) and Service Warranty (how well it does it). *See also* Warranty.

Source

See Service Sourcing.

Specification

A formal definition of Requirements. A Specification may be used to define technical or Operational Requirements, and may be internal or external. Many public Standards consist of a Code of Practice and a Specification. The Specification defines the Standard against which an Organization can be Audited.

Stakeholder

All people who have an interest in an Organization, Project, IT Service, etc. Stakeholders may be interested in the Activities, targets, Resources, or Deliverables. Stakeholders may include Customers, Partners, employees, shareholders, owners, etc. *See also* RACI.

Standard

A mandatory Requirement. Examples include ISO/IEC 20000 (an international Standard), an internal security standard for Unix configuration, or a government standard for how financial Records should be maintained. The term Standard is also used to refer to a Code of Practice or Specification published by a Standards Organization such as ISO or BSI. *See also* Guideline.

Standby

(Service Design) Used to refer to Resources that are not required to deliver the Live IT Services, but are available to support IT Service Continuity Plans. For example a Standby data centre may be maintained to support Hot Standby, Warm Standby or Cold Standby arrangements.

Status

The name of a required field in many types of Record. It shows the current stage in the Lifecycle of the associated Configuration Item, Incident, Problem, etc.

Strategic

(Service Strategy) The highest of three levels of Planning and delivery (Strategic, Tactical, Operational). Strategic Activities include Objective setting and long-term Planning to achieve the overall Vision.

Strategy

(Service Strategy) A Strategic Plan designed to achieve defined Objectives.

Supplier

(Service Strategy) (Service Design) A Third Party responsible for supplying goods or Services that are required to deliver IT Services. Examples of suppliers include commodity hardware and software vendors, network and telecom providers, and outsourcing Organizations. *See also* Supply Chain.

Supplier Management

(Service Design) The Process responsible for ensuring that all Contracts with Suppliers support the needs of the business, and that all Suppliers meet their contractual commitments.

Supply Chain

(Service Strategy) The Activities in a Value Chain carried out by Suppliers. A Supply Chain typically involves multiple Suppliers, each adding value to the product or Service. *See also* Value Network.

Supporting Service

(Service Strategy) A Service that enables or enhances a core service. For example, a directory service or a backup service. *See also* Service Package.

System

A number of related things that work together to achieve an overall Objective. For example:

- A computer System including hardware, software and Applications

- A management System, including multiple Processes that are planned and managed together. For example, a Quality Management System

- A Database Management System or Operating System that includes many software modules that are designed to perform a set of related Functions.

Tactical

The middle of three levels of Planning and delivery (Strategic, Tactical, Operational). Tactical Activities include the medium-term Plans required to achieve specific Objectives, typically over a period of weeks to months.

Tag

(Service Strategy) A short code used to identify a Category. For example tags EC1, EC2, EC3, etc. might be used to identify different Customer outcomes when analysing and comparing Strategies. The term Tag is also used to refer to the activity of assigning Tags to things.

Technical Management

(Service Operation) The Function responsible for providing technical skills in support of IT Services and management of the IT infrastructure. Technical Management defines the Roles of Support Groups, as well as the tools, Processes and Procedures required.

Technical Support

See Technical Management.

Test

(Service Transition) An Activity that verifies that a Configuration Item, IT Service, Process, etc. meets its Specification or agreed Requirements.

Third Party

A person, group, or business that is not part of the Service Level Agreement for an IT Service, but is required to ensure successful delivery of that IT Service. For example, a software Supplier, a hardware maintenance company, or a facilities department. Requirements for Third Parties are typically specified in Underpinning Contracts or Operational Level Agreements.

Threat

Anything that might exploit a Vulnerability. Any potential cause of an Incident can be considered to be a Threat. For example a fire is a Threat that could exploit the Vulnerability of flammable floor coverings. This term is commonly used in Information Security Management and IT Service Continuity Management, but also applies to other areas such as Problem and Availability Management.

Threshold

The value of a Metric that should cause an Alert to be generated, or management action to be taken. For example 'Priority 1 Incident not solved within four hours', 'more than five soft disk errors in an hour', or 'more than 10 failed changes in a month'.

Throughput

(Service Design) A measure of the number of Transactions, or other Operations, performed in a fixed time. For example, 5,000 e-mails sent per hour, or 200 disk I/Os per second.

Total Cost of Ownership

(Service Strategy) A methodology used to help make investment decisions. TCO assesses the full Lifecycle cost of owning a Configuration Item, not just the initial cost or purchase price. *See also* Total Cost of Utilization.

Total Cost of Utilization

(Service Strategy) A methodology used to help make investment and Service Sourcing decisions. TCU assesses the full Lifecycle cost to the Customer of using an IT Service. *See also* Total Cost of Ownership.

Transaction

A discrete Function performed by an IT Service. For example transferring money from one bank account to another. A single Transaction may involve numerous additions, deletions and modifications of data. Either all of these complete successfully or none of them is carried out.

Transition

(Service Transition) A change in state, corresponding to a movement of an IT Service or other Configuration Item from one Lifecycle status to the next.

Type I Service Provider

(Service Strategy) An internal service provider that is embedded within a business unit. There may be several Type I Service Providers within an Organization.

Type II Service Provider

(Service Strategy) An internal service provider that provides shared IT Services to more than one business unit.

Type III Service Provider

(Service Strategy) A Service Provider that provides IT Services to External Customers.

Unit Cost

(Service Strategy) The cost to the IT Service Provider of providing a single Component of an IT Service. For example the cost of a single desktop PC, or of a single Transaction.

Usability

(Service Design) The ease with which an Application, product, or IT Service can be used. Usability Requirements are often included in a Statement of Requirements.

Use Case

(Service Design) A technique used to define required functionality and Objectives, and to design Tests. Use Cases define realistic scenarios that describe interactions between Users and an IT Service or other System. *See also* Change Case.

User

A person who uses the IT Service on a day-to-day basis. Users are distinct from Customers, as some Customers do not use the IT Service directly.

User Profile

(Service Strategy) A pattern of User demand for IT Services. Each User Profile includes one or more patterns of business activity.

Utility

(Service Strategy) Functionality offered by a Product or Service to meet a particular need. Utility is often summarized as 'what it does'. *See also* Service Utility.

Value Chain

(Service Strategy) A sequence of Processes that creates a product or Service that is of value to a Customer. Each step of the sequence builds on the previous steps and contributes to the overall product or Service. *See also* Value Network.

Value for Money

An informal measure of cost effectiveness. Value for Money is often based on a comparison with the cost of alternatives.

Value Network

(Service Strategy) A complex set of relationships between two or more groups or organizations. Value is generated through exchange of knowledge, information, goods or Services. *See also* Value Chain, Partnership.

Variable Cost

(Service Strategy) A cost that depends on how much the IT Service is used, how many products are produced, the number and type of Users, or something else that cannot be fixed in advance. *See also* Variable Cost Dynamics.

Variable Cost Dynamics

(Service Strategy) A technique used to understand how overall costs are affected by the many complex variable elements that contribute to the provision of IT Services.

Variance

The difference between a planned value and the actual measured value. Commonly used in Financial Management, Capacity Management and Service Level Management, but could apply in any area where Plans are in place.

Verification

(Service Transition) An Activity that ensures a new or changed IT Service, Process, Plan, or other Deliverable is complete, accurate, Reliable and matches its design specification.

Version

(Service Transition) A Version is used to identify a specific Baseline of a Configuration Item. Versions typically use a naming convention that enables the sequence or date of each Baseline to be identified. For example Payroll Application Version 3 contains updated functionality from Version 2.

Vision

A description of what the Organization intends to become in the future. A Vision is created by senior management and is used to help influence Culture and Strategic Planning.

Vulnerability

A weakness that could be exploited by a Threat. For example an open firewall port, a password that is never changed, or a flammable carpet. A missing Control is also considered to be a Vulnerability.

Warranty

(Service Strategy) A promise or guarantee that a product or Service will meet its agreed Requirements. *See also* Service Warranty.

Workload

The Resources required to deliver an identifiable part of an IT Service. Workloads may be Categorized by Users, groups of Users, or Functions within the IT Service. This is used to assist in analysing and managing the Capacity, Performance and Utilization of Configuration Items and IT Services. The term Workload is sometimes used as a synonym for Throughput.

Index

Index